The Essential Jill Johnston Reader

The Essential Jill Johnston Reader

Jill Johnston

Edited by Clare Croft

Duke University Press *Durham and London* 2024

Printed in the United States of America on acid-free paper ∞
Project Editor: Bird Williams
Designed by Courtney Leigh Richardson
Typeset in Freight and Cronos by Copperline Book Services

Library of Congress Cataloging-in-Publication Data
Names: Johnston, Jill, author. | Croft, Clare, editor.
Title: The essential Jill Johnston reader / [Jill Johnston]; edited by Clare Croft.
Description: Durham : Duke University Press, 2024. | Includes bibliographical references and index.
Identifiers: 2023057412 (print)
LCCN 2023057413 (ebook)
ISBN 9781478030904 (paperback)
ISBN 9781478026679 (hardcover)
ISBN 9781478059943 (ebook)
Subjects: LCSH: Johnston, Jill. | Feminist art criticism—United States. | Dance criticism—United States. | Feminism and the arts—United States. | Lesbian feminist theory—United States. | BISCAC: PERFORMING ARTS / Dance / General | SOCIAL SCIENCE / LGBTQ Studies / Lesbian Studies
Classification: LCC NX640 .J54 2024 (print)
LCC NX640 (ebook)
DDC 070.4/493054—dc23/eng/20240511
LC record available at https://lccn.loc.gov/2023057412
LC ebook record available at https://lccn.loc.gov/2023057413

Cover art: Jill Johnston, 1970. Photo by Diana Jo Davies. Courtesy the Manuscripts and Archives Division, The New York Public Library.

Contents

Embedded Writing | 105

Profiles | 119

Travel Writing | 157

Coming Out | 173

A Note on Transcription

Jill Johnston's experimental approach to writing makes re-presenting her writing in the format she intended a sometimes complicated task. This is further compounded by the fact that, as Johnston sometimes lamented in public, her main publication platform, the *Village Voice*, had, at best, a sometimes haphazard approach to proofreading and typesetting. At the level of the sentence it is sometimes difficult to discern the difference between a stylistic choice Johnston intended and an errant typographical error.

With these factors in mind, all transcription for this volume was first done from, whenever possible, the original publication of the piece and then cross-referenced against later publications of the writing that Johnston oversaw. Through these comparisons, it usually became clear when Johnston made intentional creative or structural choices for stylistic reasons versus when errors beyond her control were introduced. This comparative process also revealed the instances in which Johnston allowed changes to be made to reprints of her original pieces of writing, usually in the case of adding diacritics to names (something the *Voice* rarely did) or correcting the spellings of names and/or titles. In compiling this volume, the only intentional changes made were in the vein of those Johnston made for earlier collections of her writing. I would like to thank Sophie Allen for her tireless, detail-oriented work to render Johnston's writing as accurately as possible. That said, the final responsibility for the transcription rests with me, and any errors in the published volume are my own.

Introduction

Jill Johnston (1929–2010) was a writer.[1] She was a writer who understood writing as an action that could create a world of sensation and possibility for both writer and reader. As she once described it, riffing on her lesbian writing predecessor Gertrude Stein, "... by written I mean made. And by made I mean felt."[2] Reading work by Johnston is a combination of the visual, kinesthetic, and sonic, an experience so full that the reader can imagine they are—or even actually can be—transformed.

Johnston is best known as a dance critic and lesbian feminist provocateur, yet her writing from these two locations actually sends readers tumbling among a wide array of topics. Her writing shows that both dance and lesbian feminism—sites often seen as marginal—bring important insights and frames to social questions more broadly. In the column that Johnston wrote for the New York alternative weekly newspaper the *Village Voice* from 1960 to 1980, she wielded the tools and tactics of performance analysis and gender analysis in a manner that simultaneously educated, challenged, and confounded her readers. The boundary crossings Johnston relished in New York's avant-garde art scene of the 1950s and 1960s materialized anew in her writing, leading readers into unexpected arenas or giving them fresh ways of encountering already well-worn paths. By the 1970s, Johnston had developed a signature writing style that she used to chart another set of boundary crossings, bringing readers with her as she moved among the overlaps and frictions of the women's and gay liberation movements.

No matter the topic, Jill Johnston's writing is a performance itself. She drops a reader into a moment, an event at an art gallery or a protest for women's rights or gay rights, and then floods the scene with vivid details. She has little interest in explaining context, but intense interest in presence—an interest she often invoked through attending to what French theater director and theorist Antonin Artaud referred to (and Johnston often quoted): how live performance can present people "signaling through the flames." In Johnston's engagement with Artaud, to "signal through the flames" meant borrowing from theatrical means to elaborate how being alive is an experience of rhythm and cadence, action and heat. In later writing, Johnston used the Artaud-ian frame of fire and flame even more specifically—to invoke the iterative, sometimes frightening, sometimes enthralling experience of coming out as a lesbian.

Johnston's emphasis on presence and its sensorial dimensions upends any notion of reading as a passive act of consumption. Reading Johnston's writing involves far more than just scanning eyes across words on a page. As one reader put it in a "letter to the editor" published in the *Village Voice* in 1974, the best way to read Johnston's column was to "listen" to it.[3] Johnston went further, describing language as an "ongoing battleground" where meaning is simultaneously made and contested, never settled.[4] Writing is not merely a practice meant to make an idea legible, but rather a site to convey multiplicity and contradiction. To read Johnston's writing is to navigate a flood of words and ideas that demands an activated, even turned-on body. Johnston brought the practices that so shaped her, writing and dancing, close enough to touch.

WHO SHE WAS

Jill Johnston was a writer and woman created by the American white, middle-class, post-WWII suburbs of the East Coast; the New York modernist and postmodernist art scenes; and pre-Stonewall and pre–women's liberation New York City. Born in London in 1929, to an American mother, Olive Johnston, and British father, Cyril F. Johnston, who met on a transatlantic voyage, Johnston spent her first two years of life in a London suburb before moving, with her mother, to live with her grandmother, Pauline, in Little Neck, Queens. Upon returning to the United States, Jill was largely raised by Pauline, with Olive, who worked as a nurse in nearby New York City, joining Jill and Pauline on weekends. To shield Jill from her status as "illegitimate," Olive took Johnston's name and gave it to Jill as well, but told her daughter that her father had died before her birth.

When Jill reached adolescence, Olive took a nursing position in Europe and sent Jill to boarding school in Peekskill, New York. In the first of her four autobiographies, *Mother Bound* (1983), Johnston describes her time at the all-girls Episcopal school as something of a lab for experimenting with ways to be a girl, even as all the experiments were limited by the constricting codes of 1950s white, middle-class girlhood, including the necessity of acquiring a boyfriend from the nearby boys' school. An avid athlete in high school, Johnston turned her attention to dance as she entered college at Tufts University in Boston. There, two events (that eventually became intertwined) shaped Johnston's college years: discovering the truth about her father and having her first female lover. Johnston's father actually died while she was in school, and her mother—afraid Jill would learn the truth from his *New York Times* obituary—sent college-aged Jill a copy of the newspaper and a letter explaining the realities of her conception "outside of marriage." Shocked by her newly revealed origin story, Johnston turned to her mentor and dance professor, who eventually became her first female lover—and the person who would introduce Johnston to the New York dance scene that Johnston moved into as an adult.

After more schooling, first in Minnesota and then in an MFA program for writing at University of North Carolina at Greensboro, at the time, another all-women's school where Johnston had a first glimpse of nascent lesbian community, Johnston landed in New York City in the early 1950s. The move was one meant to provide Johnston a place to study philosophy and dance, the former at Columbia University and the latter at the school of foundational modern dance figure José Limón. Obviously aware of Johnston's attractions to women, her Tufts dance professor suggested that the normative femininity of the modern dance world would help Johnston find a path toward heterosexuality. Johnston came into her adult life in New York as a dancer and as a woman who had experiences with a lot of secret-keeping: one that she felt had exploded on her (the news of her father) and one that she was trying to keep (her attraction to women).

Johnston danced professionally in the city and continued to train at the Limón school, until a broken foot halted her dance career. She then got a job at the New York Public Library's Dance Collection, where she worked briefly, and, more importantly, where she met modern dance impresario Louis Horst, who offered Johnston her first opportunity to write professionally. Johnston published her first piece, an essay about the state of concert dance, in 1955 in Horst's *Dance Observer*. The piece grapples with the state of the modern dance field and what Johnston called the *new dance*, a sea change in choreography for the stage that would eventually become known as *postmodern dance*, a movement based in downtown New York City and usually associated with Merce Cunningham and the Judson Dance Theater. Johnston loved the emerging postmodern scene's commitment to reimagining definitions and categories. She tracked these developments across galleries and stages uptown and down, even as she still sought to abide by more conservative and expected categories in her personal life. In 1956, Johnston married a man, with whom she had two children, Richard and Winnie. In her autobiographies, she records those years as ones full of abuse and frustration, leading her to eventually move with her two young children to Manhattan's East Broadway community in 1961 (and officially divorce her husband in 1963). By 1963, Johnston was emerging into the roles for which she first became best known: a visual arts and dance critic—or "cricket" as she was fond of describing the profession.[5]

The pun, critic as "cricket," is one of many examples of Johnston's play with the visual and sonic in her writing, and it also produces a metaphor suitable for understanding the writer that she became: a woman accomplished at creating a buzz. As a *Voice* writer covering the avant-garde performance scene, including the beginning of postmodern dance and Happenings, she chronicled an artistic revolution-in-process. In the late 1960s, as she moved away from reviewing staged performance and brought her critical eye to life more generally, the *Voice* retitled her column from "Dance" to "Dance Journal," finally retitling it again in 1971 simply as "Jill Johnston." By the time of this last shift, Johnston had moved fully into examining her life as a lesbian and her life as someone who had been diagnosed with schizophrenia, experiences she wrote about by using the sensory-rich prose for which she had become known as a dance critic. As Johnston attended now full-time to gender and sexuality, she was just as likely to write about her often provocative takes on women's and gay liberation as she was the psychoanalytic writings of Freud and Jung. Her 1970s writings, along with a series of stand-offs with figures like the onetime *Voice* owner and writer Norman Mailer and liberal feminist Betty Friedan, launched Johnston into public view. A 1971 *LIFE* magazine story about gay liberation described her as "a full-time polemicist for sexual liberation."[6]

Johnston's prolific production as a writer made her a public intellectual for the arts, for feminism, and for lesbians. In addition to her column for the *Voice* and writing for other periodicals, including *Art in America* and the *New York Times Book Review*, Johnston also published ten books. Most notable among these are *Marmalade Me* (1971), a collection of her writing about performance in the 1960s; *Lesbian Nation* (1973), a collection of slightly revised versions of the *Voice* columns, press coverage of Johnston's writing and public appearances, excerpts from her personal journals, and correspondence with readers; and *Jasper Johns: Privileged Information* (1996), an example of the psychobiographic approach she took to her writing about artists later in life. In these examinations of artists, Johnston was often supported and assisted by her wife, Ingrid Nyeboe, her partner from the late 1970s until Johnston's death in 2010.

WHAT SHE WROTE

Johnston made fantastic use of the episodic nature of her (mostly) weekly newspaper column, where she covered dance, lesbian life, and what she eventually termed the "theatre of life."[7] Drawing on the kinetic force she learned to infuse her writing with through her focus on dance, Johnston bravely demonstrated what it looked like and felt like to be a woman and a lesbian during the social movements of the 1960s and 1970s, a perspective much debated at the time but one almost never narrated by a lesbian herself. Through Johnston's writing, readers got to experience what it meant to live as both a woman and a homosexual, to be seen as a lesbian and to see as a lesbian.

The Essential Jill Johnston Reader displays Johnston's panoramic intensity as both an arts critic and a foundational voice in struggles for women's rights and gay rights. The larger contexts in which Johnston wrote are explored in greater detail in this book's complementary volume, *Jill Johnston in Motion: Dance, Writing, and Lesbian Life*. This anthology lets Johnston speak for herself. It is organized around the wide array of writing genres Johnston contributed to (and often reimagined): theory, performance reviews, "embedded writing," travel writing, coming-out stories, personal essays, and reflections on writing. For the first time, Johnston's writings about art, women's and gay liberation movements, and lesbian life appear side-by-side in one book.

The volume begins with works of theory, pieces in which Johnston makes generalizable claims about larger questions of art and gender. It begins with theory because that's where Johnston began: writing broad treatises for the *Dance Observer*, including offering rationales for arts criticism and questioning what constituted abstraction in the field of dance. History has best remembered Johnston for how her writing always attends to specificity and detail. Recognizing theory as the site through which Johnston-the-writer entered public view highlights another of her abiding interests: how larger ideas delivered via art and protest bring people together (or don't). Reading Johnston's theoretical writing, both pieces focused on art and those focused on gender, also emphasizes that there is one thing that always held Johnston's attention: the body. In the six pieces of theory featured here, Johnston grapples with what it means to communicate with the body, how bodies are understood and misunderstood, and how the body can be a platform for moving theory into practice. Starting with Johnston's theoretical writing and its labor toward generalized claims also clarifies some of her writing's limits, specifically how thinking about "the body," rather than about bodies in particular contexts and histories, risks the very homogenization of society Johnston critiqued later in life.

From these broader theoretical perspectives, the anthology turns to the most specific of Johnston's writing, the genre for which she is best known and the genre sometimes imagined as theory's opposite: performance reviews. The twenty-plus examples of Johnston's reviews are but a tiny sliver of the hundreds she wrote, yet even this relatively small selection is stunning in its range. The featured reviews cover multiple disciplines, genres, and mediums, among them sculpture, painting, ballet, and modern/postmodern dance. Regardless of discipline, Johnston approaches art as an event, considering the works' formal characteristics, how works index the process by which they were made, and the audience's experience of encountering each work. Johnston weaves these layers to a variety of ends, which this anthology elaborates through six subcategories. The "on criticism/on watching" category includes reviews that question the role of the critic, what it means to be an audience member, and what it means to watch. The next group focuses on description, a category that might seem self-evident but that Johnston renders as a vast expanse, demonstrating just how many kinds of actions could be described in any one event. Next among the reviews come Johnston's wildest experiments in writing, where she pushes the limits of what words can do on a page. In the final subcategories of reviews, Johnston focuses on one event but then contextualizes that event within three different areas: historical legacy, patterns in contemporary art, or the state of the dance field.

Across all these many types of reviews, Johnston undoes what the word "review" can mean, posing myriad ways that both the writer and her readers "re-view" art through and with language. With incredibly fleshy details, Johnston attends to what happened at any given performance, but she never—even in her most descriptive reviews—merely travels back through the event in order to evaluate it. Instead she takes up the act of reviewing much as she does all her writing: an opportunity to make something. Johnston's writings about art and performance confirm that encountering others' art can propel audiences toward new thoughts, modes of expression, and perspectives. In Johnston's writing, writing about others' artistic creations becomes its own act of creation. She displays how criticism might itself be an art form, as her fellow critic and close friend Gregory Battcock credited her with doing in his introduction to the best-known collection of her writing, *Marmalade Me*.

This volume's third category, termed "embedded writing," highlights Johnston's refusal of clear distinctions between being inside or outside an event. In these pieces, even when she is technically an outsider, Johnston always writes from within and elaborates how being "inside" is still an experience of multiplicity. Readers gain a sense of what it was like to be present at an event or a scene—a feature that often draws comparisons between Johnston and New Journalists, like Tom Wolfe and Hunter S. Thompson, who borrowed techniques from fiction to enhance their long-form journalism. Yet, unlike those associated with New Journalism, Johnston refuses to equate a sense of "being there" with notions of legibility or full comprehension. She does not seek status as superior expert, but rather proves herself to be an intense observer from within the milieu—an approach to watching shaped by performance that later anchored her lesbian feminist politics. Three lengthy accountings of events—some explicitly performances, others better understood as what Johnston called "theatre of life"—represent her "embedded writing." In the first, Johnston describes performing in a 1964 performance/Happening, cast as a "free agent" by director Allan Kaprow. In the next piece, set at an Avant Garde Festival organized by performer and musician Charlotte Moorman, Johnston moves from her more usual mode commenting on the audience at a theatrical event into being part of an audience that refuses to remain an audience. In the third and final piece of "embedded writing," she disrupts a feminist fundraiser, going for a partially nude swim to interrupt a scene of elitism and respectability.

The fourth section of the anthology features Johnston's profiles of individuals, usually artists. This section might prove to be the volume's most surprising. Johnston's interest in writing as an opportunity to create a phenomenological scene often elevates her experiences over those of others. Yet these profiles reveal her intense interest in other people and how they use their bodies to build worlds and communities at the intersection of arts, politics, and society. This profiles portion gathers Johnston's sensitive, often humorous portraits of artists, including James Lee Byars, Mark di Suvero, Gertrude Stein, and Agnes Martin. The outlier among the profiles is Johnston's writing about feminist icon and New York congresswoman Bella Abzug. The Abzug piece, which charts Johnston's encounters with the congresswoman in both Washington and New York, provides a rare glimpse into a meeting of feminists from decidedly different wings of the movement, liberal and radical, with neither shying away from their differences nor using those differences to refuse to see the other's contributions.

Whether she was visiting subjects she wrote about or exploring for both research and pleasure, Jill Johnston was often on the road. Her chronicles of traveling form the subject of the anthology's fifth section. Reading Johnston's column, one could wonder if she was ever at home—she's often reporting from cars, speeding along in them or, as is the case with "Three American Pennies," one of the best pieces in this section, trying to get a broken-down car to start. What is notable in reading these travel pieces is not so much that Johnston should be equally known for this genre as much as she is for arts criticism or feminist critique, but rather that her travel writing highlights another lifetime fascination for Johnston: motion. An emphasis on motion is what her writings about dance, travel, and her developing lesbian and feminist identities all share.

While "coming out," the subject of the anthology's next section, might be more easily understood as a topic than a writing genre, it is absolutely a writing genre for Johnston. Indeed, she made an art form of the coming-out narrative. Her iterative announcements to the world about her gender and sexuality return again and again in the *Voice* as she toys with just how much to share about herself and other lesbians and with whom she wants to share. While coming out was something Johnston arguably did over the course of decades, this anthology focuses on her most intense moments of doing so, which are also among some of her most experimental columns: a series of versions of coming out that she published in 1970 and 1971, culminating in her infamous March 1971 triptych, "Lois Lane is a Lesbian."

Johnston's coming-out narratives are followed by a section titled "Personal Essay," a perhaps misleading title. Given Johnston's propensity (and skill) in describing her presence in her writing, everything in this volume could be termed "personal essay." Yet the pieces collected explicitly within this category are ones where Johnston is at her most musing. These columns exemplify her kaleidoscopic approach to any idea of an "I"—a perspective perhaps informed by her lifelong study of psychoanalytic theory, from Freud and Jung to R. D. Laing's more experimental ideas. In these most personal essays, Johnston reflects on her relationships with women and her childhood love of sports, among other topics. The section concludes with what is perhaps Johnston's opus, "On the Death of a Mother/Twelve-Part Variation on the Death of a Mother," a column about her mother's death that is even more so a meditation on how loss lives in the body. The 1979 piece is the most frequently anthologized piece of Johnston's writing . . . as it should be. Finally, as seems fitting for such a prolific writer, the volume ends by giving Johnston the last word on her writing, closing with an essay she wrote reflecting on her writing, "Fictions of the Self in the Making," published in the *New York Times* in 1993.

Enjoy the writing that Jill Johnston made.

Notes

1. All writing by Jill Johnston reprinted in this volume appears courtesy of Ingrid Nyeboe, who owns all rights to writing by Johnston.

2. Jill Johnston, "Stein: Affectionately Obscene Poetry," *Village Voice*, May 4, 1972.

3. Adrienne Vashon, "Letter to the Editor: Case Study," *Village Voice*, August 1, 1974.

4. Jill Johnston, "Making of a Lesbian Chauvinist," *Village Voice*, June 17, 1971.

5. Jill Johnston, "You Got Me," *Village Voice*, February 20, 1969, 28.

6. Michael Durham (text) and Grey Villet (photographs), "A Direct Assault on Laws and Customs," *LIFE*, December 31, 1971, 64–69.

7. Jill Johnston, "Of This Pure But Irregular Passion," *Village Voice*, July 2, 1971.

Theory

THOUGHTS ON THE PRESENT AND FUTURE DIRECTIONS OF MODERN DANCE

Dance Observer, August/September 1955

There is a prevailing opinion in dance circles which regards the whole modern dance movement in very dismal tones. In fact, there are those who believe that this branch of the art is in the throes of its last gasp. Criticism of the negative sort—complaining, nagging, devoid of hope—indicates a narrow perspective and a concentration on the worst efforts in the art. No one will be foolish enough to deny the justice of many of these complaints. The failings are real and of a varied nature.

It is time to attempt a look at the whole—for an understanding of the present directions of the dance, and the kind of future that may be fulfilled by these directions.

There are two main currents to be observed in the present course of activities. The energies of one group are directed toward the expansion and development of movement ideas and materials bequeathed to us by the pioneering geniuses of the field. The second direction is just as natural—if perhaps less successful—the way of the rebels, not content with the new forms (and they are new after all), seeking more uncharted ways. And, of course, many shades exist in between.

An all too common criticism is that a static position has been reached. The art is not moving forward. We may safely assume that this criticism is aimed at the group carrying on the work of the pioneers—or the pioneers themselves who are working within their own established style and craft.

What do we mean by "moving forward"? What is the criterion for judging progress? If we mean by progress that each artist must exhibit a new force at work, new underlying principles, daring originality; then this group is most certainly standing still. But such requirements are admittedly extreme criteria for progress.

Since the artists within this group vary in appeal, inventiveness and sincerity, it may be another safe assumption that the "standing-still" criticism is leveled chiefly at those who are lacking in the kind of conviction, style, personality, and craftsmanship that will win our audiences. But is there justification for criticism based on the similarity of an artist's technique and methods to that of the masters?

Let us explore the idea of progress. A survey of the history of art forms through many centuries will quickly reveal an ever recurring pattern of birth, growth, mature development, disease and death; death here meaning natural exhaustion, giving way to the new. Every living organism, from the simplest animal through the most complex political structure, partakes of this cycle.

Progress rests upon two conditions: discovery, or birth—and the exploitation of the potential inherent within a discovery. Conversely, any discovery is the realization of a potential within the very nature of things. Thus the two interact and provide for us the inexorable course of novel combinations. This course constitutes progress. *How* materials are exploited, and for what purpose, is another matter—in the realm of skill and morals.

The materials of all art forms have always existed. But the materials did not emerge as art media until simple aesthetic foundations were laid. The laying of a foundation is a discovery based on the potential of materials which are natural phenomena. Tones, for instance, are the natural materials of music. When tones were organized into meaningful patterns, an art form was born. Concentration on a pattern because of acceptance based on aesthetic prejudice would be enough to set the form in motion.

The property of a new discovery provides a suggestive springboard. When the rich potential of a property is not exploited it remains for posterity an isolated phenomenon. Fortunately, this is a rare circumstance. What we see in the course of art's history is a succession of daring innovations followed by the gradual flowering of these seeds, gathering momentum towards a climactic culmination. Also, a movement dies hard, as exhibited by the decay which precedes the birth of new values. Nor does it ever really die. The characteristics of each movement live on, dimly perhaps, cropping up in strange places, the ever-present links in a growing chain. The real change consists in the replacement of dominant characteristics.

There is no time formula for the cycle of development and perishing. Too many factors are at work—those within the arts, those connecting all the arts and those connecting the arts to every other living activity. Within one art, while a single area of a technique may reign and evolve for some 500 years, other areas may be unfolding in new directions within the same period. Thus an intricate network of novelty and tradition is always at work simultaneously.

Progress, then, is not only the discovery of new techniques and methods, but the development or exploitation of them. The next 50 to 100 years may produce dance artists of incomparable stature who have worked patiently to plumb the depths of original suggestions. There *are* at this moment serious young choreographers who feel the immensity of the impact of the pioneering ideas and techniques; seeing within them the large potential for development. The barren imitators do exist. But on the positive side are those strong enough to utilize their heritage without expending their own individuality.

To determine the present and future significance of the rebel group is a more difficult problem. They elicit from us an admixture of scepticism and admiration. The label of rebel may be too strong a description, but individuals they are, seeking independent directions. Here and there in this boiling pot of arm waving, choreography by chance, egos in vacuums, and styles of all descriptions may be detected snatches of original inspiration, and an occasional work of breadth. To some observers this group represents the real "forward look." Others would ban them if it were legally possible. The great variety of approach within this direction, and the large range of ability in technique and handling of materials makes a general appraisal difficult. Because no figure of startling proportions has emerged as yet from these activities, we must consider this current as a bystream to the bulk of established work by the masters, with their perpetuators. This does not diminish its importance, or its right to be reckoned with. Who can tell what seeds are being planted there for tomorrow—or how the future's backward glance may account for today.

For novel experimentation and upheaval in the arts, our generation—and perhaps many to come—has seen its hey-day. The challenge to perpetuate the vitality of the dance becomes increasingly evident. The first excitement engendered by a whole new movement afoot cannot be recaptured—nor is it realistic to dwell on that excitement.

Reflection on the pioneering scene reveals the power of exemplary forces—forces of spirit and aesthetic convictions. They are both an inspiration and a challenge. Without ignoring the obvious failures about us, it cannot be too much to say that there *are* positive examples of this challenge being met. And no matter what the disagreements, all parties must join forces in a spirit of encouragement. The danger of immediate criticism lies in its circular perspective. The eyes of observers must travel along linear paths, which radiate in many directions—paths relating to each other in many diverse ways. Criticism (both lay and professional) alongside the creators and performers must also meet the challenge, not only in its offer of constructive diagnosis and suggestion, but by its positive and kindly tones.

ABSTRACTION IN DANCE

Dance Observer, December 1957

Shall we take the proverbial bull by its ancient horns and discuss that *mot terrible* of the dance world, *Abstraction*? Certainly the existence of the dance world is not seriously endangered by such theoretical nuisances—but the high prevalence of the word hereabouts, with all its various uses and abuses, would lead one to suspect that the term bears a certain charm.

Nor is the word without its formidable aspect. Consider the group of American painters who actually brandish it in their unofficial title: the Abstract Expressionists. Formidable indeed! Yet the unpoetical sounding description has been applied and accepted with seeming ease by the plastic arts. Music of course is generally exempt from any controversy. But for the dancers the word has always possessed a fatal attraction, like a forbidden oath.

Abstraction is most obviously applicable to the plastic arts, but since analogies between the arts, and transferences of terms from one art to another are inevitable, the dance early contracted some of the definitions and terms that caught the people's fancies and satisfied the critics' craving for order.

It appears that the basis of the dancers' objection to the transference of abstraction to dance was, and is, this: that the body is itself on the stage, that it is no other (likewise, movement is itself)—nor is a group of dancers anything but itself. In short, the dancers *are*; they are *not* abstractions. I confess that this is all I have been able to make of the argument.

And if this really is all, the rebuttal is embarrassingly simple. In fact, there really is no rebuttal, for the argument, as expressed above, is quite correct. It would take a zany sophist indeed to prove that the dancers we see before us are abstractions of themselves.

Ridiculous.

But now let us investigate the source of the misunderstanding, and by the by establish the meaning of abstraction. The misunderstanding is just simple enough to be exasperatingly slippery. The dancers have taken the term, *Abstraction*, to be applied to the dance movement itself and to the dance *performance*. Whereas the correct and accurate application of the term is to the process of *composition*, and then, as a description of certain types of composition.

To clarify things at the beginning—the word, *Abstraction*, derives from the Latin *abstrahere*, meaning to draw from, to separate. —*abs*, away + *trahere*, to draw. Keeping this definition in mind, on the elementary level all forms in art are abstracted forms. Forms are separated, abstracted from material existence and given the new life we call art. This preliminary definition should take care of the *process* of composition. But *Abstraction* has gradually become the acceptable term to describe the tendency to eliminate conventional subject matter in so much modern art. For this development and the accuracy of our word to describe it, we may borrow an apt sentence of A. N. Whitehead's: "To be abstract is to transcend particular concrete occasions of actual happening." What these concretions have been and how they have been transcended is the pervasive interest of modern art. Perhaps the early invasion of -isms on the critical scene was, and continues to be, an attempt to sort out and distinguish one method of distortion from another. Painting affords the best illustration of the modern drive toward abstraction. We are all familiar with a particular type of distortion known as Cubism, an analytical method which at first stayed within the limits of representational elements and which had its logical dénouement in the geometric space forms of Mondrian, Ben Nicholson and Naum Gabo.

The important question in this essay, however, is—What constitutes particular concretions in the world of dance, and what does the choreographer do to transcend them, if that is his desire. How does dance become abstract?

First things first. The instrument is the body, the human body. That is the first premise. The human body is a functional (working), social (relating to other people), emotional (feeling), rational (thinking) entity. That is the second premise. The human body moves in space (creating designs), in time (creating rhythms), with energy (creating a range of force or dynamism), and with gestures (which are a means of subsistence, of communication and of personal expression). This is the third premise. The first fact and the following two sets of qualifying facts constitute the raw material of the choreographer.

Since abstraction is the transcendence of concrete details, movement itself does not offer the means of abstraction. We cannot transcend movement, as the dancers have correctly argued; we only select and organize movement. Movement is what it is. Or, of course, we can think of movement as being abstract to begin with since it precludes subject matter. But that is jumping the gun for we come now to the crux of the matter. The basis of abstraction in dance is its proximity to or distance from *dramatic* subject matter, the carrier of which is *gesture*. And gesture is movement invested with meaning. Thus, while representation in painting and sculpture means more or less fidelity to visible objects, representation in dance means more or less fidelity to dramatic character and situation. When drama is eliminated movement in its spatio-temporal and dynamic aspects (divested now of gesture) becomes the sole aesthetic focus. The audience becomes a collaborator in a play of muscular forces, of tensions and resolutions—the drama of interacting forces themselves. In much the same way lines, colors and areas in abstract painting express vitality and convey emotion in what they themselves seem to do.

But even aside from the extreme position of pure, undramatic movement, dance also progressed toward greater abstraction in its dramatic element alone. The naturalism of the story ballet with its pantomimic action and narrative progression of events suffered the same eclipse that naturalism in the other arts endured. But added to this dance was afflicted with its own peculiar paradox, a kind of absurdity. Throughout its history the ballet has teetered precariously, and with small resolution, between its dramatic possibilities and its musical, or pure dance potential. The problem was: how to tell a story and dance at the same time! And, of course, they did it by alternating dishes, doing first one (the story), then the other (the divertissement)—and we can still see this intriguing historical curiosity on our modern stage. Not only that, but the third acts of many ballets abandoned the story pretense altogether, having the entire corps arrange themselves prettily around the sides of the stage while one duet, trio and quintet after another went through its paces.

It remained for modern dance to solve the problem by eliminating the story narrative and finding methods of stylizing gesture which kept it within the bounds of a rhythmic foundation—the long desired fusion of dramatic action and movement. We must also keep in mind Balanchine's resolution (foreshadowed by Fokine's "Les Sylphides")—the elimination of both the narrative *and* the dramatic gesture, except for the overtones of meaning in a work like "Serenade." These overtones are always present in Doris Humphrey's abstract work.

Gesture undergoes several transformations before it loses its more explicit, dramatic meaning. Think first of the physical action of an actor. Imagine him walking on stage in a normal street walk and shaking hands in a normal handshake with another normal appearing actor. Now imagine a stage personality mincing on stage and shaking hands in a jerky manner with an imaginary friend. We would call this stage movement mime. The simple gestures used here, the walk and handshake, are stylized, removed, exaggerated. He has become a character. The next step is to stylize the gesture rhythmically. This usually involves a repetitive treatment of the gesture and increased spatial organization, and, of course, it is now dance. To retain its explicit dramatic meaning, however, the import of a greeting must remain evident. Now—for a further removal, imagine the arm of our dancer extended forward and moving up and down rhythmically from the elbow (without an opposite dancer and without inclining the body forward in a greeting manner) and slowly, keeping the up and down motion, moving the whole arm overhead, then bringing the other arm into play, perhaps twisting the body while the arm is moving overhead, and then perhaps changing the rhythm and dynamics of the up and down motion so that strong accent occurs on one beat. Well, the possibilities are endless, but the point was that we now have "pure movement." The up and down movement of a greeting gesture has been repeated and stylized for its own sake; the greeting is no longer evident or intended. José Limón's dance is full of stylized decoration that may originally have been specific dramatic gestures to fit specific dramatic situations. And, to make another analogy, primitive art is full of geometrically stylized figures, such as animals, which often become further transformed into geometric crystalline shapes, remote in their linear purity from their representational origins.

This essay is a bare outline of what *Abstraction* means in dance. If the reader has been patient he may feel that our *mot terrible* is not so terrible after all and that, though dance is under no obligation to use the word, it is still an accurate description of a simple fact—the absence, to greater or lesser degrees, of dramatic subject matter.

WHICH WAY THE AVANT GARDE?

New York Times, August 11, 1968

In an essay called "The Politics of Revolution," an interdisciplinary thinker, Harvey Wheeler, defines a well-known process of cultural upheaval in terms applicable to modes of activity within the larger political framework. All revolutions, he says, are tales of two cities. The society of the future is the "second city" which lives and flourishes inside the Establishment. The second city is sometimes hard to see and even when it becomes visible, the Establishment tries to hide from itself the authenticity of the second city.

For some centuries now, the art world of the West has been involved in cyclic patterns of subversion, overthrow and replacement of one sort of Establishment after another. Many have pointed out that these patterns have increased their tempo in recent years. The dance world tends to linger behind in its reluctance to accept the inevitability, if not the necessity, of revolution.

The avant-garde choreographers of the sixties number a mere handful and their audience is nothing next to the droves who turn out for everything conservative; but they and their dedicated followers (many of them artists with similar concerns) tenaciously cling to the principle that revolution is not only inevitable but essential. Actually, their revolution, in its original delirium of a sprawling rebellion, is over. It all happened at Judson Memorial Church from 1962–64. Democratically assembled, the choreographers included painters, sculptors and composers as well as dancers. Within a positive assertion of old creative values was the negative idea of the annihilation of all preconceived notions about dance. In retrospect it was a beautiful mess. Within that mess certain hard-core positions were taking shape and certain works were undeniably extraordinary.

After a period of some confusion and dispersion, the movement regained its momentum and is now in the process of enlarging, elaborating and consolidating the dimension of its early promise. It is no longer so much a rebellion as a serious extension of novel positions. Having undermined some cherished presumptions about dance, the choreographers are internalizing the struggle to maintain and to stretch the scope of their new esthetic.

If the most revolutionary proposition of the new dance was that any sort of movement, or action, and any kind of body (non-dancer as well as dancer) was acceptable as material proper to the medium, it was also true that certain choreographers remained in some dialectical relation to tradition, retaining a technical basis for movement while seeking to transform the outmoded structuring of conventional techniques: One of the most encouraging aspects of recent developments is a reassertion of a concern for such movement—as it is still understood in the context of the dance tradition—in a programmatic effort to define it in truly contemporary terms.

Yvonne Rainer, one of the original and most prolific members of the Judson vanguard, set the pace for this development with her "Trio A" of 1966, a short section of pure dance activity which gradually snowballed into a magnum opus called "The Mind is a Muscle." "Trio A" constituted a minor revolution in itself. The idea was to reorganize (or to eliminate for that matter) the traditionally conceived dance phrase with its alternating dynamic of high and low points, or its plot-like structure of a beginning, a middle, and an end. The result was a duration of action characterized by a smooth unaccented continuity, each phrase receiving equal emphasis, each movement projected at an energy level that never seemed to change. This was an all-over dance. It was totally de-focused. Its innumerable discrete parts blended into a continuum rendering a sense of the dance being at rest, static, even as it constantly moved.

Two other charter Judson choreographers, Deborah Hay and Lucinda Childs, have recently attacked the problem of advancing the medium within a sphere that lies somewhere between ordinary action (anybody can do it) and a more dance-based idiom. Their choreography, like Rainer's, encompasses both realms. Deborah Hay used five non-dancers in two closely related works, "Group I" and "Group II." The choreography was simple and blasé, both informally dispersed and schematically patterned, with an overall bland consistency and a deadpan, anonymous performing quality.

A trio of a new work by Lucinda Childs, informally presented this spring, involves some exquisite permutations of about five simple actions which anyone could do, but which require, at the same time, the finesse and mild athletic strength that only a trained person could manage. For all its simplicity, it's an extremely precise and structurally complex piece of work.

Beneath individual differences in these dances are a few common denominators. They are making it clearer than ever that formalist structural concerns were always an issue and that the future of dance rests on these concerns rather than on any new cult of personality or new schools of technique. As a historical example, I would contend that the formal contribution of an incredible composition like "Primitive Mysteries" of 1931 by Martha Graham far transcends the myth of high-priestessdom that Miss Graham became, or the institutionalizing of her technique that followed in the wake of her success. Both processes obscure the real issues.

Implicit in the work of the three artists discussed above is an attack on this very elemental premise of traditional Western dance: the projection of a star supported by a hierarchal imperialist organization (e.g., the kings and queens of the ballet, the tragic heroes and heroines of the modern dance). While I'm at it, I should mention a few other correlative notions that are also under attack. These are, of course, the trappings of any hierarchal system: the pomp and splendor and glamour and spectacle and seduction and virtuosic accomplishments required by aristocratic expectations.

Every underground movement is a revolt against one authority or another. The dance underground of the sixties is more than this natural child-parent affair. The new choreographers are outrageously invalidating the very nature of authority. The thinking behind the work goes beyond democracy into anarchy. No member outstanding. No body necessarily more beautiful than any other body. No movement necessarily more important or more beautiful than any other movement. It is, at last, seeing beyond our subjective tastes and conditioning, always admittedly operative, to a phenomenological understanding of the world.

The inclusive character of the earlier Judson days remains ultimately significant. The attitude was nowhere perhaps so perfectly demonstrated as in a recent dance by Steve Paxton, another charter member, in which about 32 any old lovely people in their old clothes from our any old lives walked across the large performing space, occasionally standing still or sitting down. For all his training and credentials (several years in Merce Cunningham's Company), Paxton takes the most extreme liberated positions. He likes people for what they are and believes in their physicality (their shape and way of moving) for what it is. The tyranny of the ballet, by the way, lies not only in its institutional authority (it commands the field in numbers, in financial support, in critical acclaim) but in its insistence on the superhuman; on the claim that only a streamlined body of extraordinary prowess is worth our time and money to look at.

I've just barely touched on the activities of the avant-garde dance in New York. Meredith Monk, for instance, is one of the most interesting younger choreographers around. With her multiple concerns she has been exploring the possibilities of dancy dances, of "found" dances, of environmental dances, of "still" images and of intermedia work. Also dealing with imagery in an intermedia framework is painter Robert Rauschenberg. I think the question whether some of these things are dance or not is irrelevant to the vitality of a movement which, in any case, has questioned the entire fabric of traditionalist dance—both structurally and philosophically.

THE UNHAPPY SPECTATOR

Village Voice, October 17, 1968

The "late" John Brockman said that anyone who gets up and does something these days is liable to be shot. He was right, although this is no truer for our time than any other time. Dionysus, for instance, was annually murdered and resurrected. To be successful means not only to "get up" (and do something) but to "get it up"—to erect oneself and then properly ejaculate. When the actor and spectator embrace in the ritual copulation of theatre nobody is satisfied unless there is mutual ejaculation. The actor who fails to bring it off is executed. When the girl in the Living Theater's "Frankenstein" fails to levitate (to become soaring phallus) she is executed. If she had in fact levitated she would have been executed just the same, as Icarus must fall in his presumption to fly. The program note for "Frankenstein" stated that if the girl, the center of attention in a hypnotic meditation to accomplish the miracle, did indeed levitate, the program would be consummated. The show would not go on. The girl would be the first and last erection. Once erected she must fall (ejaculate) in the consummation of self-execution; and the spectators would ideally participate in the ritual death. To ejaculate is to expire, to die. The consummation of a mountain is a volcanic eruption in which the lava falls and consumes all the inhabitants. After the ejaculation everyone goes to sleep, dies. The people leave the theatre and go home to bed, to sleep. When they arise they look again for the ritual of their own execution. If they don't find it there's hell to pay—a literal murder. "The world is governed by the badly fucked" (G. Brecht).—"There is no way to avoid murder except by ritual murder" (Brown).

Since mutual ejaculation (catharsis) in the theatre is very rare, and in fact impossible in any total sense, the antagonism between actor and spectator is an acute unresolved tension. Who's going to get whom? It becomes a sadomasochistic dilemma, a deadlock of mutual hatred. The actor, the hero, is the sadist screwing the passive spectator. Yet the actor sacrifices himself in the fiery outstretched arms of a greedy audience which desperately wants what it has for centuries denied itself—the right to act itself. The actor is that part of the organism audience projected outside itself to unfold the misery of its own self-alienation. If everybody is an actor there is no longer any need to act. We're all in it together. The revolutionary theatre of our time is an attempt to expose the farce of this separation between actor and spectator. When the collective authorship is understood, the projected author (leader, hero, actor) might also be understood as merely a practical expedient in a situation requiring a transient spokesman. In their playground games the children know exactly what they're doing when they alternate leadership as a formal expedient. The child who becomes a bully because of an acute daddy problem (daddy gets me at home so I'm going to be the daddy here) is expelled, exiled, executed by the rest of the group. If the demands of the bully are accepted and complied with the children are doing precisely what we adults do in the larger political arena. Mutual hatred (sadomasochism) is the only outcome. And the bully, the leader, will murder the people if the people don't get him first, or we all go down together, which is the genocide, or giant suicide, now facing an unhappy world.

The theatre must go. There is only one theatre. We are all actors and spectators simultaneously upon the stage of the world. The argument between actor and spectator is no more no less than an attempt to dominate the proceedings. When the argument evaporates the actor and spectator become one.—The audience at Loeb Student Center of NYU, on Sunday, October 6, 1968, got the idea very quickly. The confusion was very intense. Last spring six of us agreed to collaborate on a performance to take place on October 6. I'm hazy on how it actually originated. There was a phone conversation with Janet Solinger of NYU about a possible panel. I suggested a "panel performance." For three years I've nursed the notion of a "panel caricature" without any specific idea of the form it might take. I asked sculptor Les Levine to participate and Levine and I then asked Allan Kaprow, Gordon Mumma, and dancers Barbara Lloyd and Meredith Monk. When Meredith couldn't do it dancer Trisha Brown Schlichter agreed to collaborate. Each person would contribute his own thing involving all of us simultaneously in one way or another. It was quite vague. A month ago we met to bat it around. Les said he'd bring in his videotape equipment for some sort of television feedback. Gordon said he'd manipulate the voices with his electronic gear. Trisha talked about doing something outside the windows. Barbara wanted to manipulate the audience somehow. If they were in groups designated by number or letter she would suggest a shifting from group to group. Allan was thinking of engaging the Telephone Company to pipe in some of their public service numbers as answers to questions. And I said I'd provide the script, the written stuff comprised of questions and answers. We were still searching for an overall form to the event. At the first meeting I believe it was Allan who picked up on Barbara's audience involvement idea to push it into the brilliant conclusion of the audience replacing us as panel members. The key word became "disintegration." We had no idea the extent to which a disintegration would be fulfilled. If we had we might have worn bullet-proof vests. But as one of those Kennedys said, there's no safety in retreat.

No doubt the initial question was: What is a panel? The word panel is derived from pane, meaning a piece, and pan, meaning a part. A panel is a piece of somebody or something. Panels are a big drag, that's what they are. They're a tribal council of elders meeting to decide the fate of their subjects. They're a corporation board meeting to do likewise. They're an official organ mouthing the dogmas of the current style. A few people are erected, elevated, to pontificate the agenda of the day. They're the authorities, the experts. They're the publicity agents for themselves and what they represent. The people come to get a "fix." The people are antagonistic but they submit the way a child submits to the classroom situation. A teacher up there is going to tell you where it's at and if you're well behaved you'll get a chance at the end to be a Mickey Mouse yourself by asking a question which has already been asked. If you're not polite you'll challenge somebody and then the whole place gets up-tight and perplexed. Everyone starts looking for the exit. If the teachers stand their ground a battle is in the making. The issues are irrelevant. What's at stake is the question of authority. Traditionally a panel is a serious affair. People expect serious answers to serious questions on what everyone has tacitly agreed to be momentous issues.

So I suppose the idea of our panel was to undermine its seriousness (in terms of settling any issues) by exposing the emotional roots of any authoritative situation. The panel is a conventional public structure as good as any other for revealing the raw nerve of the unhappy spectator and the presumptuous authority. I must say that I don't believe the mob of people who came to Loeb October 6 expected a panel of any sort. The final publicity for the thing simply identified it as a "program" to be given by those six people. But there we were behind a long table on the stage looking like a panel. So I can't say if the convulsion that threatened to finally seize the event was in part a result of an initial disappointment over a structure (panel) that a lot of these people, like myself, don't ordinarily attend. It might be a moot point. There was a huge crowd. I could swear that 2,000 people were there. Enough for a political convention. I asked Janet to close the gates before the Fire Department descended on us. As moderator I introduced the panel members, forgetting to introduce Wilhemina, a sweet friendly pig whom Barbara had brought along to participate by being there. Les, by the way, was invisible to the audience, although he was sedated at one end of the table. When I introduced him he turned on his image in the form of three television sets arranged in pyramid in front of him on the table. He also had a French interpreter with him. After introductions I asked each member a conventional (somewhat impertinent) question related to their respective professions. To Gordon: Would you comment on the axiomatic advantages of electronic sadomasochism? To my own confusion my collaborators began immediately to reply with the prepared nonsense of the script. I had hoped the thing would begin more conventionally. So we were plunged into our own confusion at the outset. The more I pressed for a conventional reply the worse it got. Moreover, with Gordon's electronic sound-modification system, our voices were turned on (up) or off, and sometimes made unintelligible through distortion.

The script was in two parts. There were about eighty short answers which members could speak or yell at random at any time in response to a question or to another answer. Samples: It strikes me as absurd; Let's start from the beginning again; You're interrupting me; You're full of shit; You trumped up that question to confuse me; You must be out of your mind; Let's change the subject; Phrase it differently; I was always vague on that issue; Do you think you're ideally suited to ask these questions; That's not a real question; That's an interesting question; I'll give it some thought, etc. There were also some longer involuted answers providing the opportunity for an oratorical delivery. Each member had an identical script. Deviation from the script was possible at any time. I had a separate script of questions, although some of the questions were answers (or statements), just as some of the answers were questions. Samples: Can anyone else add to that?—You're repeating yourself—You're putting me on the spot—I'll try to clarify the question—I'd like to get a concept of the whole before we go any further—Do you see anybody in the audience you'd like to make it with—etc. Some longer questions, like the longer answers, were convolutions, plays on a single subject, like about exits and entrances. The short answers and questions were the kinds of clichés that people often speak in these situations, sometimes as preface to a serious remark. Or they are the unspoken clichés of an emotional response that people feel and don't express. They were loaded on the side of repressed hostility.

To compound the responses were a set of about 35 gesture possibilities, identical for each member, from which to choose as the moment seemed to dictate. They were the physical counterpart of the verbal material. Tyrannize someone on the panel; crawl across the panel table (Trisha did); embrace someone; pretend to have a headache; make wild oratorical gestures; look omnipotent; yawn extravagantly; wrestle somebody on the floor; become confused, etc.

Trisha had abandoned her plan for action outside the windows. Allan was unable to secure the cooperation of the Telephone Company. And Barbara had abandoned her plan for manipulating the audience, although we retained the essential idea of gradually relinquishing our panel positions. In any case the audience became involved almost instantly. The first invitation for license was my announcement at the outset that a vacant chair on stage at the end of the panel table was there for anyone from the audience to occupy at any time to ask or answer questions, etc. Even the explicit invitation was probably unnecessary. After several minutes of our own confusion, both real and planned, and my constantly stepping into a real or imagined vacuum with a commandeering aggression that might have unnerved an elephant, the audience assumed its proper role of the enraged spectator. I'm speaking in general, knowing that there are always some, especially your friends, who will come celebrate anything you do as your thing of the moment, offered in a spirit of celebration. I'm speaking of the general sickness of the resigned passive spectator, rendered impotent by his own repudiation of responsibility to act, to participate, to become himself the center of his own attention. Who has never felt this impotence and the repressed rage which accompanies such a helpless condition? To be enchanted and mesmerized by a special theatrical event is not an answer to such a sorry plight either. We've all been thus pleased. This is the romantic illusionism of a mutual ejaculation which creates the next anticipatory anxiety for a successful conclusion. You out there, the better part of me projected to fulfill my fantasies, you'd best not let me down, etc. The critics are always murdering some poor bloke who doesn't quite make it on the stage. The critic and actor alike are educated to expect a successful conclusion. The critic is the angry spectator wielding a wicked pen on behalf of his fellow spectators. The critic is the medium between actor and spectator to convey to each the success or the disaster of the attempted copulation. The critic is as screwed up in his presumption as the actor is in his role of the sacrificial lamb and the spectator in his role of the suffering nobody.—The theatre must go.

Someone said the situation at Loeb October 6 was a historic occasion. If so it was only because a breakdown of actor-spectator boundaries took place under the guise of a panel idea, and through an agony of extreme confusion in which an audience encouraged to express its hostility had to fight its way through to the recognition it has always been primed to reject. (If you cease to be the authority, who are we going to attack, and so on.) We didn't make it that easy. Nor was it easy on us. I can't speak for the others, but I felt on fire from the intense concentration of dealing with flak from every direction, and converting the flak (by the reversal we had planned) into the absurdity of an antagonism that had no place to go once the antagonist found himself recognized. As an exercise in emotional conversation the situation was different in kind from certain participation events in which the artist instantly recognizes the spectators and robs them of their passive role by seducing them into a game of total participation. Moreover, the panel event remained symbolic from the view of total participation. The take-over was incomplete. Ideally, if literally enacted, the panel which succeeded us (whom we found at random to supercede us) would have been replaced by another panel, and another, and so on until the ritual was completed. The murder of each successive presumptuous authority. The irony was too much. Barbara found our first panel replacement. He was Willoughby Sharp. He couldn't have been better. I'm not sure how long he was with us when he lunged, and I didn't know what hit me as Willoughby, my chair, and I went crashing to the floor. I'd forgotten that gesture instruction to wrestle somebody to the floor. I returned askew to the mike and announced I'd been raped. Earlier, in response to a panel question about who gets screwed in the theatre ritual, a man in the audience yelled "We are." After the event Les remarked that perhaps everyone stayed to see who else might hump the hostess.

But Willoughby wasn't done yet. At some point I was dimly aware of a white form looming up next to me. Willoughby was standing on his chair removing all his clothes. Again, I'd forgotten there was a gesture possibility called "undress." Everybody applauded the beautiful gesture and I think at that moment we were going into the final phase. Wilhelmina the pig was being much appreciated. The children were wandering onto the stage to be where the action was and to add their two golden cents. One small boy toward the end took charge of a mike and called for order and asked the man shouting "Fire" to shut up, among other things. The mix-up in people's heads over what was real and what wasn't was as perfectly expressed in the continuous fire episode as by anything else. The man incessantly yelling "Fire" might have been immoral in the situation, but he was saying the word which struck him as no other word might have. Fire means to be burned up, inflamed, angry. Fire means to be fired from the job. Fire means to fire the cannons. Fire means execution. Fire means sex and war and total holocaust. Fire means to be immolated altogether in the flames of disintegrating boundaries. Fire is the word of panic when everything is at stake. Yes. Then there was a real fire on stage on the panel table. Gordon put it out with two glasses of water. Earlier he had gone into the audience to give the "fire" man a glass of water and to light his cigar to boot. Back at the table he told a story about his grandfather who once fell in an old outhouse hole on the farm and shouted "fire" to attract the attention of possible rescuers. Later, asked why he yelled "fire" grandfather said, "how in hell far do you think I'd have gotten if I'd yelled Shit."

But the fire which must have moved everyone was the unhappy desperate girl who mounted the stage at last to burn the place up in a plea for love. She was absolutely for real. She was signaling through the flames. Steve Paxton and Barbara Jarvis became her immediate rescuers, finally easing her down between them, after encouraging her to let it all out, holding her hands and rubbing her back. She was everybody's transfigured sacrifice. She was the crucible of the day. If she wasn't in fact, resurrected, I think we all wanted her to be, to be resurrected right there out of the center of her own catastrophe.

She was the real echo of Trisha earlier following instruction at the table by "leaving the proceedings angrily and returning with denunciations." Trisha screamed and crashed her chair down and left. Again the confusion. Two days later she called me to say she was following instructions, since she had heard I thought she might have been actually upset. And that's true, I thought perhaps she was. Perhaps she was.—And Barbara, by the way, was very involved in the mythology of the pig, which was a sacred animal accompanying the Greek earth goddess Demeter.

The pig, the children, the dog. My moderator replacement, David Bradshaw, has a lovely dog called Sumi. They're very close friends. In between moderating, I think, David was lying down on the stage in front of the table being humped by Sumi, who enjoys humping her close friends. This was near the end, which you might hardly call a conclusion. I recall that a lot of people had left, but the place still seemed jammed. Allan, Les, Trisha, Barbara, Gordon, and I shook hands with and congratulated our panel replacements the way they do after *The Tonight Show* or something and gradually at this point much of the crowd appeared to be massing toward the stage, and in fact the stage became a swamp of people, talking, talking, and looking over the equipment and making off with some of it. The milk and yogurt I'd consumed during the event was sustaining me in a dizzy spell of exhaustion and exhilaration.

HEADS—TAILS

Village Voice, November 14, 1968

November 3, 1968, Meredith Monk gave an afternoon called "Co-op" at Loeb Student Center of NYU. Meredith had a few simple oppositional ideas in mind, but I think the afternoon was basically united as a body show. Strange to speak of a dance event as a body show since what else ever is it; but aspects of Meredith's presentation concern the show of the body as a body more related to the body as seen perhaps by a painter, a sculptor or a lover than by a dancer or a dance-goer. As a medium idea dancing can become quite removed from the everyday functioning body; so much so that it begins to look like dancing and people forget to see the body which is doing all that stuff. Possibly the dancers forget about their bodies too. Thus I see the three aspects of Meredith's body show as three contemporary ways of revealing the solid shaped-as-it-is body and the body as an essentially erotic being. Other than how I see the bodies around me from house to street everyday, I've been thinking sometime how a body looks better to me in an old-master painting (an Ingres, say) than in a modern traditional piece of dancing. Maybe Robert Morris had that in mind when he set up the nude female as replica idea of Manet's Olympia in his dance piece, "Site." She was all body and didn't move around thank god. Morris did a lot of static and relatively static body things as perhaps in part ironic commentary (and reaction) to dancing as an art seemingly involved with disguising the real body in a whirlwind of movement and technically distorting configurations. There's a new demanding realism in the dance art of the '60s.

Meredith had two static presentations of the figure in her "Co-op." In the main theatre auditorium were four cubicles, two on each side of the room flush to the walls. Each wall of cubicle consisted of stacks of ten beach umbrella boxes, six-feet long by eight inches square. Within each cubicle a clothed person or people assumed ordinary relaxed positions which they occasionally changed. A striking idea was the cubicle filled with people, maybe ten, all standing and facing the wall. As the audience freely mobilized around the room, like a bazaar, they might at some moment be standing behind the ten cubicle figures, and I don't have to make the visual irony explicit. The single or double figures clearly cut a sculptural idea in a space partially enclosed to set them off in that fashion. But perhaps Meredith's dominant idea in this exercise, bodies notwithstanding, was to reverse the actor-audience relationship by immobilizing the performers in a space where the audience would have to mobilize in order to see the presented objects. Extending the informal idea, Meredith hoped the people would feel they could leave, have coffee, come back, etc. As further extension: downstairs in the Loeb lounge was a six-and-a-half-minute movie going forward and backward to run continuously for the hour and a half of the total performance time. The movie consists of six body sequences alternating with five ball bearings. Three nude men and three nude women are the subjects of the film. One sequence is seen as a single body in the same reclining position in each of four frames, but they're facing different directions in each frame compartment.

The formality of the cubicle and film presentations was offset by the informality of free mobilization by audience. Yet a limitation was superposed on this particular situation by the program indication of specific shows taking place on stage at precisely 3:17, at 3:41, at 4:05. If you wanted to see the shows you had to watch the clock and interrupt your nonchalant itinerancy. So there was this theatrical thing mixed up with a bazaar thing.

The theatre shows were of three elements. Meredith did her hippie love dance (in front of a psychedelic backdrop) with William Dunas, originally performed last summer in San Francisco as a nightly night-club act. Meredith here conformed to the crazy New York State laws about not moving or touching while naked. They did a lot of straight charged sex stuff avec clothes, then stripped to G-strings and stalked each other a bit, then dressed quickly and attacked with a pelvic grind and thrust that looked as much like the real thing to me as being properly undressed. Simultaneously, a movie of the original San Francisco version was shown below the stage on the floor in the middle of the audience. In that space the film was postage-stamp size. Not many people saw it. But it was shown three times. The second time, at 3:41, with the second show on stage: Meredith and Bob Wilson bouncing lightly on a long low board suspended a foot or so above the floor and between two boxes, wearing winter hats and heavy long fur coats. The juxtaposition was funny and good. Who cares about clothes or not if you know what they're for.—The third time, with the third show, at 4:05, the hippie love dance again.

The hippie love dance is a corny name for where dancing is at for a lot of people these days. I meant to say above also that a body not only makes more sense to me in an old-master painting (not that either really) but also in any discotheque where the body as erotic being is displaying itself even if straining after this erotic heritage denied it by the bullshit of Western body sickness. Maybe the best of it is the best black dancing and the white dancing which most looks like black. The white Negro. I saw a black chick at Max's one night knocking me and a friend of mine out, and this friend said to me what would you do with her in bed. Clearly she wouldn't have too much truck with a stiff white.—As an artist Meredith is trying to resolve a conflict between concept and physicality, between art and fucking. She says she's tired of lying in bed conceptualizing a dance. She's a pretty bubbly open-ended girl anyhow. I never thought of her work as spineless or juiceless, no matter how static or conceptual or imagistic. But now she wants to be more physically direct, meaning in part not to set a dance into a piece recognized as an indeterminate moment (the complexity of a spaghetti heap) caught in an angle and a step the same forever. The hippie love dance is as indeterminate in this manner as a body in a moment or an evening at a discotheque, or a body in a moment or a night of fucking. They could only be immortalized on film. Who wants to immortalize anything. It's all over. Why do you think that the very thing that holds our society together is the most appalling aspect of living here. As for your concepts, etc., Meredith, I gotta assure you that as Yvonne said of Martha Graham—What's between your legs is no more interesting to me than what's in your head. You're good because you have an interesting head and a healthy body. Did you know that the French never got over the loss of their head? And the Africans in America are suffering the loss of their bodies?

WHAT SEX?

Village Voice, February 19, 1970

Sex Power Politics Property Economics Culture Religion. Politics is the struggle for power to control the sex objects through the manipulation of property and economy, and the persuasion of culture and religion. Power is sexual latitude, whether employed or not. Rap Brown and other black militants perfectly explain the black bid for power to accomplish what Eldridge Cleaver passionately describes as the black drive to possess the women of his former masters. Equal or better opportunities in the business of living mean ultimately that sexual latitude. The plantation system, like any feudalism, contained a harem for the master. The black grievance runs deepest at its consideration of the historical control over its prime property: the body. Cleaver's contempt for homosexuality (i.e., Baldwin's) could be read as a fear for black potency in accomplishing any task of redressing its grievance.

What do the women want in the exercise of power through politics? What property do they want to acquire? Whose religion can they accept? Whose body do they want? What sex? All movements are political, wishing to usurp the power of real and/or imagined oppressors. The cry of equality is a euphemism for the drive to power. Equality exists only in the head and will never exist in any material reality on earth. All men and women were created with possibly one leg and one eye. The conception of a drive to power is a declaration of war. No incumbent power can afford to refuse the challenge. The war between men and women who continue to want each other was waged light years ago in the dusk of some unisexual animal. Men and women reenact their primeval struggle in which they created their own sexual differentiation and complementary roles through the rituals of courtship in which they advance and retreat in patterns of aggression and resistance only dimly suggesting a once violent encounter resulting in the penetration and submission of one of the combatants. The agreed upon union then transcends the struggle of opposition as a moment of hermaphroditic truth. Warfare when not ritually enacted is the violence of resistance and rape. The wars between men and men, between the brothers, are either the eruption of sexual energy deprived of its object, or the protection and acquisition of and competition for property to sustain and/or enlarge the hunting grounds. Territory and the body of the woman are one and the same. Evolutionary biology is deep in our archetypal unconscious. Biology and the social structures cannot be understood apart from each other. We are in some unalterable senses locked into our history. The social structures in every way support our sexual polarity achieved in some critical adaptation to new conditions attending one of those oceanic upheavals. Viewed as a catastrophe, the bisexual situation remains the tragedy that it once was in its disturbance of a more harmonious form of existence in which the organism was self-sustaining, self-reproducing, the autonomous being. The illusion of romantic love is the veil that nature (within and without) throws over us to effect the passing union with a lost member essential for reproduction and for the transitory recovery of that lost sense of well-being, of being the One indivisible or the divisible One in the continuous Many.

We know truly that the great illusion is the physical reality of our separate sexual selves. It is the mystical tradition in all cultures which carries forward the project of uniting ourselves within ourselves by recognizing our fate and renouncing the desperate search to complete ourselves by possessing another. It is the drive to possess which places the societies at all levels at war within themselves and each other. The warfare on the battlefields is merely the visible public form of what goes on in the private agony of every family. Who suffers more, in particular or in general, seems irrelevant to the prime condition of animals living out their tragedies in varying degrees of successful adjustment. The power of projective thinking is such that we generalize quickly from our particular existential despair. The possessor is also the possessed. The oppressor is also the oppressed. Revolutionary movements are never motivated by pleasure. They say "I want what you've got" instead of "I want you to have what I've got." The drug and flower movement dissipates in the anger at material inequalities. Yet desire begets desire and there is no end to desire. The apparently powerful never rest content in their power. Beyond power is the ultimate power of inner power. Perfect inner containment. There is now a young woman of 23 or so walking about in frayed velvet pants giving light. She is not a woman or a man and she passes through properties as a medium through transparencies. Pure being neither wants what it could think it has not, nor wants for others what it imagines somebody else should have that they have not. All is as it is. Thus a movement motivated by pleasure would be the celebration of being in all its forms. That would not be a movement in the political sense but a radiating outward light energy from the light sources.

The women's liberation women want correction of social ills specifically involving women. Abortion laws and less defined discriminatory practices for reform, repeal, etc. All these things. But the true issue is the sexuality of women. Any apocalyptic revolution toward a utopia would involve the dissolution of sexual identities liberating the social structures dependent on those identities; the physical reality of separate sexes. The women's liberation people face a critical dilemma in their program. Already some of them have crossed over into the militant GLF, Gay Liberation Front, recognizing possibly not that they want their own sex but that open social recognition of homosexuality and encouragement of latent homosexual needs is the pivot upon which their liberation as women would turn. The same should be true for men. For they are as bound in their roles and identities as the women. For the women, the cry of lesbian from a stud male is enough apparently to wither up the most militant woman in women's liberation. The fear of the label and the prejudice behind it is not so fearsome as the realization that they are really saying they no longer wish to be the quarry in the female quest for the possession of the mother in all her forms. She then sees sexual renunciation without the traditional refuge of a nunnery. Or the psychotic ambivalence of struggling against the domination of the animal she continues to have relations with. Or that the ultimate political act would be a declaration of homosexuality.

Sexual liberation in this century in the West has until now meant the loosening of heterosexual restrictions, moralities. The fear of homosexuality is well-founded. It is the absolute challenge to every facet of the social structures as they continue to exist in defiance of our sexually polymorphic and hermaphroditic natures, and in support of the heterosexual institution. As a challenge, in any case, it is doomed. Any bid for power to achieve the sexual latitude of the successful male in the quest for the same object would be suicide. In the Gay Liberation Front the men and women are working together to liberate men for men and women for women. Clearly the female project of partial or total renunciation of the male, for greater autonomy and expression of her own needs for the mother, depends for its outcome upon the active and declared renunciation of the female by a portion of the male population at last convincing enough to clarify our multiple sexualities and shatter the institutional myth of the one institutionalized possibility. The first order of business in this movement resembles the black program at its initial psychological stages. Black is beautiful. Gay is great. Etc. Affirmation of identity. After that I part company. For I see this affirmation as the first and final order of business. Militant tactics provoke militant repressions. And political concessions under pressure don't alter the fundamental psychology of resistance. The issue is acceptance. Sexual latitude in all its forms. Waged as a power struggle to wrest some control over the sex objects they feel deprived of the movement is doomed. There is militance enough in the affirmation and celebration of a sexuality that would undermine and topple the institutions it seeks recognition from. Angry aggression is not a proper means to an end envisioned in any way as a cessation of the very sex-politico-property games of a warfare society which they have felt oppressed by in the first place.

DANCE JOURNAL

Village Voice, September 24, 1970

If the situation is hopeless we have nothing to worry about. I should say who said that possibly but I just told a Viennese artist recently I don't suck cock any more although I did very little of that even in my life as a critic unconsciously I supported my own sex for the better whole. Still, I never actually realized that dancing is the only organized cultural institution in which women are preeminent; nor that the reason for this is rooted in attitudes toward the dance as a frivolous entertainment in which a lady is encouraged to exhibit her charms, her grace and deportment, her bodily attributes, her seductive powers, in the formally sanctioned theatre of a man's license for approved general voyeurism. The maître de ballet, the master of old who ruled the situation by his choreography and direction, still obtains in the contemporary dance theatre notwithstanding the recognized accomplishments of Graham and Humphrey and Holm and Wigman or the younger Rainer and Monk and Tharp in developing that aspect of the art which by intellectual authority gives the body a reinvented frame within which to perform and justify its continuation as a body exhibiting more than its crude appeal to sex. The singing virtuosic body. Considering the male dominion in matters of finance and organization and criticism and choreography and even areas of the virtuosic performance itself I wonder at my judgment of female preeminence in the field. Yet Graham is equally honored with Balanchine. Pavlova with Nijinsky. Fonteyn with Nureyev. St. Denis with Shawn. De Mille with Robbins. Etc. Which is more than can be said for the leadership in any other cultural institution; and I have an unstatistical feeling about a matriarchy in dance based probably on my own entry into it through the legend of Isadora and Loïe Fuller and even St. Denis whom I never saw and who meant more to me than her partner Shawn. Then too, in the '40s Balanchine was still a Russian immigrant and Cunningham was unheard of and Limón was still a student of Humphrey's and Nijinsky was insane and the men were still trying to convince somebody that dancing could be as masculine as basketball. I entered in the '50s when you were doing well to obtain a ticket for a last row seat in the top balcony at Carnegie Hall to watch Graham do a solo number before the most prestigious symphony orchestra in the world. Or be able to congratulate Humphrey after a new uproarious standing ovation for her latest choreographic efforts. Or win a place at an audition for Holm's "My Fair Lady." Or go to Germany to study in Wigman's post war reconstituted school. Or in other words become a part in any significant way of the matriarchal dance world. I went to Limón only because he was the husband of a Pauline who was a friend of another Pauline who was my lover and he was under the artistic direction of Humphrey who was my heroine who was restricted by her crippling arthritis just to teaching courses in choreography (which I took) and because I was unable to spring my crotch for the demon dragon mother Martha. At Limón's you had to be a Venus or a Helen to survive the attention lavished on any male student from the sticks who could raise a deformed leg five inches off the floor. Since I wasn't a Venus or a Helen my strategy was to be a Valkyrie and consign the men to their graves by leaping higher and consuming more space faster, but I didn't survive anyway. Limón was pressing forward the earlier fraternal projects of Shawn and Weidman and was probably happiest when he and his boys exclusively performed his Judas and Christ work "The Traitor." Limón himself was projected into his eminence by the female support of his manager wife Pauline and of Humphrey who had withdrawn support from her original partner Weidman and whose protagonists in her dance works increasingly assumed the form of her male model protege Limón. The days of the '30s and early '40s when she herself danced and figured as the heroine in such works as "The Shakers" were over. The hegemony of women I had sensed on entering the arena was quietly and invisibly shifting toward a more male dominated scene as Graham fell apart and Humphrey aligned herself with Limón and Holm seemed permanently captive of musical comedy and Tamiris had faded out and bemoantimes Cunningham (and Waring too) appeared as the new outraged and Balanchine became a successful institution through the efforts of Kirstein and Robbins became popular and Tudor and Ashton were recognized as geniuses from England and so forth. A final blow was the introduction of another Englishman to be our most powerful critic—overlooking the gentler more androgynous thinking feeling American (male) they already had as well as one of our own outstanding female scholars and observers in the field. The Englishman they got is the type of heterosexual who has little respect for women. Prior to him our male critics had been bisexually oriented. The heterosexual man who is not offended by his own homosexual inclinations. The homosexual man who naturally sucks cock but who can also appreciate the woman at her idealized aesthetic distance as in any case the body upon which so much of the technique and choreography of stage dancing is modeled. Still, my present unstatistical feeling about a scene I am no longer directly involved in is that the women are preeminent if not equal to men in the world of dancing. The financial poverty of the female dancer choreographer is proof of the permission she is granted to be eminent in a field considered to be relatively harmless in the social scheme of profit and power through tangible property. Choreography is property in the most minimal abstracted sense. The body is property only on the premises of her husband. The female as painter and sculptor is everywhere discouraged and excluded. The female gallery owners suck cock. Likewise the female art critics. And the successful female artist has become so by doing same if not independently wealthy. Also: the female will be encouraged and supported in whatever medium her exposure as body is most directly facilitated: i.e., dancing, acting. Writing too, as a form more explicit than music or painting, the latter medium in its erotic exposures traditionally arrogated to the male artist who enjoys a captive female model in the studio for such pleasures as he then sells to his patrons to continue this type of voyeurism for himself and his patrons. The female innovators in choreography in this century have always by correct instinct initially in their inventions denied or strictly curtailed the erotic seductive aspect of their medium. Thus begging or demanding a serious appraisal of the work. Attention to the invention. The body as medium for the invention. Not as the object itself. Many a choreographer has succumbed to the tacit requirement to be seductive. The still low regard for theatre dancing generally is the feeble recognition of the intellectual rigorousness by which the form has any status at all beyond its operatic splendors or its music hall titillations. Isadora was not a great choreographer but a fine dancer with an eccentric personality and a scandalous love life. She sucked cock all over the world in order to buy the opportunity to be a free lady—a life that could in those times only be supported by ever wilder and wilder excesses of exhibition for which she paid heavily in distress and suicides. She was beautiful and courageous and the nature of her work remains of little interest to a continually curious public. Only her life. It seems to me remarkable actually that the raw exhibitionism of the dance was transcended in this century in this country at all by a serious choreography developed out of a determined academic approach to a defunct medium. But our American women who got it all going were no kitchen molls or vaudeville floozies. They were the daughters of the sons and daughters of our straight-laced Victorian puritans. Well read and virtuous and accomplished and ambitious, they sought to make a medium that was immediately open to the female for all the sex objective reasons (and closed to some for the same reasons) highly respectable by application of male (role defined) standards of intellect and aggressive adventurousness. As a critic naturally I was not immune to the charms of my sisters and mothers but it was the formal choreographic aspect of the work which commanded me, like them, consistently, in our conscious or unconscious collective project to do and be what the women's movement is broadcasting as essential on a big scale. The ironies of female preeminence in the dance has occurred to a lot of people. I don't know if it has. Probably I am through being interested in it having explored a few of my own ideas about it. Then anyway in all cases if the situation is hopeless we have nothing to worry about.

Reviews

On Criticism/ On Watching

CUNNINGHAM IN CONNECTICUT

Village Voice, September 7, 1961

The annual Dance Festival at New London this year (August 17–20) employed eight choreographers, four older, four younger, and the warring camps remain as decisive as ever in their convictions as to who is really it and who isn't, but that's what camps do. For myself, Merce Cunningham, his dances and dancers, are greater than ever—like aging wine they taste better every year—and I consider myself fortunate to be a spectator in this era of a dancer-choreographer with the genius, integrity, breadth (all those words) to keep alive, in touch and to be making always experiences which ask no more of the observer than a desire to see.

NOT EASY TO SEE

It is not easy to see. Outside the theatre, living as we do, most of us see very little with our eyes wide open. In action the eye absorbs space forms to function; in repose the eye becomes a facial decoration as sight turns inward. And our training is such that when we do look for non-functional reasons, it is usually at something huge and spectacular, like cathedrals or sunsets. And even then it is rare to see more than a general outline. Or to see more and still *enter*. That is the crucial transition, from seeing to entering. Not only crucial but mysterious, so I won't say any more except to note that I think most people who go to dance concerts don't see very well, not even dancers, sometimes dancers especially, and most often the critics, who must attend special classes in becoming blind.

Mr. Cunningham presented a new dance, "Aeon," almost 50 minutes long, to a score by John Cage and with décor by Robert Rauschenberg. "Aeon" is a dance of great scale. It moves through so much, in range of quality, physical force, the human condition, that the whole thing is staggering to think of in retrospect. Human events: the activity of dancers on a proscenium stage. Other human events: the ways people communicate with each other, or speak for themselves. Exterior events: explosions, clouds, lights, a machine, sounds. And always the dancing, the superb dancing. The stillness too, which is never a mere choreographic stop, but an act of undaunted containment, of simple yet magnificent composure, of not-being which is the essence of being. A complete act, not a choreographic or dramatic transition. Yet Cunningham the choreographer is a man who certainly knows what to do next. It is downright satisfying to participate in a sweep of tremendous agitation, like the sequence near the beginning of "Aeon" of high jumps and falls—the whole company moving off stage right as they jump and fall, the arms and head also involved in side-to-side movements, the bodies heaving up and down in counter rhythms—which leaves just Cunningham on stage standing, looking at one fallen girl in a silent aftermath.

Cunningham's own range in this dance is fantastic. Not only those typical sudden shifts from motion to stillness, but the subtle gradations of energy (I have a vivid recollection of an "incident" originating as a vibration in the thighs, transferred to the stomach, traveling upward to the arms and shoulders and exploding like a geyser at the top); not to mention all the complicated coordinations, and the wordless drama that every movement event secretes.

Cunningham is a great dancer, and you know it not by his technical range and command alone; you feel it in the whole man, the whole man is in it every time. You may see a procession of selves and the man never makes a move not true to himself.

The Cunningham style of composition has exerted its influence, with some interesting results, but none so interesting as a dance on the Festival by Ruth Currier titled "Resonances." Miss Currier evidently decided to solve her "problem" (a tragedy involving four people—it is impossible to follow these plots without explicit program notes) with two solutions: the first in the grief-stricken velvet-and-gown style; the second, I take it, in a Currier version of Cunningham—leotard, tights, Non-Objective. This curious imitation revealed a long miscalculating attitude of many artists toward Cunningham's work, that his dances are de-humanized, de-personalized, abstract, non-objective if you will. Take the red blood of a living style and inject it with pure doses of Idea. Result: poison, disease, a de-humanized abstraction. What a buckling irony!

Anna Sokolow's kind of expressionism is direct, immediate, and, in a dance like "Dreams," hypnotic. Miss Sokolow doesn't pull any punches. The tension is right there, bam, raw, undistilled. I think you feel it that way for two reasons. Once she draws out a movement image she pulls every bit of juice out of it—through hypnotic repetitions and intense performance. Second, the image itself is usually a primordial product; it has a kinesthetic power corresponding to deep springs of tension—the self-preservative emotions of attraction and repulsion. (I am reminded of T. S. Eliot's Objective Correlative for poetry.) Miss Sokolow makes a high concentrate of one image, dwells on it, makes it go, sometimes propels it into an orgasmic release. The hypnotic effect breaks down only when the choreographer is too impressed with an image to let it go.

UNTITLED (RESPONSE TO ALLAN KAPROW)

Village Voice, July 26, 1962

Not too long ago I received a letter from Allan Kaprow concerning his "happening" at the Maidman Playhouse on March 22 and my review of it in the March 29 issue of The Voice. He complains that I am "beginning to join with many in denouncing 'meaning' in art and favoring 'no-meaning,' or purely-existent-situations-for-themselves." And further, that my interpretation of his happening was completely off-base because I had called it a fertility rite, whereas in reality it was a "service for the dead (composed in memoriam for a friend)." I had no idea there were many who were denouncing meaning in art and favoring no-meaning, but I think the problem, if there is one, is of general interest, so I sketched the following poem, mostly questions—with regards to John Cage and Edith Copley.

How does one go about denouncing meaning?
How does one go about denouncing the effect anything might have on you?
On Monday a Mondrian might look to me like rectangles, lines, and colors.
On Tuesday a Mondrian might remind me of boards and fences, or a clear day in the country.

On Wednesday my children won't let me look at anything.
Thursday I'm ill.
Friday we make castles in the sandbox and so life goes on.

What do you mean by meaning?
Are not all things existent-situations-for-themselves?
Isn't everything a subject matter?
What is the meaning of a subject matter?
What does a moon mean?
Does it mean the same thing to you and me? One thing to you and another thing to me? Different things to you and me on different days and nights?
What does it mean to a rabbit? a tree?

Should we talk about signs and symbols?
Let's not.

When does something mean itself or something else? Can it mean both? Can it mean itself when the something else is not known? If the something else is not known does it still exist for itself? Does it require that something else in order to exist for itself?

Who decides what a thing should mean? If you decide that a thing means itself or something else or both will I agree with you? If I don't does it still mean what you decided it should mean? If I do does it mean that somebody else is foolish if he doesn't? If many people agree does that make them happy together?

The last time I saw Paris it looked green.

I like my hot dogs with mustard, no relish.

War is basically a semantic problem.

And I don't understand peace either.

Concerning Art, I like it quick with sauce, or over and well done, any old way actually and I don't usually care much what it's all about but I care very much how it's done and if I like the way it's done I'll care what it's all about.

As for the meaning of meaning and related subjects I refer any body to the catalogue under A (esthetics) in the New York Public Library.

(P.S., to Mr. Kaprow: Dear Allan Kaprow, Apologies for confusing a fertility rite with a service for the dead. I have a small suggestion. Next time you have something definite in mind provide an advance program note; or ask the school children (who were there you said and knew what it was all about) to enlighten the adults. I think school children are smarter than adults. They know when a thing is dead or alive.)

WARING—RAINER

Village Voice, May 6, 1965

On St. Patrick's Day I tried to get from 53rd Street to 57th Street on Fifth Avenue, and I had to go through two buildings (between Fifth and Sixth Avenues) because of police barricades, but on my way back I looked at the parade and waited for some bagpipers, who did come, and I walked one block with them, then ran back to the subway entrance on 53rd Street in order to retain the sound of bagpipes and avoid watching a group of nurses or old veterans or something; thus thinking for the nth time how nice it is not to go to a parade (not knowing about these holidays in advance) but to hear the commotion a block away, and to ask somebody what the holiday is, then look at it for a minute and go away happy about parades.

I don't care for subways much, but upon entering a car I often glance around fast at the people in my half of the car to position myself with respect to whoever I think will best sustain my interest for the duration of stops.

I suppose that most people who put themselves out to go to the theater, especially if they pay for it, expect to be entertained. A lot might be said about the personal nature of entertainment. Naturally I can only speak for myself; at the same time anyone can see that certain things elicit general approval and others reduce the majority to boredom and/or other unfavorable conditions. The responses are often clear and simple. The expectations that create the responses are vastly complex from any cultural point of view. The responses themselves, speaking individually, can be just as complex in their subtle gradations according to how the various appetites (from person to person and within one person) are appeased or frustrated.

TWO SIDES

Recently James Waring gave his concert of the year at Judson Memorial Church. As an entertainer Waring has two sides. He always presents at least one "serious" work and this in a style crystallized over the past few years, notably since "Peripateia" of 1960. By that time I think Waring, who has been a choreographer since 1946 and created some 50-odd dances, had assimilated what he liked about ballet and Cunningham, and he combined these influences with his own idiosyncrasies to project the abstract ensemble of a certain breadth and dignity. The movement is often right out of a ballet studio, or it looks like ballet via Cunningham (meaning whatever there is about Cunningham that is in the turned-out, attenuated classical tradition, minus the virtuosic orientation and the enchaînements of steps that constitute the balletic phraseology). The space is often the Cunningham space of decentralized activity (i.e., the dancers holding an independent course such that the values are equalized). And the gestural details are the poetic absurdities of Mr. Waring. They are his personal calligraphy in a field of generalized movement quickly identified by Western tradition. The gestures may be tenderly lyrical, as in a duet from the new "Three Symphonies" (I recall specifically a passage in which one listens to the other's body with his head and then she listens to his with her hand, etc.), but more typically they are a pantomimic charade of a deftly brittle quality with satiric overtones.

FANCY STYLES

Lifted from the context of this "serious" and abstract works, these charades become the focal attraction of Waring's other side, his everlasting humor, which I first saw in "Dances Before the Wall" ('58), and later at his campiest in "Extravaganza" ('59), then on a large scale in "At the Hallelujah Gardens" ('63)—a dance over an hour long), and most recently in a massive dance of 10 comic episodes called "Musical Moments," dedicated to Gracie Allen. I like Waring's wit at its subtlest and most intimate, when I'm amused by a series of incongruities that I only vaguely comprehend from any realistic vantage point. "Musical Moments" contained this aspect of his humor, but it also extended into a broader realm of theatrical entertainment utilizing the props and fancy costumes and styles of old film, song, popular dance, that intrigue Waring as material for adroit showmanship. Whatever Waring absorbs, he becomes the instrument of his own ingenious invention. For that reason I think he is a brilliant eclectic artist, never interested in paring influences to create the single indelible image associated with artists internally obsessed.

From the earlier days of his intimate quasi-narrative dances, and what he says Louis Horst called his "shuffling and huggling" period, and what I would call his underground camp appeal (to name three aspects of his work), Waring has moved into an arena of popular attraction beyond which I can only imagine more funds to support the kind of fantastic and spectacular endeavor that an institution like the New York City Ballet should be happy to inject into their repertory. For myself, a Waring production at Lincoln Center would make the trip uptown a more alluring prospect. From a downtown contemporary point of view (my personal downtown view), his work doesn't interest me too much right now.

PEOPLE AND MATTRESSES

From any Waring standpoint Yvonne Rainer's new work for 10 people and 10 mattresses (presented at Judson on a concert shared with Robert Morris) called "Parts of Some Sextets" must have been a striking bore. The piece consisted of 43 minutes of dancing and 59 minutes of sound, which was a tape recording of Rainer reading excerpts from a diary of daily observations (1780–1819) by one Reverend William Bentley. The only break in this interminable drone of dry facts occurs about one-fourth of the way through, when Rainer opens into a beautiful chant of nameless origin. Except for this brief interlude, the tape functions as "furniture" music: aural background that fills our lives like interior decoration and asserts no special claim to interest. In this case I thought the furniture was too obtrusive. I wished the volume was lower so I could tune in when I felt like it and not be irritated by the sound of it when I didn't want to hear the sense of it.

The dance itself has a curious slack in its structure. Dynamically, the action levels off after about 15 minutes and slides into a steady low key with an occasional thrust that doesn't matter once the audience succumbs to the repetition of material at a seemingly uneventful pace. I saw the work four times (twice in New York and twice in Hartford, where it was premiered as a commissioned work by the Wadsworth Atheneum Museum), and the audience never failed to settle into a pall by the 30-minute mark if not sooner.

TIME CHART

In making the dance Rainer decided upon 32 movement possibilities and set them down intuitively within the spaces of a time chart, each space representing a 30-second interval. If more than one activity came up for an interval, she would decide who would do what and so on. The movement consisted of simple and complex dance phrases and action that any healthy, or in certain cases sickly, individual could manage. One action was to lie down for a spell on a mattress. Another was to bend over and put a piece of paper or other light object on the back. Another was to be shoveled along on the hands and forearms of several other performers who would line up, hands palm up at waist height, to facilitate this worm-like progress until a pile of mattresses terminated the journey. More strenuous, athletic activity included running and walk-racing and things with the mattresses that kids might think of if they were in a room with a pile of them: squirming through them, flying leaps onto them, surrounding them and pulling in different directions in a kind of tug of war, etc. These were a few of the 32 possibilities, and the audience saw them over and over again in various group and spatial combinations.

Dance and tape together, the work is a tour de force of factual information. The dance is tough and pure and unrelenting in its constant reiteration of material. At some point the success of the dance considered from any norm of desire for the maintenance of tension within a certain time span (How much of what? And how long?) was out of the question. Just so the tape. How long would you listen to the Reverend Bentley's pedestrian observations before you flaked out or began to daydream or excused yourself or told the good man to take a powder? On the other hand, why not, and why not look at the interior decoration which is a polka-dot expanse outside important trips from bed to icebox? Existentially, why not anything? Nothing matters, not too much anyway, because everything matters, equally. I can tell you how and when my bed or icebox is more important to me than my wallpaper, and I can tell you how I might love my wallpaper if it were better looking, and I can imagine how important wallpaper must be to those who manufacture it, and I could go on and on about the personal nature of entertainment, but I'll agree with anybody who tells me that the diary of an obscure minister is just as momentous as the diary of another obscure minister. However, to continue along personal lines, I assume that any artist who takes the trouble it takes to assemble a work for presentation wants to please an audience. It is difficult enough to please people on a daily improvised basis. Always the question is: how far can you go in pleasing yourself when your own pleasure is in any way dependent upon the pleasure of somebody else? For the vanguard artist this is no simple question. I have no clear idea myself, as I've circuitously suggested. But I have a couple of specific ideas about "Parts of Some Sextets."

The action in the dance had that straightforward punch and clarity that those who have been pleased by Rainer have come to associate with her work.

Also there was plenty of variety in the action. Also... etc. But finally I think the material was strangled by a static time structure. The repetition of the action was beside the point (the device is quite familiar in any case and has its own integrity and purpose), and so was the dynamic slack into a low key that I mentioned above. The problem was that the performers were bound hand and foot by the cue system of responses to the tape at 30-second intervals. Thus everything began to look and feel like it was happening in a large experimental cage for conditioned responses of some sort. There is something even slightly grotesque about playground activity subjected to signal commands at regular intervals. The audience should not be conscious of these cue-responses. I only know because I asked, and I'm using the information to suggest a possible reason for the suffocation of excellent material. One of Rainer's fortes has been the excitement she can generate by the "spontaneous determination" of set material. The sleep-love duet she made and did with Robert Morris was a closed and set dance all the way round, and the structure was suitably tight. The new work projects an uncomfortable contradiction. It is delightfully open and sprawling, but it's like telling your kids to go and have a great time in the backyard and standing at the window with a whistle to regulate the possibilities. If Rainer had decided to use the tape simply for its "furniture" value and had not depended upon it as well for her sequence-cues, she might have applied another sequential device more appropriate to the kind of action that seems to require the elbow room finally provided at the end of the dance when Robert Morris and Lucinda Childs did a "rope" duet in which they spontaneously determined where and in what order they would perform their set movement possibilities. The rule-games incorporated in the structure of "Terrain" (1963) similarly functioned as agents of freedom in a work also containing "real" play and also committed to the reiteration of set material. "Parts of Some Sextets" was an ambitious and impressive work with a structural flaw that might be construed as a daring assault on the tolerance-attention of any audience.

HELLO YOUNG LOVERS

Village Voice, September 19, 1968

Thursday, September 5, 1968, 7 p.m., go to the Delacorte Theatre in Central Park to see the Harkness Youth Company and Rod Rodgers and Richard Kuch and Lotte Goslar. It's windy. The sky is overcast. I see big possibilities here with the lake water beyond the stage and a piece of city panorama beyond that. But then we're all stashed up tight among the dance enthusiasts. The trees outside the amphitheater are incidental. They want our attention for what we agreed to come for. That's fair I guess. It's chilly so I'm snuggling into my seat and trying to overhear three fags behind me talking about what they had for dessert. You have to prime yourself for these things. When the business on stage begins I'm craning around admiring the flags of all nations or all festivals blowing about from positions ringing the outer limits of the theatre. Now I'm admiring five barechested sleek huskies doing a Spartan routine based on karate exercises. They're very serious about it. Mostly I'm conscious of the pretty torsos. The head of one boy lolls about more relaxed than the others so I'm thinking he might be the best one to go home with after the show. Next there are three routines based on swimming, skiing, and tennis. In the *entrée* for the first, two couples make like swimming, in bathing suits too, through some gauze of chiffon stretched from wing to wing upstage and undulating in the breeze. I suppose people are aware of the lake somewhat reflected by city lights behind the swimmers. But this is very unusual swimming fare. When the skiers come on I'm still thinking amphibiously. Now I have to adjust to a slope-and-snow situation. Next a tennis situation. This is a stage for all seasons. It's nice to be everyplace at once without being there or waiting for the seasonal cycles.

The audience apparently likes its sports spiced with its flirtations. Sports be damned. The love game is out in front. Cute teen-age stuff. They could be auditioning for *The Ed Sullivan Show*. Especially since the dance people are showing us how integrated they are. I don't think the Black Power people would appreciate this at all. That black boy in the trio tennis game is already looking lighter than he is. He seems to be enjoying it too. I'm interested to see who'll get who, forgetting momentarily they'll have to end up the happy trio they started out to be. Clearly the two boys want to screw the girl in any case. She seems to be up to it. They're all healthy. Jesus what are they thinking about. At one point I'm rooting for the black boy, imagining he might be deprived of his innings when the white boy is jealously guarding his catch, leaving his competition to display nothing better than his splendid technique. I detect a bit of prejudice here. The white boy takes his turn, after all, for exhibiting his special tricks, but at that moment the black boy isn't as close to the girl as the white boy was when the black boy was doing his stuff. This is interesting sociology. Clearly the next step in trios is to have a black boy and a black boy, or a white boy and a black girl and a black girl, etc. It's very confusing.

The next sequence, the skating act, looks much safer. Lots of people. More possibilities in a crowd. I think skating is sexier on ice since the velocity is greater. Ballet might be the bastard child of skating. They say the skaters imitate the ballet dancers although it's obviously the other way around. But perhaps the skating profession could improve its costuming. I never saw a male skater in those almost transparent white tights so well made by the ballet designers. The white jock straps are nice too. White on white is always a pleasant surprise. I know the three guys behind me are digging that. Also, there's an outstanding trick in this number, as good as anything I've seen on ice. This fellow spins around in the air and at the same time his legs are going through some extraordinary pretzel mutations. I like that a lot. I never see the girls in these situations. Or else I wonder why they don't have any tits. My theory is that they have to be as toplight as possible to sustain their weight on the toes of one foot, which they do so often. They get rid of the extra baggage in school or maybe in a special place for that sort of sacrifice. It goes down into the calf muscle or something. Parts are shifted about to do the job. Dedicated kids. In the finale one chick loses her white hat too. They take everything in stride.

Well, I'm really involved in this performance. I've almost forgotten the trees and flags. The mopping up of the floor between the acts is especially interesting. They keep the lights dim for that. Not so dim you can't make out how the moppers are as integrated as the dancers. I'm getting color blind from all this integration. I like my black black and my white white. If they integrated the stop lights we'd be in trouble. Still, it's nice to see people getting along well together. One number on this program is all white and they don't get along together at all. The four of them are really angry about something. It's called "The Brood" and the choreographer is Richard Kuch. I never saw such an unhappy crew. The audience loves it. There's an old lady in it, and a young girl, and two strapping fellows. They're made up ugly as sin. A two-wheeled cart which belongs to the old lady is also quite involved in it, whatever it is. Sorry I can't transcribe the plot. I think it's about the end of the world. A real disaster. They're terribly mean to each other. One of the boys even seems to be raping the old lady. Anyhow he's sucking on one of her nipples. And she doesn't like that a bit. Obviously nobody's gonna be satisfied here so I concentrate on the lit-up top of a building off in the distance around Park Avenue. There're psychedelic possibilities wherever you go. The last thing I see, they've got the old lady slumped on a wheel of the overturned cart. I'm sure that's the end. It is. The audience applauds wildly and I recover during the intermission on a box of popcorn and other oral satisfaction available at the stand outside the theatre.

The next is a relief. A Black Swan or Aurora or what pas de dukes. The guy is a real queen. He's wearing a little pastel green skirt that almost covers his ass and a cross-torso sash to match. His hair is orange or straw yellow. He's strong too. The showstopper is a lift where he carries the girl off on one hand stretched straight overhead on a rigid arm. She loves it. They sprang right out of the head of Zeus, these two, or maybe a UFO, which has recently been identified as swamp gas. This is what all of us slobs could be like if we just tried harder. At the curtain call the girl gives her green Samson a pink flower out of the bouquet delivered by an integrated stagehand. This is going too far. We're being infiltrated. Or else it's a regression. They have to keep reminding us of our past. Really if the dancers are white the stagehand flower boy should be very white or at least computerized.

Never mind. They come into their own again in the final number. Lotte Goslar and Company. This is what I came for. I've heard she's very funny. She is. She's a riot. She's a stocky little middle-aged lady with a face of great putty mobility who could be anybody's peasant immigrant mother verging on the ridiculous. It seems I spent an evening with her last spring in the presence of mutual friends and I didn't know who she was and she didn't mention it either. In fact she didn't say anything at all. She got lost in the wallpaper. She must be a delightful friend to people. Maybe she saves it all up for her art.

They do about 12 short numbers under the general title, "Clowns and Other Fools." Situation comedy. Lotte is most of the show. She even steals it standing stock-still as a "mushroom" in a scene involving the classical prince looking for his classical maiden in the classical forest assisted by classical hunters. One scene is Lotte enacting the life of a flower on a green mat, and in another solo she enacts the life of her grandmother as a lady who "danced her way through life" from cradle to heaven. I guess my favorite is the dancing lesson where a gorgeous siren of a girl tries to teach a recalcitrant Lotte the elements of grace and deportment. She's really a brilliant mime. It's clearly in the dance-mime tradition peculiarly American in the sense that Charles Weidman was at one time a famous practitioner of it and he came from Nebraska. Charles put the European mime tradition together with the American modern dance tradition (which he was helping to create) for a curious hybrid at once Charles and nobody else. Later, Katherine Litz, who emerged from the Weidman-Humphrey company, did her version of it: a somewhat nostalgic female humor, exquisitely subtle and delicate with shades of meaning impossible to catch and define. Lotte Goslar's humor is unabashedly theatrical. The comedy is often out in front with a slap-dash extroversion nobody can miss; but she's subtle as well, and a slow-motion film of a gamut of her expressions and gestures in just a short sequence would reveal a lifetime of arduous labor to accomplish what they call the mastery of a craft. Also, she has a keen grasp of sex types. She's got 'em all mixed up. A queen is a queen is a boy is a girl is a ballerina is a boy is a dyke is a fag is a butch is a boy is a girl is just a kinky son of a gun like the rest of us. Hello all you sexes. We're too good to be true.

Description

BRUCE CONNER

ARTnews, November 1961

Bruce Conner (Alan) is represented in the current Museum of Modern Art "Assemblage" exhibition. A conventional gallery or museum is a poor place to show Conner's work. Of course the best thing would be a "haunted" ancestral mansion shrouded in black bent trees dripping with Spanish moss. In such a setting nobody would be very surprised to stumble on a huge black box affair (a kind of closet) decorated with cheap beads and black gauze, or stretched and torn nylon, containing a partially visible mannikin-mummy sprouting a scared bird out of one breast. Or the sculptured child slumped on a high-chair, embalmed in tattered stocking. These old desecrated stockings are Conner's trademark. They bind, smother, strangle, decorate, and connect with a chaotically perfumed past, a past to commemorate with monuments of death, a past to exorcise by making a grotesque laughing stock of possibly once cherished mementos from a further past of foolish illusory finery. Conner is lively with diabolical schemes. The question is, how dead can he get?

CLAES OLDENBURG

ARTnews, January 1962

Claes Oldenburg rented a store on East Second Street which he plans to use as a studio and a place of exhibition. He calls it the Ray Gun Mfg. Co., and his first exhibition was a "store" containing at least eighty-five stock items. He says that when the children get out of school they walk by and look in, but if he approaches the door they run away. They might not run so fast if the window display included some of those cakes and pies, like the piece of yellow cake with white icing and strawberries reposing on a plate on a chair. (This reviewer's daughter could not grasp the significance of good food lying around that was not to eat.) The store has no significance. It really is a store and you can buy things (prices quoted below) and take them home. But there is one difference between this and other stores. If you take an item home and don't throw it away, it retains the status it had in Oldenburg's "store": an object you put someplace, to look at or fill up space or to fit with something else. But some other stores sell items for just that purpose, too. It's hard to think of a good difference. Anyway, Oldenburg's store is an environment of glossy chunks and slabs—suspended, scattered, sitting—of anything from shoes, hats and dresses to brides, cakes and sardines that you move in, around, under and see from any perspective. Oldenburg made the big shapes by covering chicken wire with plaster and painting the plaster with dripping smooth enamel so that the colors dance and bounce around like oil and sun on a hot tin roof. A gay indigestible bazaar. And quite real: no significance, an everyday affair.

DEMOCRACY

Village Voice, August 23, 1962

It was a democratic evening of dance at Judson Memorial Church on July 6. There were 14 choreographers and 17 performers. There should have been something for everybody, including a nap if desired; and in fact there was so much that special moments arose as expected and at least three dances provoked a big response from everybody.

I liked Fred Herko's "Once or Twice a Week I Put on Sneakers to Go Uptown." Herko did a barefoot Suzie-Q in a tassel-veil head-dress, moving around the big open performing area (no stage at the church) in a semi-circle, doing only the barefoot Suzie-Q with sometimes a lazy arm snaking up and collapsing down.

BUSINESS AT HAND

John Herbert McDowell is a composer. He has no dance training. He made a dance called "February Fun at Bucharest." Having no tics or tensions arising from a training and having an inordinate sense of fun, McDowell distinguishes himself as a "natural"—not a natural dancer (although you could think of it that way if you're not too set in your idea of what dancing is); I mean a natural person going about the business at hand, which in this case consisted of a few zany actions performed in a red sock and a yellow sweater.

Ruth Emerson is a tall, imposing woman who makes simple, direct, clean movement and occasionally ruins it with a gesture that doesn't look like hers. If the gesture turns up by chance it must be a problem to internalize it. Chance procedures (which predominated in this program) are useful in many ways and usually produce novel results, but in the end the only thing that matters is who is doing what. Chance procedures are preliminary controls; the chance results are subjected to the control of performance, and that means you always end up with a person expressing himself. Movement is not like sound in that respect. Movement is the person. The material and the person are One.

David Gordon, for instance. For my free time David Gordon did two extraordinary dances on that program. He did some movement nobody ever saw before. Like the body bent off center, the head awkwardly strained back, the elbows squeezed into the ribs at the flattened hands and forearms made the painful beauty of spastic helplessness. As though the body were straining, yelling, against an involuntary violence. Molloy and Malone should be so lucky.

AFTER THE DROUGHT

William Davis came up with dance No. 13, "Crayon," to some jazz: Dee Clark, the Shells, and the audience went crazy for a minute because of the dry spell that came before. I think the audience was glad enough to see Davis, too. He's a finely proportioned dancer who performs with quiet, clean, unassuming strength. And the dance was a good one. I only wish he had let loose, just once anyway.

Not that it mattered so much. And then Yvonne Rainer came on with "Ordinary Dance." It is an ordinary dance because it is autobiographical and Miss Rainer does a lot of talking while she moves, ordinary-type talking, telling you the facts (Hugo St. . . . oh yes I forgot to mention Gilroy the two wheel cart that moved the earth . . . 1941–1942 . . . let's see . . . uh . . . panhandle, early morning, white . . . I'm really not telling you much am I . . .). Poetry of facts. The title has its ironic aspect. The dance is out of the ordinary. Like Gordon she did some movement nobody ever saw before. I can't say any more now except to note the audience responded tumultuously and we had good reason.

Also on the program, and not discussed for reasons of space, were dances by Steve Paxton, Elaine Summers, Carol Scothorn, Gretchen MacLane, and Deborah Hay. I didn't mention that this was an important program in bringing together a number of young talents who stand apart from the past and who could make the present of modern dance more exciting than it's been for twenty years (except for an individual here and there who always makes it regardless of the general inertia). Almost all these dancers and choreographers were in Robert Dunn's composition class at the Living Theatre.

THE ROYAL BALLET

Village Voice, May 2, 1963

"The Two Pigeons" is a new ballet, an allegory in two acts and three scenes based on the Fable by La Fontaine, choreographed by Frederick Ashton, and with music by André Messager. The Young Man (Alexander Grant) and his Young Girl (Lynn Seymour) are working out their problems in a "studio in Paris" assisted by a group of eight girl friends who flutter down the stairs in the studio after it becomes apparent that the young man is dissatisfied with the young girl's posing (he's a painter) and her subsequent attempts to humor him with kisses and tickles. He sulks around the studio while the girls flutter up the atmosphere and until Miss Seymour introduces the "pigeon" movements of the ballet—elbow flapping, knee prancing, head pecking—at which time Mr. Grant joins her in a happy pas de deux establishing their position as pigeon-people lovers, symbolically reinforced by two real white pigeons who have been released from the flies. The eight girl friends then stop fluttering and coagulate into a climax of the pigeon idea. When they finish, the plot is advanced again as the young man recalls his original mood and droops with bad humor over the chair. Thereupon a bunch of handsome gypsies pour into the studio, and the young man arises from his torpor to become infatuated with a prototype of lust in the form of Georgina Parkinson, who dances with subtle extravagance (fiery black wig and all) in her role as the 'Gypsy' Girl. Naturally Miss Seymour gets quite upset. She hangs on the young man; jostles between him and his weakness; pushes all the gypsies around; does an attractive shoo-fly solo; and engages her new competitor in a show-off duet of fast, nervous action in which the pigeon idea somehow stays intact, and the feet are important messengers of anger (the Royal feet are exquisitely trained).

PIGEON DESPAIR

The first act concludes as the young man follows the departed gypsies, mounting the stairs with a mixture of reckless abandon and traces of regret for his better half, who languishes below in romantic pigeon despair. The second act shows the Prodigal Son having a great time in the "gypsy encampment near Paris." With the girl friends and the early plot developments out of the way, the ballet becomes quite lively. The gypsy men make fancy, colorful patterns in a virile folk-stomping style, looking more masculine as a group than the boys over here. Mr. Grant and the gypsy girl display themselves with sporting fertility and wind up the orgy with proper lust as he pin-wheels her legs in a lift and circles around her with a serpentine torso to a bit of fanfare music that often emerges appropriately from this kind of confectionary score.

CHRISTIAN CYCLE

Well, so the prodigal pays for his merriment in hell. The gypsy boy takes him on, the rest join the assault (a rope is dramatically employed), and the young man is on his way back home, in front of a stockade scrim, bearing one of the white pigeons (again released from the flies), disheveled but chastened, back to Miss Seymour—who is happier to see the deserter than you might think, considering all she must have suffered. But as the fable goes

"... Three days at most will give my whim its run/
And then I shall be back to tell/
All my adventures one by one/
'Twill cheer you up, and be the greatest fun."

Actually, the choreography and performance of the reunion is rather touching, so I don't believe Mr. Ashton intended anyone to take this escapade lightly. In fact, reading between the lines (of both La Fontaine and Ashton), I see simply another enactment of the Christian cycle: apple, fall, atonement, redemption, purity—and where the devil are we after several thousand years? Would all these people get up and leave if the cycle were reversed? Or do they just go to see the Royal Ballet? I guess that's it. The story doesn't matter. It's just a game, a device to perpetuate the action. Nobody cares about those old stories any more. Or do they? Maybe the British do. They can make pretty spectacles out of them, anyway. Next time I hope the pigeons fly out over the orchestra and up into the boxes and peanut galleries. And God Save the Queen.

AGNES MARTIN

ARTnews, April 1965

Agnes Martin (Elkon; April 10–30) continues to make extraordinarily lyrical geometric paintings. She makes graphs, on paper in small ink drawings, or on canvas with pencil and/or crayon on a white Liquitex or white gesso ground, with white and off-white oil washes. The all-over rectangular schemes (evenly spaced intersecting vertical and horizontal lines) are absurdly simple—yet the result is the quiet intensity of a perfectly contained image that moves in and around itself without moving at all. The image is penetrating by virtue of its recession within a rigid format. The pencil and crayon lines are faint, and irregularly grained in their straight course. The pictures are, as the artist says, like tranquilizers. They leave you no place to go except further and further within their linear symmetry and harmony. One large canvas does something more. There are no verticals in it. The canvas is a single mass of closely spaced horizontal light red crayon lines. From a distance you can't tell what it is because the lines blend and blur to become a kind of pink suffusing mirage.

RAINER'S "MIND IS A MUSCLE"

Village Voice, June 2, 1966

Progress on a year's work. Positions, changes, settlements. In a text written for a recent issue of *Tulane Drama Review* about the inception and development of "Parts of Some Sextets," work for 12 mattresses and 10 people ('65) Yvonne Rainer said she felt she "could no longer call on the energy and hard-attack impulses that had characterized (her) work previously." Nor did she wish to "explore any further the imitations-from-life kinds of eccentric movement" also typical of earlier work. Repelled by certain entertainment values in the theatre, including I presume her own seductive exertions, Rainer made special efforts to purge her new work of the idiosyncratic (emotion-laden) gesture and dynamically varied movement—both keys to an accessible form. Easy access makes a pie-happy audience grow sleepy. Jamming avenues of expectation creates a deprivation requiring efforts to discover new routes of involvement. Rainer is very concerned with her audience and thinks among other things that people should go to see a choreographer's work the way people go to the galleries—to see an artist's current interests, precluding standard theatrical aims of endearing exhibitionism. Get off my wagon have a look at the structure. Begin with a muscle. "The Mind is a Muscle" is one way of saying the dance is about movement.

First time I saw "The Mind is a Muscle" it was a solo fragment (work in progress) performed by Rainer at R. Rauschenberg's loft as part of a little concert for Joan Miró. Next time it was a trio performed with Steve Paxton and David Gordon in January at Judson. The trio, about 10 minutes, was accompanied by sound and sight of sticks falling steadily one by one from balcony to floor, timed to begin and end with the dance. Before going to Washington, D.C., May 8th in a roller rink concert (part of Arts Festival there) the completed dance was presented for friends in the gymnasium at the church. William Davis replaced Paxton in the trio. The dance was in five parts: Trio A, Trio B (Becky Arnold, Barbara Lloyd, Peter Saul), Trio A1, Horses (ensemble), and Lecture (solo by Peter Saul). Additional accompaniment included a tape of galloping horses and the Greenbriar Boys singing "The Lament for Amelia Earhart." In Washington there were mirrors set behind the dancers and the Earhart song was eliminated. In New York at Judson May 22–24 there were no mirrors and the sticks fell with the solo at the end. Also, in final form a slide projection (by Hollis Frampton)—a treescape with antelopes—appeared in the ensemble of six with the galloping horses. In this section the dancers themselves are like a herd. They begin walking or standing still with one of the two mattresses from the previous section (Trio A1) on their heads (antelope-people in tree-mattress terrain). About three other actions, in unison, most obvious as a herd when they take off suddenly and run like mad, on somebody's cue, changing directions, following each other or whoever takes the lead (no animal out in front).

Section 2, Trio B, is a very sophisticated herd. Basic action is a springy space-consuming run, in "trained" unison, shifting directions sharply on counts like 5, 3, 5, 3, 6, 3, etc. Other movement included—dip, twist, turn, hop, a cartwheel, slow walk at the end—this section is broad, expansive, on an even-tempoed keel, with an exciting thrust and focus, notably on a diagonal bias. Dynamically too it must be said it works in dramatic juxtaposition to the opening Trio A, in which the three figures move in isolation, doing the same movement but in the space of their choice and at their own speed, such that each one is slightly behind or ahead of another. Moreover, many movement fragments, or segments, comprise a section, which is repeated, to complete the approximate 10 minutes. Much detail of movement makes a situation of varied individual performance. As a continuum of movement loaded in detail (in gesture, focus, level, direction), with a relatively uninflected surface dynamic the effect obtained is kind of a liquid "all over" mosaic. The pieces are quite distinct, the continuity is abrupt from any conventional view of organic phrasing (there are no phrases), yet the pieces articulate like well oiled joints. Sculpturally, with the slight discrepancies in speed, notwithstanding differences in performance and body structure, it's like looking at three identical works revealing three aspects of its complications (as intricate mobiles) simultaneously. Also, like certain objects, there is no "presentational" concession to the audience. The dance has no eye, doesn't look at anybody. I got this idea from noticing that the innumerable focal changes are always, with maybe one or two exceptions, up, down, side, diagonal or back, never directly at the audience, as though consciously designed to withdraw that contact which is the performer's traditional tradetool of seductive involvement. It is suggested the audience find the eye in the dance, not on the faces of performers. The face is a muscle.

Another view of Trio A appears in the final solo: the same two sequences but with some variation in speed and some virtuosic additions. With his extra technical equipment Peter Saul highlights the material by a crisply extended razor edged delivery. Same object with a chrome coating. The first version is almost languid by comparison. About the raining sticks I have no special comment except they underscored the basic intention of a superficially tedious continuum, they put the audience into a twit the first night (a man in front waved a truce flag), and I could personally take them or leave them. Which may not be beside the point. Like the mattress and diagonal section of Trio A1: Rainer, Gordon, Davis go back and forth on one diagonal from mattress to mattress (in the corners): walk, trip each other up; runs arms swaying overhead; run backward; run, lift up middle person; run, barrel-roll middle person; hike up on someone's back; roll somebody over in a mattress. Taking it or not, altogether, is one good pressure point of a stance not bent on captivity. There's no great urgency. The machinery is around to witness. In dance there is not enough of this machinery, I mean choreographers working out an artistic game from one move to the next in a climate of mutual theft. Choreography still has a lot of bells on its toes.

CANCELLED

Village Voice, November 30, 1967

Fun City is picking up. I must congratulate Elaine Sturtevant on her revival of Satie's "Relăche." It was a total success. A cancellation can't go wrong. Things are always going wrong. Absence is perfection. "Thou ceaseth to be something thou hadst done better never to become." Life is a raincheck to oblivion. If we could earn a living on cancellations we might forget ourselves when we leave the house and go straight to the sandbox. "Relache" does mean "suspension of performance." I refused to look it up in the dictionary before going to the theatre. Someone told me there would be a performance. Someone else said there wouldn't. Rumors of Elaine and Bob Rauschenberg appearing naked. Rumors of omission. A friend said he wouldn't miss what Elaine does because she comes to his things. "But you'd better look it up in the dictionary before we go, Jill." In "The Banquet Years" Shattuck says that "Relache" was scheduled on a Thursday in November of 1924 and the people found the theatre tight shut. A week later there was a performance. Both evenings were scandalous.

There was no scandal Monday night, November 20, at the School of Visual Arts. Westchester might find it disgraceful, but not the people I know, for whom scandal is a way of life. Well—a few of us in the lounge were mildly enjoying the joke and the good company. Niceties all around: "That's what you get for having a smattering of French." Or, "How long shall we stay to experience the cancellation?" We exit and appreciate the fine lettered poster pasted on the door: "Sturtevant–Relache." Two people get out of a taxi and approach the door. It's Marcel Duchamp and his wife. We have a few words. Yes there's no performance. Yes "Relache" means cancellation. Yes he appeared nude in the original production. They've kept the taxi waiting. I watch his diminutive figure retreat in the night. Beautiful. Wouldn't have missed it for anything. From Paris to New York and 43 years in between. Nothing is deleted. That which is deleted has always existed. Whatever is is constantly in deletion. Existence and deletion the same thing.

Cancellation art: demonstration of the void in the thing and the thing in the void. Also a demonstration of subjective continuity. Monuments in the mind. Easy come easy go. In Chicago a home for the elderly is being built on the site of the landmark of the garage where the St. Valentine's Day gangland massacre took place in 1929. Last Thursday, November 16, James Byars, itinerant artist of the world, paper expert, commuter to Japan, laid out a 500-foot paper man on 53rd Street between Fifth and Sixth Avenues. Fifty

St. Thomas Choir School boys stretched out flat along the edges of the man to hold him down. The head was at the Modern Museum, the crotch at the Craft Museum, the feet at the CBS Building. Flusher trucks from the Garbage Department moved in with 20,000 gallons of water. They slid and skid, confounded by a sheet of paper. It took 100 hours to make and 10 minutes to destroy. The exhibit ended at noon exactly. The Donnell Library was playing a movie: "No Reason to Stay." The half mile of paper was furnished by Gilbreth International Company which makes this dissolvable paper—a recent biochemical discovery. Spy paper. It's a sterile edible material. Spies can now eat their information. A fat man in a gray flannel suit protested the papershow by tearing up his *New York Times*. "This paper has undone me."—"Shut your mouth dame or with this paper shall I stop it." (Shakespeare)

PAXTON'S PEOPLE

Village Voice, April 4, 1968

"Like the famous tree which is uncertain if it will be heard should it fall in a forest without people there is a way of looking at things which renders them performance." That's the first line of Steve Paxton's taped lecture accompanying a piece for man, chair, and dog presented in the gymnasium of St. Peter's Episcopal Church March 22 and 24. I asked Paxton what he meant by the line and he wasn't sure but we agreed it was poetic. I've been twisting it around looking for a key to open it. "Like the famous people who were uncertain if they would be heard should they fall in a forest without trees. . . ." etc. In '63 Paxton did a concert called "Afternoon" in the forest surrounding Billy Klüver's house in New Jersey. There were six performers in the piece, or more correctly 11 since five trees were singled out to wear costumes. More correctly beyond (or within) that an indeterminate number of people, the audience, "whose shape and figure moving from place to place determined much of the timing, the forms, the ideas behind the dance." And of course the trees, all the infamous trees without costumes. Not to mention the sky, the ground, the leaves, the shrubbery. When and where does a performance take place and who are the protagonists? "I think theatre is like everything else. Any time you want theatre you just turn it on in your head."

One day I was rounding a corner with Paxton and Robert Rauschenberg. Paxton spied a truck rumbling off a bridge. He took off flying to examine I guess what he considered to be its unusual shape. I turned to Rauschenberg and said I thought it was unfashionable to get so excited about things in the street. (An affectionate joke.) Paxton brings the street into his theatre. Or puts the theatre back on the street. "Like the famous person who is uncertain if he will be heard should he fall in a forest without other people who were uncertain if people. . . ." Change that to "Like the ordinary people who were uncertain if they would be seen if Paxton didn't put them in one of his dances" and you have a more or less inaccurate idea of what transpired at the concert at St. Peter's. I mentioned the man-chair-dog dance. This is a dance for dog mostly. Paxton accommodates himself to a sweet black haired dog. Laika may not be an ordinary dog. But this is an ordinary dog dance. No tricks I mean. It's like well here's a dog and he'll do his dog thing which is just being a dog, under any street or living room conditions, and we could take it or leave it from there, the dog quality of this particular dog. Now for Paxton's people, who appear under similar conditions. "English," a revival ('63), is not the best example of this tender attitude toward the special thingness of things (not, however, invested with anything special, that is "with problems or relationships or fantastic techniques" or the like). For all its ordinary aspects it's a rather stiff formal piece and I guess I'm partial to the recent more casual explorations of the familiar. "English," for nine performers in black tights and leotards, combines movement derived from photo sources (photo scores, mostly of baseball action, interpreted by several dancers) and the pedestrian forms of walking, standing still, and pantomiming routine activities.

"The Atlantic" is a talk piece. Four people choose spots to sit close to the audience and speak in off-hand conversational style, a kind of bland domestic intimacy, about (1) the colors of any situation (Simone Whitman); (2) a personal story (Tom Gormley); (3) important movement experiences (Paxton, Deborah Hay). The voices are heard simultaneously, with pauses by one or two or more for relocation; so you hear snatches of one or the other or combined snatches or an unintelligible garble depending on your place or point of view and all that.

Returning to "English" a moment—I think when this dance was done originally the performing bodies were as a whole more like Paxton's, like the "trained" ideal type body. Maybe not, but I don't recall being impressed as now by the incredible assortment of bodies, the any old bodies of our any old lives. And here they all were in this concert in the last dance, 32 any old wonderful people in "Satisfyin' Lover" walking one after the other across the gymnasium in their any old clothes. The fat, the skinny, the medium, the slouched and slumped, the straight and tall, the bow-legged and knock-kneed, the awkward, the elegant, the coarse, the delicate, the pregnant, the virginal, the you name it, by implication every postural possibility in the postural spectrum, that's you and me in all our ordinary everyday who cares postural splendor. Like the famous ordinary people who are certain they will see and be seen whether they fall down or keep walking in a forest with or without other famous ordinary people there is a way of looking at things which renders them performance. Let us now praise famous ordinary people.

Experiments in Writing

FLUXUS FUXUS

Village Voice, July 2, 1964

Fluxus flapdoodle. Fluxus concert, 1964. Donald Duck meets the Flying Tigers. Why should anyone notice the shape of a watch at the moment of looking at the time? Should we formulate the law of the fall of a body toward a center, or the law of the ascension of a vacuum towards a periphery? The exposition became a double bloody mary. Some Fluxus experts went to the Carnegie Tavern also. Fluxus moved into the street and on to my typewriter. Polyethelene and people everywhere and some of them have all these voices, Soren Agenoux said (that). The voice of being kind to your fine feathered friends. Put your favorite sounds in a tube and see how they come out at the other end. Be kind to Your Fine Feathered Friends was never so palatable. Take a loaf of tip top bread and try constructing a staircase. What did George Maciunas mean by saying that "all other pieces have been performed whether you notice them or not"? I noticed George Maciunas enter formally (what is the name of the high round collar you see the men wearing in those old photos, sitting stiffly for posterity) with a french horn but I couldn't determine from the balcony what fell out of the horn when he bowed. Stones or marbles. They rolled. The sound of stones or marbles rolling. It might also be amusing to see the King in his finery walk down the aisle formed by his silent obedient courtiers, turn to prepare to be seated on the throne, and retch. For that to which we are accustomed, prepare to die. What could anybody expect from a french horn in a Fluxus concert at the Carnegie Recital horn, uh, hall. Horns and halls. And the orchestra seated as well known, leader, conductor, immaculate in tails, Kuniharu Akiyama, famed possibly for his interpretations of contemporary music. Silence, order in the court. Arms uplifted. The signal. The single sound. Curtain. The sound of one sound sounding. Another an historic occasion. No, it is not like the baby crying I hear now outside my window. It is exactly like a sound made in the Carnegie Recital Hall made at approximately 10 p.m. Historical as a pumpkin pie. What do my expectations have to do with rolling marbles? Consider Nam June Paik, Korean expatriate active in Europe. I knew about his violin piece. I knew he stood behind a table holding a violin in two hands and raised it so slowly overhead and at the zenith brought it down to crash and be destroyed by impact with table. That was the form I expected. But Paik might have surprised himself as well as me. The audience was already giddy from making their own music (laughter) apart from what they might have thought to be the absence of it where they had any reason to expect it from a historical setting of elegant high purpose. Already they had witnessed the wind music of five musicians watching the air from the wings blow gently some sheets of paper off their music stands. And George Brecht placing a vase of flowers (later at the Carnegie Tavern) on the grand piano. And Alison Knowles explaining her Child Art Piece which had been done in Paris and Düsseldorf but which was cancelled here to conform to the tenets of the Society for the Prevention of Cruelty to Children and replaced by Version 2: Exit in a New Suit. And Philip Corner at the piano submitting the image of himself, precise placements of hands, no sounds. And a piece for three, four stringed instruments by Congo, chimpanzee from London. So that if Paik did not want to surprise himself he might have done his work of taut concentration at the outset. A stringed instrument can cost a fortune. Everybody knows that. How much can it cost to change your mind? Paik changed his mind when his arms and violin were extended parallel to the floor. At the moment he stepped aside, spoke briefly, possibly in a white fury, and if so smashed the violin out of a present need, more present than the fulfillment of a planned action. Pure Fluxus. Did La Monte Young know he was going to burn a violin in a concert at 91st Street several years ago? Modes of destruction and positive statement. What about the excellent fad of college boys which began in Derby, England, and moved on to California where the boys organized a Piano Reduction Study Group to reduce the piano in the shortest possible time to such a state that it may be passed through an aperture of 20 cm. in diameter? The record time was 10 minutes 44.4 seconds. What is to be said about this or about the gradual erosion of a piano left to nature's design in a junkyard? One could observe and record the phenomenon in either case. Is Child Art on the stage any different from Child Art in the home? Of course it is, and Fluxus fux any notion of value attached to staying home or going to the theatre. Fluxus composers are contemporary Pataphysicians. Pataphysics is the science of particulars, the examination of laws which govern exceptions: The world is composed of exceptions, and it seems a shame to the Pataphysician to reduce the universe to unexceptional exceptions by discovering laws of the correlation of exceptions. All things being exceptions it follows that each thing is a law unto itself, thus how could there be any competition for value among things which have no meaning beyond their own particular design? There can, therefore only be indifference to value and not to the performance of a particular duty. Value resides in the performance. That is the elegant high purpose of it. Not indifference, but engagement. Fluxus composers are not pro-art or anti-art. How could they be for or against anything when the thing to do on the program is to eat the hot dogs distributed by the conductor who caught them as they flew down to the stage on a rope from the balcony? The action was also clear in Ay-O's "Rainbow Piece for Wind Orchestra" in which the conductor stabbed the bubbles made by instruments and a toy store bubble maker with his baton. Nor do I care about Fluxus one way or another. Going to Fluxus was another engagement. It was a delightful occasion. Next time I might stay home, or contemplate a hot dog at Coney Island. Meanwhile, I salute you and fux Fluxus from the 42 keys of my typewriter.

ROBERT WHITMAN

Village Voice, September 8, 1966

Robert Whitman presented a beautiful happening or theatre thing rather he would prefer maybe (to call it) in East Hampton August 27 and 28. The location was fantastic although I couldn't see it too well. It was a NIGHT TIME event. The location was fantastic. Whitman lit the place up for tripping the lights. I thought I was in a metaphorical paradise. I was. I couldn't find my seat, which was in a field. The field was full of grass and other weeds and there was also a swamp and nobody stepped on it (except the performers). But first of all (and last) I walked through an alley of paper bags glowing candles. They made a curving country path leading from the road where two guides (policemen) led the performing spectators with their flashlights, down to three enormous plexiglass sheets sprayed with copper to make them into mirrors and situated so as to form a kind of room (enclosure). I found myself in the mirrors. I thought I was a clown at a country fair, or an amusement park. I was. Distortions are a riot if it doesn't bother you. From there I watched a number of other distortions, although I didn't get it at first. This is what happened: a young dancer named Deborah Hay stood or danced, in the room between the mirrors; actually she imitated (she told me) the kinds of distortions these mirrors make—by shifting her weight slowly from foot to foot and making other subtle gestures with her head, hands, shoulders, etc., and at some moment she was reflected in herself by a young man who stood directly opposite her (body) and did or seemed to be trying to do exactly what she was doing. Meanwhile a number of children (and other people) were entering the boat tent, for real I mean the swamp-field, for the journey through this outer space Antarctica (later) and as they passed by Deborah between the three mirrors, we spectators by now enjoying ourselves on lovely blue pillows, smiling along as it were, I noticed these children—who were entering—reflected (like Deborah) on another big sheet or screen located directly in front of us. Whitman somehow connected (transmitted) these images from one place to another. It reminded me of closed-circuit television where you look at yourself in store windows. It was great. Okay. Next. By this time I was so comfortable I didn't feel like moving but a gentlemanly neighbor suggested we pick our bodies up off our pillows and take a stroll to our right where events themselves in this boat of a Happening theatre seemed to be moving. The water became more apparent. I saw myself reflected in it. After all it was a swamp. As we moved along I saw what I had already seen which is to say another large screen (in the trees) upon which (the screen) a naked lady was robing and disrobing. The other performers (spectators), or most of them, didn't move along with me and my neighbor. They must have liked the screen lady. The sky was also voluptuous. It was night time. After the Happening I mentioned to a friend that I thought the sky was El Greco (Toledo) that weekend and we agreed. But as for the happening itself: there were literally two more screens in the trees, moving always to the right as it were. On one of them I heard some sound, which was coming from a noise box situated someplace in the swamp. On the screen itself Whitman made a journey to Antarctica (mentioned earlier) utilizing icebergs, boats, penguins, and other paraphernalia that I'm having difficulty remembering since so much was going on all at once, including the crickets in the thickets. The noise box was transmitting a man's voice talking about what we were fortunate enough to be looking at on the screen. I liked the connection. It was almost osmotic. On the fourth and last (to the right) screen another film appeared but I couldn't make it out so I thought about it. A few children standing nearby, close to the water swamp, mentioned that this screen looked like a whale or a cloud or a balloon and I instantly (later) remembered Moby Dick, which to my surprise was not an original thought because one of the performers (Julie) told me it looked closer to a whale of a Moby pillow. Wow. Bemeantimes I was standing as far to the right as was possible (without keeling over) when along came about six penguins or girls in plastic bags sort of waddling by the grass. Then they disappeared. Now I recall seeing (earlier) a number of phosphorescent figures at a great distance from our blue pillows who also retreated into the forest. June bugs. Lightning flies. The night was still clear and while I was noting various other phenomena in my trusty notebook I spied a tent (tabernacle) deep in the forest. I was beginning to think I should go there (the next stop on the right see) when a confident performer notified me that the lit-up tent was actually a supply place for the theatre event and I could go there if I wanted refreshments. I didn't. One of the last things I saw in this "metaphor" was another young dancer by name Tony Holder paddling about very relaxed in something in the reflected water—towing behind him an incredible white sculpture construction. I didn't mention all the colors in this event but I'm sure you can see for yourself. White stands for Moby. Soon I wandered back over my path to the left thinking a great deal about how nice it was to be there. The crickets were sounding off. So was a finale noise box interpreting the sounds of the swamp. Simone (Whitman) told me it was more truly the sound of paper crackling through the trees in the wind. At that point I couldn't have cared less.

P.S. Norman Brown is a genius. This revue could be transcribed as a parody of Brown. Synaptically speaking. If you saw something I didn't see, sorry. Oh, one more thing: when Tony (Holder) was in his rowboat someone behind us tossed up firecrackers (maybe flashlights) which landed all around Tony especially for him to fish for. The noise was *Fantastic*. I guess Whitman is a genius too.

DANSCRABBLE

Village Voice, August 15, 1968

The dancer stops short in her initial flight track, a full open run of high expectation, steps back slowly, a hand at the chest. Look down first, Madam, before stepping up, your hat is slipping. You're not supposed to smile when I enter the room. But I thought . . . You thought. . . . All my trains left ages ago. Just because you imagine you've nowhere to go. Why don't you write a book called "Supply and Desire: An Introduction to Economic Psychology"? A woman who wants to show off her furs will cross by the North Atlantic route; her figure by the South Atlantic. Does it hold your attention? Do you like to look at it? Do you dip the scent in the bottle before uncorking your pleasure? The least gesture is permissible. Walking on straight knees, on flat feet, twisted torso extended at a right angle from the hips, elbows sticking out from fists plastered against the ears. Her veined hands ran quickly over her pearls and the feathers around her neckband. She has a special way of cutting off an impulse with a fragile dab or jerk so that the continuity is oddly disrupted. She could be hanging herself—one arm stretched above hunched shoulders, head and neck pressed with tortured tension against the left clavicle. We even need volunteers to tell you how badly we need volunteers. I blow my whistle once for my butler, twice for my valet, thrice for the maid, six times for tea. When I blow something may happen, or it may not. I experimented with chance briefly and found that the possibilities are infinite, and that I am no more interested in infinity than I am in one given thing or another, or in no thing at all, than in a single way of arriving at one thing. I never noticed the clock lying in the crate and the lady who kept coming and going without saying goodbye or hello. Does the world live in order to develop the lines on its face? Do women see a uniform as a symbol of death? I can assure you I feel the visual image to be two inches behind the bridge of my nose. The torso and head thrown back, held there a moment, the arms angled, bent at elbow and wrist, up over the face, to reinforce the ecstatic arch. The romantic attitude is nowhere so clear as in the fall from that effort, for while the legs take the weight of the body into the floor, the arms remain stretched, the gaze follows the arms, and the torso sinks to one side, still hoping for the impossible. Advance token to the nearest railroad. Is this the way the world will end? I didn't get kissed nearly enough. What an old maid I'm getting to be, lacking the courage to be in love with death. Of course I couldn't risk opening the door. I try to reflect the flow and concentrated variety of the music through the interlaced bodies of the dancers rooted to a central spot on the stage. Don't music up no gravy on my spoon. I measure out my life in coffee cups. Genius is a faculty for clever theft. Martin Luther sat on a privy to tell the world the truth. Einstein had his in a bathtub. I'm reading Wittgenstein with great pleasure, not understanding a word. And I couldn't read a goddamn comic book until I was almost in seventh grade. Are you hip to it? I have nothing to add or subtract: I mean what you say that I mean. The Ostiaks of the river Ob. The boobies of Fernando Po. Any time is a good time for a letter from you. He flashes a smile in all directions. She raises her hands with the palms outward and turns in profile. She says the police will never die properly until they are permitted to make obscene remarks like the others, inside the room with an unobstructed view of the landscape through the windows. They put her cat out on the street but fortunately she brought back a dying rabbit. It's impossible to please a satisfied woman. In her final pose, her head resting against the angle made by her upraised arm, there was the intimation of the acceptance of isolation. Should the raft be abandoned after the stream is crossed? It's wonderful the way I'm not interested. She does things like hitting herself into staggers and distorted backbends, or examining her feet as she lets her heels roll dangerously to port and starboard. Not much she can do to stop what's been done. She makes several footprints in dirt or coffee grinds by stepping in a small pile of it and using a brush to sweep off the excess to create the outline of foot and to push the dirt ahead for the next imprint. Mark a neutral area extending six feet on both sides of the net and prohibit throws and scores in this area. The player will find that the places in which he performs his actions will be determined by the wanderings of the other players. Did you realize that the Greeks dreaded the idea of a life everlasting? They never walk through doors, they pass through walls. Was my visit through a window an affront to your definition of a door? Should we reduce the universe to unexceptional exceptions by discovering laws of the correlation of exceptions? This whole business has been complicated by people who say all smart things. Look man, mind yer beezwax, I like to walk piggyback. They put platformate in my banana daiquiri and I crawled five miles further.

Historical Lineages

NEW "HAPPENINGS" AT THE REUBEN

Village Voice, June 23, 1960

The evening of "Happenings" at the Reuben Gallery (which Jean Robinson reviewed in *The Voice* June 16th) no doubt comes close, in spirit and method, to the "Dada" in Paris after World War I, which was really a joke, but with serious underpinnings. It was funny because it usually makes people laugh when they see materials brought together that are not supposed to go together in ordinary life and which are arranged in a bizarre fashion. It was serious because it came out of a thoughtful revolt against a world in chaos that was pretending order.

But whatever its political significance, it was also an important new aesthetic. It said: "Why shouldn't this go with that and be called something else." Why not, indeed? And the "Happenings" at the Reuben demonstrate this premise very well.

LOUD STAPLER

Especially the opera "E.G.," by Robert Whitman. The two female characters looked like huge roly-police from Queen Xixi of Ix. There was a guy clothed in a messy bush who started off feverishly making something with a loud stapler. Another guy, with paper balls painted colors all over his body, set the tone of violence by hurling an object or two against the wall. There was a lot of stalking around, an activity that became noisier as the floor became messier. There was an incident of crushing one guy down against the wall and throwing a bucket of water on him. The author himself took honors with spectacular dolphin leaps, landing the length of his body with resounding smacks. By the time of the final scramble—the floor a bloody battlefield of great wads of paper and all the junk that had dangled from the ceiling—I felt dazed, shattered, sickened, and convulsed (with laughter).

Brecht's "Gossoon," with movement by James Waring, was not shown to best advantage in the jammed gallery. It needs more space and fewer heads to look over and between for better vision.

JUICY WADS

In this "Vaudeville Collage" Jim Dine appeared on stage of a narrow construction like a puppet theatre and tore off juicy wads of cotton from around his neck. Two girls on either side at the top dangled lovely big cabbages; then poured a pail of red paint each over the sides of the theatre. For the finale, Mr. Dine made like a vaudeville dance with two painted cardboard girls under each arm. The crowd really liked it.

Jean Robinson is a bad boy. He doesn't know how to enjoy himself.

NEW LONDON REVIVALS: PART II

Village Voice, September 10, 1964

Last column I talked mostly about Martha Graham's "Primitive Mysteries," one of the revivals at the American Dance Festival in New London. It would have been interesting to see an early work by Doris Humphrey on the same program to note certain striking similarities in the ideas of these two artists who, along with Charles Weidman, emerged from Denishawn in the late '20s to create new forms and techniques, laying the foundation for all future developments. The American idea was basic to the early efforts of the three pioneers. Like Miss Graham, Doris Humphrey's heritage is the lock and stock of the proud immigrants who cleared the land. Her grandfathers were Congregational clergymen, one of them a descendent of Elder Brewster, and her father's step-mother was a daughter of Ralph Waldo Emerson.

Parallel to "Primitive Mysteries" was Humphrey's "Shakers," made in the same year, 1931. "Shakers" was derived from the religious attitude of the

New England Shaker sect, their belief in celibacy and of literally shaking off their sins. The counterpart in "Shakers" to the Virgin in "Primitive Mysteries" was the matriarchal leader, the central figure of invocation and exhortation. The design of the dance adhered to the design of the Shaker ritual, the men and women divided into separate groups on either side of a rectangular floor plan. Its strict linear and circular patterns followed from the plan, and are close, in essence, to the square formality of design in Graham's dance. Although Humphrey's technique differed in important respects from the technique of Graham (something I can't elaborate here), there was also the similarity of making vivid contrasts of design in gesture (as in "Shakers": a vertical kneeling position, in profile to the audience, with the hands clasped in prayer close to the chest, followed by a strong diagonal as the arms extend straight downward and the torso leans back in one piece), a technique of composition developed most consciously by Humphrey as one of her theories of theatrical effectiveness.

TO A HIGH PITCH

Unlike the Graham work, "Shakers" progresses dynamically from a quiet beginning through an accumulation of energy to a high pitch of exstasy, in keeping with the Shaker idea of shaking sin. The more energetic sections of "Shakers" are remote from the contained intensity of "Primitive Mysteries." But if one were to superimpose an image from other sections of "Shakers" onto the Graham work, or vice versa, one might see quickly the historical affinity of the two dances. An obvious example is a section in each dance in which the central figure acts in the passageway created by two lines of kneeling penitents. Comparing these works I am also reminded of other parallels, not only in the earlier forms, but in later developments, such as in the work of the now famous protege of Humphrey, José Limón, whose repertory represents a culmination of the early era. From a 23-year distance, a passage in Limón's "The Traitor" (1954) is curiously like the two just mentioned from the Graham and Humphrey works. In the Last Supper scene the Christ figure leans over the symbolic cloth to bless the disciples, who form the same parallel lines, divided on either side of the cloth, extending downstage to upstage, as the audience views it. The big difference is the relative mobility of Limón's passage, characteristic of his style, in which the percussive accents of his predecessors were smoothed out in fluid articulations. Limón's Baroque extension of the Humphrey-Weidman technique was beautifully exemplified in his "A Choreographic Offering," set to Bach, a premier at the Festival, in memory of Humphrey. This gigantic dance of solos, duets, and ensembles for 28 dancers contained motifs from 14 of Miss Humphrey's works, but the piece was all Limón in its massive opulence and orchestration of both movement and groups of dancers, reminiscent of his "Missa Brevis," but without the Gothic aspiration of eternity, unity, brotherhood, etc., a dance of pure movement and design close to the Baroque music that he admires the most. It is not so far-fetched to make an analogy of Limón and his predecessors to the transition in painting from High Renaissance to Baroque. With Limón the classical symmetries and four-square arrangements of the earlier works for large group (a generalization marked by exceptions) have dissolved in a sensual flow of movement whereby the architecture is constantly leaning and shifting, one image melting into another so that the eye is never permitted to settle on a single noteworthy picture.

TRADITIONAL

Limón's new work is a grand symphonic dance in a tradition of plotless ballets dating from Fokine's "Les Sylphides," the comparatively crude music visualizations of Denishawn and Massine, and, more to the point in Limón's ancestry, a work like Doris Humphrey's, "Passacaglia and Fugue in C Minor." On the same program at New London was a revival of "Lament for Ignatio Sanchez Mejias," choreographed for Limón by Humphrey in 1946, a dance typical of the more prominent interest of early choreographers in literary content. "The Lament" may be a schmaltzy dance from a contemporary point of view, overwrought with passion of life and death, but there are three solos for the bullfighter in this dance that remain exquisite examples of choreography by a woman who put her principles of choreography above everything on her scale of artistic values, and whose work was a constant test of these principles. Here Humphrey combined her craft at its best with an inspiration from the García Lorca poem and a style especially suited to Limón's great weight and refined Spanish arrogance and Mexican-Indian brutality. The death solo, which begins just as the doomed bullfighter pitches prone at the feet of the Woman of Destiny (Letitia Ide) and the Woman of Compassion (Patricia Hammack), rushes downstage at the edge of the pit to bellow the Lorca line "I did not want to see it" ("the blood of Ignatio over the arena")—the death solo is one of the most exciting solos, death or otherwise, including the suicide of Giselle, in my personal vision. Ignatio gets up and begins with a hair-raising rhythm, the top of one foot, this foot crossed behind the supporting leg, beating the floor in a desperate syncopation (coordinated with an eruption of drums in the score), arms spread-eagled but dangling as if broken feathers, the beating foot like an externalization of a wild heart beat, the whole action a kind of embattled limp—trapped animal in a final ritual of proud if hopeless assertion. Limón bequeathed his role to Louis Falco for this revival, and Falco, much lighter (and younger) than Limón, made something very beautiful out of it in his own way. His agility and phrasing and modulations of intensity are extraordinary. Falco is what some people sometimes call a "born dancer." Also, he carried himself like a Spaniard and satisfied my fuzzy ideal concept of a classical matador. I also liked Patricia Hammack's guttural melodramatic delivery of the Lorca lines. She belted them out as though her life and everybody's literally depended on it.

MEXICAN HERITAGE

"Lament" is one of quite a few dances in the Limón repertory derived from the content of his Mexican heritage. "La Malinche," for one, choreographed by Limón in 1949, is about the conquering Cortez, the vanquished people, and the woman of the title who betrayed her people as mistress and interpreter to Cortez, but in legend comes back as a spirit to lead the people against their conqueror in expiation of her sins. I mention this dance because it brings me back to parallels again in its similarity to another Graham revival at the Festival, "El Penitente" (1940), based on the fanatical rites of the Penitentes, a religious sect which came to Old and New Mexico from Spain with the Conquistadors. Like "La Malinche," "El Penitente" is a trio, and the form of both dances is that of a group of strolling street players who make a processional entrance and then assume their characters to enact a mystery play. The Mary figure in "El Penitente" relates to the woman of Cortez in "La Malinche," but chiefly as a prime mover, for in her role as sinner La Malinche is like the penitent figure in the Graham work. The characters in each dance represent different things, but the subject matter is the same.

EXCESSIVE MOTION

"El Penitente" was originally created with Merce Cunningham as Christ, Erick Hawkins as the Penitent, Miss Graham as the Mary figure, and I can imagine it was quite a different dance. I didn't get much from this performance with Gene McDonald, David Wood, and Marnie Thomas in the corresponding roles. The Flagellation of the Penitent, for one thing, which initiates the action directly after the entrance, was done with excessive motion, writhing, and no credible intensity. Nor did I feel any agony when the Penitent pulled the Death Cart (a wooden construction in the original production, here a flimsy rope affair) on his hands and knees. I've seen photographs of Erick Hawkins in the part that look much closer to the masochistic fervor which inspired the sect from which the dance is derived at least in spirit. Having such a specific content the dance is more than its formal arrangement of parts and gestures. I would look for the exorcism in some degree that I gathered from a curdling description of the actual rite, written by a first-hand observer, printed in the *Frontier Times* (1941): "It was like being on the rim of Hades listening to the screams of the damned."

GRAHAM'S "FRONTIER"

Miss Graham's third revival at New London was "Frontier," a solo choreographed in 1935, another classic of the '30s, another example of the spare delineations that marked an early period of rigorous formality in design and simple integrity of gesture. "Frontier" is the dance of American Woman in her pleasure of expansion over herself and the great American plains and all that. The focus of the dance is the straight positioning, vertical and horizontal, done on a centrally placed fragment of rail fence, a V shape of ropes extending from the fence to infinity. The gestures are broad and open. Ethel Winter performed the role with delightful naivete, probably without the demonic flavor Miss Graham must have given it originally, but strong enough to give me the sense of Whitmanesque grandeur and proud stability of pioneering woman.

TIME TUNNEL

Village Voice, February 8, 1968

Recently someone I know turned to someone else I know and told them that my original entry into dance was through José Limón, or words to that effect. The tone of the statement was: "Can you believe it?" I can't believe it myself. But at that time I wasn't living in this century at all. I was living in a museum. Education is a museum game. The dance part of it for me ended quite naturally. One day I broke my foot and left the studio feeling greatly relieved of the necessity to go on. In that manner at least. When the foot mended I was happy to possess two good feet in condition for nothing better than getting myself from one place to another as I was accustomed to doing before seized by a zeal for astounding myself with feats of unusual locomotion.

Of course I didn't at that moment emerge from the dance museum I had entered upon delivering myself all innocent to be educated. No, I remained devoted. José was a King. I honored his presumption. I just waited, characteristically, for other accidents to indicate what century I was living in. Actually,

I went back even further (I've placed José in the sixteenth and/or seventeenth century) and spent a lot of time in the library translating a book by a French musicologist called "The Court Ballet in France Before Louis XIV." I was pretty hot to be educated. I'm not going to enumerate the accidents that led me eventually to the time I'm living. I've lost track of it all anyway. At some point travel accelerated and I think I woke up one morning and stepped out the door into the twentieth century. Nothing looked different. My head was just suddenly empty. Naturally one of the first things I did was to privately depose the King. Thereafter I viewed the master's concerts with clinical detachment and even conceived the idea of a thesis expounding the psychology of a man whose face was so often tilted in a position parallel to the sky. It seemed significant. Even off stage: my memory is of looking up at a chin upon a daily greeting.

I began to be very interested in the novel phenomenon of dancers looking me straight in the eye. A reasonable attitude. I didn't like to see them groveling around on the floor either. Up or down seemed excessive. The dead center thing was what I first remember liking about Cunningham. Of course he went up and down. His head too. But with a difference. He didn't have his head in the clouds and he wasn't hanging it between his legs either. I mean you didn't have to feel sorry for him on the one hand, or hope for his redemption from the powers above on the other. Quite considerate. With all this and other things in mind I'd go back to see José and puzzle over his intractable habit of looking so remote. He was certainly sincere. Well, I went through some changes. First I deposed him, as I said. Then I became an academic investigator. Next I denounced him as a stuffed museum piece. Then I saw what seems very good about him, never mind his century. At last I lost interest. And now the other evening I had another attack of curiosity (or responsibility) and went to the Brooklyn Academy of Music to see "Missa Brevis" and a new work, "The Winged."

Both works are skyborne. "The Winged" is a kind of birdlore study set forth in a long series of divertissements (solos, duets, group, etc.) to a nice score of "incidental music" by Hank Johnson. The bird action is a lot of surprisingly inventive detail (especially for five girls in an angular predatory sequence) embedded in or welded onto the basic Limón vocabulary. Always the large fluid gliding weighted articulations of a body appearing in group form in swelling opulent, well-crafted symphonic orchestrations.

That applies to "Missa Brevis" though the dancers here move in the upper atmosphere without benefit of metaphor. The tilted heads were all there as I remembered. The group begins in a cluster stage center peering upward, possibly through a hole in the "bombed out church" where the dance takes place. José stands apart looking on his "flock" with paternal benevolence. José is sixty now. He doesn't look so much the King as the father-of-us-all type of thing. I'm still intrigued by his head. Imagine a history of the transition of style and attitude based on carriage. The proud Spaniard. The arrogant Conquistador. The stricken aristocrat. The Mexican-Indian underdog. The imperious matador. Jesus and Judas, Adam, Othello, Agamemnon, the Emperor Jones. He's played those roles. And he'd be delighted I'm sure to be a guest on "TV's Time Tunnel"—be sent back in time for tea and conversation with Bach, El Greco, and Michelangelo. He's a walking history book. The background might actually be more religious than I ever suspected. I thought of that as he lay prostrated in "Missa Brevis" in the form of a cross. He's probably simply a God-fearing man, but not in the American Puritan tradition, rather in another bygone manner of the exalted tragedies of saints and martyrs per Jesum Christum Dominum Nostrum.

Artistic Patterns

JACK MOORE

Village Voice, March 8, 1962

Jack Moore is some kind of middle man on the dance scene. He makes emotional dances, but his poetic sensibilities lead him to a lyrical condensed style that is as far from pure dance as it is from the records of joy and grief exposed relentlessly in the annual concerts of the dead.

Like his former teacher and director, Anna Sokolow, Moore can make a simple direct gesture that says something simple and direct without being banal. That is not only because the gesture is simple and direct (real), but also because there is no concern with logically developed drama; only with the passage of states of being, and these connected by the ambient mood of the dance. Thus the real gestures have an evocative power rendered through reduction, or elimination of context. Evocative also when they turn symptomatic—an externalized equivalent, sign, of an internal stress. What the gestures rarely do in Moore's or Sokolow's work is turn symbolic. Symbols may have their place and power, but in the work of contemporary choreographers eking out the past, the gestures are transformed (malformed) by artful exaggeration, dilution, idealization, into those generalized social and symbolic forms that *represent* states of being, and which are acceptable to an audience not interested in seeing itself nakedly reflected.

PRECARIOUS WIRE

Moore treads a precarious wire between his psychology and his medium. In "Target" and "Songs Remembered" (given at the YM-YWHA on January 28), through restraint, economy, directness, and whatever means, the artist binds the medium and his psychology in a tight little island of successful Art and moving expression. The looser construction of "Excursions" invites questions about the future of both elements. How long can this particular psychology—courting a female in a lilting dreamscape, delicate frustrations, fragile readjustments—be interesting? And how long will the Horstian type of composition—theme and development—bear up?

No dismal prophecies intended. Hopefully anticipating the growth of an honest man.

ROMANTIC DANCERS

August 22, 1963, *Village Voice*

I'm never sure what anyone means when they call a thing romantic or classical. I know what they mean when they refer to historical periods, but when it comes to specific works, especially those that penetrate me, I usually think of them as both romantic and classical. What could be more romantic than the classical Ingres? Or, what could be more classical than the romantic Pollack? I'm not even interested in the classical or romantic aspects of art, except in so far as the description of a particular style leads me to include these terms as convenient cultural pegs. The reason I'm indulging in these remarks at all is that I wanted to write about a few contemporary dancers who have developed lyrical individual styles, and I don't mind calling them romantic since that term has some general viability in the critical vocabulary.

HER OWN EMOTION

I usually think of Isadora Duncan as a pure romantic, but then she was very interested in the classical Greeks: she went around in these draperies and simulated many of the poses she found on vases in her museum excursions.

If Isadora was romantic, it was because she loved men and the ocean and flowing Greek gowns and Beethoven and "The Marseillaise," and her own emotions, and she got up in the salons or on the stage and let everybody know she loved those things. The line of movement was as natural and voluptuous as she felt her desire to be. She probably couldn't think straight long enough to dream up any method of containing all that emotion, especially after her children died and her Russian poet made life so difficult. I don't know what people would think of an Isadora now, but it seems certain that if you've spent a long time in a dim interior looking at dusty academic masterpieces, you'll come out to the sun and fall in love with the trees. The people in Isadora's time must have wanted that sunlight, and she gave them what they wanted.

TOWARD STRUCTURE

There was plenty of light in the story of modern dance after Isadora. There was also a big drive toward structure. The agitation created between 1925 and 1945 in the construction of theories of movement and composition was unprecedented in the history of the art of dance in the West.

But when the energy of this big movement to dance was spent, nobody knew quite what to do. Most of the dancers who had worked with the pioneers and who struck off on their own were still too close to the original impact to think for themselves. Thus pale reflections dominated the scene through the late '40s and the '50s, and everybody began to say the modern dance was dead. Certainly very few people were ready to receive the likes of Merce Cunningham, who had a mind of his own as early as 1944. But aside from Cunningham, whose methods and attitudes were a total break with the past and who made modern dance a truly contemporary affair (related to all the advanced work since the turn of the century in the other media), there have been a few isolated individuals who disregarded the past in a different way to develop an inward, lyric style, more related to Isadora than to their immediate predecessors.

LYRIC IMPULSE

Sybil Shearer, from Chicago, was one of the first. Katherine Litz followed soon after. The recent season in New York included concerts by Merle Marsicano, Aileen Passloff, and Beverly Schmidt. These artists have little in common with each other except that they're freefloating individuals and there is a strong lyric impulse in all their work.

Merle Marsicano is the arch lyricist, for she never extends beyond her love of the continuous, flowing gesture. Her dancing is limited only in the sense that she remains obsessively attached to a chosen quality, for she explores infinite possibilities within that quality. Her work is romantic the way a Rothko painting is romantic. The image spreads and suffuses like some luminous, internal light that soaks the space with gradual, subtly persistent intensity. Miss Marsicano also expresses an ideal feminine image. I'm not sure what that is, but I can't imagine a man with the same quality, or I could but I wouldn't like it. The image is certainly more mysterious than the projection of a woman like Martha Graham, because Graham always involved her idea of herself with a literary psychological content. Marsicano begins and ends with movement. What makes her so great is the magic she exudes through the total immersion of her personality in a quality that moves from the center outward and that has the clarity of silk sheen and the transparency of vapor.

MANY STYLES

Unlike Merle Marsicano, Aileen Passloff is stylistically diversified. She has made many kinds of dances. I have always liked her solos and duets better than the group pieces, because in the latter, which combine pure movement with evocative gestures in a free space (isolated actions occurring simultaneously), the gestures usually look pasted onto the movement, or vice versa, so that the incoherency never seemed coherent enough to me. In her solos and duets Miss Passloff has ranged widely in style and image. There is the tenuous, delicate lyricism of "Strelitzia" the brisk factual walk in heels and street clothes of "Asterisk"; the slight, slurping feminine cannibalism of "Boa Constrictor"; or the extroverted romanticism of the balletic solo "Tier." In this last the lyric impulse is fully extended without expressing any specific dramatic emotion—a quality more akin to the abstracted romantic classicism of the ballet than to the internalized calligraphy of a Marsicano or the generalized yearning of a Pauline Koner, to pardon the comparison.

TRUE CENTER

On the recent series of concerts at the Gramercy Arts Theatre, Beverly Schmidt presented a high-class romantic experience. I have no sharp opinion of what made this event so beautiful for a lot of people. For myself, I think Miss Schmidt is the kind of performer who can do anything and be beautiful because she has a true center and the emanation from that center is always a palpable reality. Exactly what a center is I have no idea. It's like trying to talk about angels, and there are many things people know that are impossible to talk about. Anyway, Miss Schmidt performed several dances with simple, unassuming lyric movement, accompanied by an offstage violin, and before a movie of her own enlarged image projected on the back wall and on a smaller downstage panel. The interplay of images—the soft, majestic volume of the figure on the screen with the diminutive flesh and blood on the stage—made a shifting mirror of the kind of dimension that reached far beyond, in the past and future, the moments of reckoning on that small stage. Near the end I had the uncanny feeling of an ancient presence when her head loomed huge in an instant of immobilized totemistic grandeur. Another timeless breath lay suspended when she appeared in a long red flowered dress against the panel and the movie stopped on a lush scene of red flowers—abstract enough to be the garden of the world. And the Corelli duet, as she broke the tension of duality to dance the same solo that she was dancing on the screen, came to me like a heroic emphasis. Miss Schmidt's lyricism has a pure, straightforward quality which includes the wit of an obliquely directed humor and the courage to be nothing more than what anybody really is. The image is so substantial, so factually grounded, that the romantic tones never seem out of touch with the grey wonder of an ordinary day.

Before closing these comments on three fine contemporary individuals, I must mention a dance that I saw this winter on a program at the Masters Institute by a young dancer named Clare Lorenzi. I don't know what Miss Lorenzi plans to do next, but as far as I'm concerned she could rest in peace if she never did anything else, because "Veil," a short solo performed in white chiffon and her own resplendent red hair, was another unforgettable lyric experience—a dance of soft, contained, economical beauty.

THE OBJECT

Village Voice, May 21, 1964

Writing a short piece recently about the new dance scene, with the emphasis on works made by artists, I was suddenly confounded by the absence of a lever to describe just how the artists have been involved in dance. Then somebody mentioned the magic word "objects." So I arbitrarily decided that the point at which the artists have become performers and choreographers is the moment of transition from a static construction to the kind of construction that invites manipulation. That seems clear enough, and I had momentarily forgotten that the Happenings by the painters were mobilized Environments. The performers in the Happenings were almost always manipulating objects.

INVITATION TO ATTACK

In an exhibition at Cordier and Ekstrom this winter, Jim Dine had a nostalgic reminder of his Happenings in the form of a canvas with a hatchet on a chain stuck in a rough beam of wood which divided the canvas down the middle. The implicit invitation to attack the wood was not lost on many. I heard that the work was destroyed in no time.

Dine's hatchet canvas was one of many object-constructions shown around the galleries these past few years which invite participation by the observer. The participation changes the character of the work or leaves it essentially intact. In either case the construction and the participant become collaborators in an Event. The next step is the relative formality of presenting the Event before a captive audience. No doubt the next step after that should be an invitation to the audience to close in on this transplanted audacity, an outcome toward which we might do well to strive. Actually, this has been done, but on a selective basis, which makes sense in terms of numbers if total annihilation does not seem desirable.

SINGULAR FACTS

Two recent works presented on a series by the Judson Dance Theatre, April 27–29, reveal the extent to which the artists and dancers of the Judson group have been grappling with objects these past two or three years. Lucinda Childs's "Carnation" and Robert Morris's "Site" are impeccable object-events with a short but eminent history behind them. Objects have figures in many works in all manner of loose and restrictive handling. They have been presented and manipulated as simple, singular facts, and they have been exploited as to their associative potential. "Site" and "Carnation" are works of maximum efficiency with a high-tension charge in their concentrated economy and their power to evoke feeling behind a neutral facade. At least two previous works by Judson Dunn's "Acapulco"; the other was an earlier piece by Morris, "Arizona."

With "Site" Morris extends himself by juxtaposing three elements. Dressed in white, wearing work gloves and a skin-tight flesh-colored mask, Morris stands before a white box containing a tape recorder which makes the constant rumbling sound of a pneumatic drill (previously recorded from his studio window). To his right is a stack of three large rectangular plywood boards, painted white. He removes one and stands it up vertically a few yards away. He removes the second and takes it off-stage. After a few moments he returns, grasps a corner of the third, and pulls it away swiftly to reveal a reclining odalisque, backed with white pillows, her skin covered with faint white make-up so that she looks somewhat dewy and transparent. She is also a facsimile of Manet's "Olympia." Morris makes the famous Manet painting his "found" object as a live entity on the stage. She remains transfixed while he manipulates the plywood board, making a moving sculpture of body and object, with the additional visual effect of shifting relationships between Morris, the odalisque, the small white box, and the stationary vertical board. Morris is a workman performing a task of balance and control. The pneumatic drill corroborates his activity. Both are dramatically opposed to the ideal poetic image of the transfixed lady. After the initial shock of exposure, the slow revelation of association sets in. Nobody is immune to its cultural significance. The extreme neutrality—the visual emphasis, the matter-of-fact manipulation, the absence of contact—is the work of an artist putting different pictures, like photographs, together on a canvas and letting the audience take it from there.

Lucinda Childs worked her materials in "Carnation" with similar economy and precision, but unlike Morris she pushed the facts into a fanciful absurdity of slight horror and some pathos. She sits at a small table with a visage of contained intensity, contemplating a plan of action with foam-rubber curlers and sponges, as momentous as a call to battle. She puts the curlers between the sponges, places a salad colander on her head, pulls out each curler with a neat swift pull, and places them around her head on the prongs of the colander. That done, she sticks the sponges in her mouth, removes the curlers, the colander, gets up and dumps them with unceremonious relief into a blue plastic bag, into which she injects her foot. The next section involves a head stand, a sheet, and two socks (attached to the sheet) with some difficult maneuvering. Finally, she caps this perfect and meticulous nonsense with a meaningless assault on the blue plastic bag. After careful placement of the bag she runs toward it, jumps on it, stands immobilized, glares in frenetic silence until her face starts to cry, and at the final moment of wrinkled distortion returns to deadpan normal and prepares for another attack on the bag.

JUDSON '64: I

Village Voice, January 21, 1965

Looking back, I think the Judson Dance Theatre, the first vanguard movement in dance since the early '30s, lost its initial momentum by the end of 1963. The first concert of the Judson series was in June of '62. Within a two-year span the idea was well-established. The consolidation of talent in the early Judson concerts was a fortuitous and spontaneous affair. Nobody set out to "make" a movement. The dancers and non-dancers who had been studying composition with Robert Dunn at Merce Cunningham's studio decided they needed a place to perform, and they found the church. Such a consolidation, vital as it may be, contains the seeds of its death in the increasing independence of its members.

Yvonne Rainer was the most adventurous and prolific choreographer of the group. After she gave her first evening-long work, "Terrain," in April of '63, she found the milieu of the weekly workshops from which the programs emerged to be increasingly superfluous to her own needs. Judith Dunn, another pivotal member of the group, gave her first solo presentation a few months later. The focus of the workshops blurred with an influx of latecomers and a division of the original core through outside performing opportunities. In the spring of '63 Billy Klüver arranged a concert of selected choreographers in Washington, D.C., as part of the Pop Festival there. From January through April of '64, an even more selective group performed in New Paltz, New York, at the Once Festival in Ann Arbor, Michigan, at the Institute of Contemporary Art in Philadelphia, and in a series arranged by Steve Paxton at Stage 73 in New York.

MORE POLISH

The church was a great launching pad for new ideas and vital collaborations. No doubt most of the choreographers now feel that the need for the "democratic" ensemble has expired. The last three concerts presented as the Judson Dance Theatre (May, '64) indicated the end of an inclusive milieu and the beginning of a more political structure based on achievements to date. The assorted pieces on two of the programs added up to more polish in the excitement generated by daring invention. Actually the differences were probably smaller than I imagine. Yet the passage of time affects our vision, and the expectations in May, '64, could not be the same as they had been a year earlier.

Three trios and a solo were satisfying professional pieces, executed with technical poise and assurance by trained dancers. They were settled works relying on familiar material and easy access to an audience attuned to the pleasures of a good body creating interesting, often difficult configurations. Gordon and Satterfield's television Pop dance was in the best tradition of these two art-nouveau comedians, whose airs and ironies might be as appropriate at the tired end of a movement as they can be at the beginning, when everything goes and too much serious endeavor is off-set by anyone who can plagiarize and satirize at the same time with stylish independence. Gordon and Satterfield have been the unwitting commentators on the scene they helped to create.

ONE DIRECTION

The place for the five-above-mentioned works and two others that I selected to write about at the time (Morris's "Site" and Childs's "Carnation") would now seem to be on a highly selective program, which is the inevitable tendency anyway. Of all the works, I found what I really expected and wanted in the sophistication and ingenuity of "Site" and "Carnation," where the rigorous formality of a commanding, implacable facade was a distinctive extension of at least one vital direction within the new movement.

Ironically, one of the concerts on this last series in May was a great improvisation, with minimal restrictions on freedom, and the most impressive collection of vanguard dancers and artists (including most of the Cunningham company) couldn't get this tacitly accepted Open Sesame (free play) of the Judson Dance Theatre off the ground. Everybody was very polite except for Yvonne Rainer, who doesn't care to be assimilated in the mass, and the response to her nerve should have been pandemonium if anybody had faced the assassination squarely. I wasn't looking for a climax but for a "situation" that would develop of electric necessity out of a collective atmosphere of private slideshows. In isolation, a number of performers were interesting enough, if that was all you wanted. The conditions for the different types of improvisation at the church have varied considerably. The conditions for success usually boiled down to a viable contract between guide lines (ground rules) supplied by the choreographer and performers who were alert and imaginative enough to be exciting under any circumstances. This last group improvisation (arranged by Deborah Hay) demonstrated the temptation to loosen guide lines under the cover of previous successes where the situations were more circumscribed. (At the other extreme, greater restrictions have illustrated that the same or even better effects can be achieved when the choreographer is in complete control; at such a point the method becomes inconsequential.) Occasionally, certain external factors have supplied the motive force. The mess of objects and structures in the collaborative concert with sculptor Charles Ross was an effective trapping for extended moments of the two free-play sections. For Rainer's "Room Service" it was even more effective, because the leadership psychology of improvisation was made explicit in the follow-the-leader form of the piece, and the materials provided a setting for the three leaders, who would have to be dull as doldrums not to take advantage of such an environment.

Another sort of thing happened at the Fred Herko memorial concert. I had hoped the concert wouldn't be lugubrious, but it was rather, and the very gravity of it set the place right for a moving rush of energy at the end of it when some of the audience joined the four dancers of the last piece in a laughing run around the performing area. The dance was the beginning of a piece made by Herko shortly before he died. Speaking of Judson and '64, I am happy and sad to find the moment for saying I think Herko was an important choreographer on the Judson scene. The dance just mentioned had that charming ridiculousness typical of a problematical character whom people loved and feared for and were exasperated by in his ultimate refusal to discipline a considerable talent. Yet at certain junctures he made the kind of contributions to the Judson concerts that were essential to the spleen of the new movement. I recall with wry affection his "Little Dances Before the Gym Wall for Dorothy," in which he confronted the audience with his typical blend of audacious vanity and cynicism, then danced rings around himself in another characteristic mixture of technical finesse and baroque flourish, and finally swaggered off like the impossible renegade and accomplished dancer that he was. I thought it was too bad that Herko and the Judson group gave up on each other. But Judson was never a stable institution, thankfully, and Herko was not the only choreographer who found the concerts a casual convenience in his peregrinations around town. If some of the others were less casual about their involvement, it has become clear, nevertheless, that the entire arrangement was a momentary expediency and that the modern dance at its best remains an individual affair and not an institutional business. The milieu created by the Judson collaborations was tight enough to afford a stimulating exchange of influence, and loose enough not to constrict personal ambitions.

JUDSON '64: II

Village Voice, January 28, 1965

In early summer Robert Dunn, motivated in part perhaps by the languishing Judson concerts, renewed his course in composition at a studio on East Broadway. Naturally the unusual situation that obtained at the original course was not to be duplicated. Dunn's intention and essentially laissez-faire approach remained the same, but the fearless talents who attended his first course, several of whom attended the second, had already shot their insurgent wad, and the next historical step is development and variation. The quick emancipation of dance from its old anchorage in literature and dependence upon musical forms and idealized movement derived from the professional studios (all prefigured by Cunningham in the '50s) makes another major insurrection seem unthinkable right now. There is no collective dissatisfaction in any case. And as the excitement which drew a number of individuals into the generalized orbit of a movement has diminished, the problem of the survival of fresh methods in new or authentic modes now most clearly devolves upon those individuals who can maintain whatever measure of dissatisfaction is necessary to withstand the pressure from the tradition of this new thing.

MORE EXCLUSIVE

The collective enterprise is far from finished, as is clear from future plans, but the character of the enterprise, as I indicated last week, has become more exclusive. Without muddling over nature's course, I might suggest it would be a pity if new or outside talent were intimidated in the search for a milieu to support more adventure. The dance world is so minute in the scheme of things that a barricade around the only vanguard movement in the country seems undesirable without anybody saying so. More to the point, no doubt, is the need for better communications to publicize activities and attract the talent that ends up in the ballet studios learning about musical comedy auditions, or at Juilliard to be indoctrinated by the old regime, or at any other dreary homes for the aged.

And more painters and composers. The Judson venture at its liveliest continues to be the coordinated engagement of artists and dancers, exerting a mutual influence in the best interests of the original confusion about what anybody thinks dance ever was or could be. In this mutual undertaking the dancers remain dancers and the artists become dancers at the point where both have projected dance into what I call the Theatre of Action. Dance is action, and that includes dancing proper (proper is a good word for that which evolved under past patronage), unless you want to fight about it, and I don't care what it is so long as I like looking at it.

THE ACTION END

What I have found most interesting since Rainer's "Terrain," which was a brilliant hybrid (as was Deborah Hay's earlier "All-Day Dance"), is the action end of the movement. Morris's "Arizona" ('63) was the first distinguished piece in the new idiom, the first anyway to define the great possibilities of less activity instead of more, of an extremely simple structure devolving upon a single activity, the expressive power of a neutral presence, and the functional transaction with an object in an image of instant visual clarity. Impressive in a similar vein have been Judith Dunn's "Acapulco" ('63), Lucinda Childs's "Carnation," Morris's "Site," Alex Hay's "Colorado Plateau" and "Prairie," and Steve Paxton's "Flat"—all of '64. Paxton's "Flat" was very intelligent, but the strained performance undermined the material. A straight delivery is the best advertisement for any material. Morris couldn't pull it off without his penetrating composure. Hay strained hard in "Colorado Plateau," but the stress was a straight exertion in lugging his people-objects about the space. Rauschenberg played it safe in the dark ("Shot Put"). From what I've heard of the August Festival in Stockholm at the Moderna Museet (which included an evening by David Tudor and one by Cunningham, on his way around the globe), Rauschenberg did his first outstanding theatre piece there. It involved a cow and a descent on a rope into a barrel of water. Sounds like a detective story. Morris and Rainer also performed there (and later in Düsseldorf), and so did Hay, Hay, and Paxton.

CURIOUS ANOMALY

Winding up these facts and flights of opinions on '64 (I've been pressed for opinions lately, and I don't mind, although I think I'm always opinionated—who isn't?), there was a curious anomaly, a studio-street dance that any Yamor Fluxus champion would appreciate (even Ray Johnson might have liked it), given by Childs at Dunn's course in June. The observers were instructed by a voice on tape to look out the sixth-floor windows while Childs descended in the elevator and crossed the street to stand or sit (on a convenient car fender) in the area designated by the "voice" as the area to look at. The voice went on to describe details—signs, items in windows, etc.—within the fixed zone, and the amazing thing that happened, from behind closed windows, was that this plebian tract, much like any other stretch of jammed buildings that people ordinarily have no reason to notice, became not only fascinating in its static detail, but also a frame, stage, screen, or whatever for normal activities intensified by the theatrical illusion. A woman passing by was caught in the act. She didn't know it and neither did a fire engine which emerged at the last moment. Quite a dramatic fire engine. So, salut '64, and more rooms with a view in '65!

THE HOLY HURRICANE

Village Voice, March 21, 1968

I've been thinking about messes and conclusions lately. Who believes that he is a poached egg is to be condemned solely on the ground that he is in a minority. I saw a beautiful demented girl on a bus about to be molested by a lousy lech. Where angels fear to tread. Who knows what happened at the end of the line. Levine says he just made the first electro-energy environment. That's the world isn't it? What can we salvage in the way of property from such an environment? The world is in a mess because of its clean boundaries. A truly messy world is a consummation devoutly to be wished. When the beans are spilled somebody loses a secret. When the dam breaks a private pond becomes a public ocean. An Australian girl thought the ocean was the sky lying on the ground. The windows become glass rectangles in their stack against the cellar wall. The rectangles are the windows of the mind. I am a wall, or a lamp, or a post or a book, or a poached egg. The fucker on the bus thought that girl was a girl. She was too crazy to be so simple-minded. Lunacy is a perception of disintegrating boundaries. The solution to the problem of identity is get lost (Brown). That's one way of looking at the conclusion of Joffrey's "Astarte." I imagine Joffrey's idea was a theatrically effective finale and that it is. But I like to think of his hero being evacuated into a night of no return. If you haven't heard, he walks out through an opening made in the sheet-drop screen (upon which we've just witnessed a virtuosic mess of filmage), through two huge doors and on to 56th Street.

I'll mention two other conclusions I've seen recently before saying what I really want to say here about a positive mess. Artists periodically are seized by eschatological reflections. A kind of artistic theology. Arpino concludes "The Clowns" with a doomsday message. Excepting the hero clown, who lives to tell the tale for some reason, they are all engulfed in a mountainous pillow of inflated plastic. On the lighter side, Aldo Tambellini (in a theatre piece on an Intermedia program in Brooklyn) got his audience playfully involved in their demise by releasing a great black balloon from the stage (the whole place meantime supercharged with an electronic racket and a barrage of visual data—superimposed slides, films of light abstractions) to be tossed, pushed by any crowd it blimps into until it bursts, which is the end of the piece. I deduced the doomsday bit from the Black Power pitch: two hysterical monologues by a Negro on tape getting after whitey. I didn't know that Tambellini's "black" art was thus associated. I think Tambellini is Italian. The piece was called "Black Zero" by the way. Well, there are these various theatrical representations of a foregone conclusion. My own conclusion is Mulatto Power backed up by the poached egg principle and worldwide metaphorical confusion. A truly messy world.

I wish to pay belated tribute to some artists who've consistently strained artistic credibility (whatever that is) in dumping their mud pies on the last clean shirt. The first funky thing I saw in New York was Robert Whitman's early Happening at the old Reuben Gallery: "E.G. Opera." I was ecstatically horrified. I was converted. A few memories at random now: the great mess of old tires that Allan Kaprow threw into Martha Jackson's backyard; Young's burning violin (bonfire of instruments); Rainer's brilliant hemorrhage of screaming in "Three Seascapes" (a choreographer was born); Marty Greenbaum's books and books—children's notebooks, crammed with mementos of the day, the clippings and scrawlings, bulged out from wax drippings, gouged out with cigarette burns; Al Hansen's toilet paper and newspaper and spray-paint word jumbles and hopeless disorganization; and three people I sometimes fantasize into a collaborative festival: Anna Halprin, Carolee Schneemann, Joseph Schlichter. Three elderly flower children. The insurrection of the flesh. The descent of the spirit into the body. In the beginning was the body. A covenant of bodies. A theatre of gang-bang. Of violence. Of excrement (paper, paint, paste, excelsior, it's all the same). A world united by its garbage.

And there was Carolee after the Intermedia concert at a party gleefully naked with two of her comrades-in-arms. O Christ, she said, Jill is going to write about this. And so I have. And now I'm going to write about the latest reason for rejoicing in the possibility of getting lost and drowning in a public ocean and turning into a poached egg. The Orgy-Mystery theatre of the Austrian, Hermann Nitsch. To twist Phaedo's last words on Socrates: Of all the theatre of my time which I have known this is the bloodiest, the cruelest, and the best. Carolee's "Meat Joy" was a sweet daydream next to this nightmare of savagery. A blood bath. A bloody brutal sacrifice. "There is no way to avoid murder, except by ritual murder." The animals and parts thereof are presented as dead before the ritual begins. The altar is a clean floor of white paper, of two tables likewise covered. The priest wears black pants and a clean white shirt. The carcass of a lamb is suspended from the ceiling on a hook. Another carcass is pinned in cruciform against the wall. Clumps of brains, entrails neatly spread on the tables. A mass of liver on the floor. The Austrian takes his time. He has cans and bottles of the liquid which will drench everything in a common bath. He begins just mildly saturating each clump of gut, staining the white it sits on. I'm losing my taste or patience for a verbal transcription. The oblations are the blood; the man, the bull; the virgin, the paschal lamb. One is to the other as milkweed to milkweed. Yes there is a chorus. The ancient ancestral voice of the dithyramb. A beautiful terrifying noise. All at once of shrill whistles and screams and pots-and-pans of kitchen brass shattering cymbals. Yes the place becomes a holy mess. A holy hurricane of blood. A riot of red. A holocaust of bodies. This is a catechism and a cataclysm. The baptism by fire. The remembrance of things past. The resurrection and the life. "Drink of it, all of you, for this is my blood of the covenant, which is poured out for the many for the forgiveness of sins." This is the eye of insanity of the dissolution of boundary. A consummation devoutly to be wished. Inferno Purgatorio Paradiso.

HAY'S GROUPS

Village Voice, April 11, 1968

Deborah Hay's concerts at the Anderson Theatre, April 4 and 5, 1968, leave me searching for superlatives. I'm tempted with platitudes like "breakthrough" and "come a long way" which may not be so impossible for a starter. The three works here presented are one person's victorious fruits of a personal quest within the larger collective enterprise known originally as the Judson Dance Theatre. I bring up Judson here because I left Hay's concert feeling the same kind of excitement I used to feel when some one thing or another in the Judson scene shot through the general effort with glittering clarity, always affirming that indeed there was cause for excitement—not in any one thing but in a total dance revolution. Hay's work must be seen in the context of that revolution. I say "must" advisedly. A direct naive appreciation of things uninformed by a historical frame of reference is always a possibility. The entry has to be made someplace in any case. I'm inclined to the view that the broader the frame of reference the richer the possibilities of involvement. Passing from naivete to sophistication in any medium, our perceptions become charged with the complications of historical issues. The new dance movement has its own complicated history, which in turn evolved from other complicated histories (ballet, modern dance, Happenings, etc.). To define the movement as revolutionary is to observe simply that its deviation from precedent forms was much greater than its conformity to those structures.

My academic asides are prompted by the tiresome ignorance of those in influential places who, unable to come on a thing with that direct naive appreciation mentioned above, continue to distort the picture for a wider public in refusing to educate themselves to a splendid phoenix that has risen from the ashes they keep poking around in, perpetuating the myth that anything livelier than dancing money from the Ford Foundation is happening there. Money is traditionally poured into an ash heap. But that's beside the point here. A wider public may also be a pointless issue. Having said what's on my mind I could as easily cancel the thought. The artists will continue to do what's essential. Yet I see prospects of more making things merrier with the kind of informed and sympathetic exposure that would draw potential talent into this orbit of activity. I used to say it a lot—that such talent is continually snared and waylaid by the deathly institutions of the dance world power structure. And again, I cancel the thought. It takes just two to knock heads together to keep this medium alive. Fortunately there are more than two, and currently a surge of action is both reinforcing and expanding the various positions of the movement, all testifying that the phoenix keeps rising even if in the shadow of the monumental ash heaps of those incredible institutions.

What's especially gratifying to me about Deborah Hay's concerts at the Anderson Theatre is that this choreographer intelligently grasped the possibilities she set forth herself in a piece given earlier this year ("Group I" at the School of Visual Arts) to present a concert of unified conceptual energy. "Group I" was repeated here, although on a proscenium stage it looked quite different. Within a frame the two complementary groups—the eight static standing figures lined up elevated on a white table each holding a ten-foot white pole, and the five mobile figures below them—project a greater visual sculpturely impact, especially in its heightened verticality. The bare minimal choreography and the horizontal uninflected energy-dynamic of the piece (called boredom in common parlance) are thrown therefore into greater relief. I described the piece in December. Briefly: in a preliminary movie some twenty people walk in and out of the corner of a room. There are several variations on getting into the corner (one at a time or en masse) and on moving out of it (always in shuffling baby steps, but facing in different directions). An equal emphasis on getting there, on being there as a mass, on moving out of there. A subtle pedestrian stylization of a crowd scene. The live action of the five mobile performers may also be viewed this way. Walking casually businesslike on and off stage in no special formation they coagulate in simple linear patterns and go further than the movie in the very plain (anybody can do it) unison choreographic gesturing. I think Hay is working in an area here that lies somewhere between the outright pedestrian action exemplified in Paxton's recent concert (and earlier Judson work, including the functional manipulation of objects) and the more technical dance-based choreography that Yvonne Rainer is exploring. There are points of agreement in the three areas. It's a difference of degree and/or emphasis. The eight people with the poles, by the way, aside from their visual importance, establish a musical counterpart to the "dancers" as they shift the poles, clattering together on the shift, from upright to upright.

The blasé perfunctory choreographic style of "Group I" assumes greater individual significance in the emphatic accretion of "Group II." More of the same with unassuming vengeance. In "Group I" all performers wear black business attire. In "Group II" the shirts, pants, and skirts are in colors, some of them bright (not costumes, just the red shirt in your closet). The poles are metal and brightly painted in red, blue, yellow. The format of the piece is similar: the movie followed by two groups of live performers. An apt analogy to this variation may be a Stella black-and-white stripe painting set next to one of his vivid-colored striped works. The color here in both "Groups" is as important as the mood-tone of a Cunningham "Summerspace" as distinct from a Cunningham "Nocturnes." The analogy ends where the energy level of Hay's "Groups" remain the same. In the movie of "Group II" about twenty people on a concrete outdoor space (a flat "ground") move in and out of the picture in a paired column, walking or running, straight, in circles, diagonals, etc., with a brief cut of chaos. On stage there's the initial impact as I said of color and sculptural arrangement. The musical pole holders are separated in two groups of four each, standing in lines on a slight diagonal bias on white tables, symmetrically disposed right and left stage. The noise they make is a gentle metallic clang each time they dip the poles into a meshed contact on cue from the conductor. The choreography below them is both informally dispersed and schematically patterned. It's a deceptively simple choreography. It looks "right" to me—just the right bland consistency. And I'm impressed by a simplicity which adumbrates the obvious while pushing us into a new realization of the obvious. A feature-less, diversion-less work energized by much more than meets the eye—by a tenacious aggressive concept. The intellectual pleasure of the concept is complemented by the physical pleasure of involvement in revelations of the ordinary. The work is feature-less in one sense but full of peculiarities in another sense—how, for instance, five people doing ostensibly the same simple thing look infinitely different in every aspect of their bodies.

All this is brilliantly clear in the third work, "Ten," which includes the rock group, the Third Eye. I think it's a smashing piece. The rock people are ranged out upstage behind a low metal bar stretching from wing to wing. Left of center and a yard or so downstage of the bar a pole stretches from floor to flies. Bar and pole are "home base" constants for the ten dancers, all in white shirts and pants, who do nothing more (which is a great deal) than position themselves in contiguous relation to these properties throughout the forty minutes of the piece. They're in three groups: five men, three girls, a man and a girl. Each group alternates leadership in determining the position, or design, to be assumed in relation to bar and pole. When the leader arranges himself the others assess the exact disposal of the body and align themselves next to him in the same shape in accordance with their observations. The variations are interminably beautiful. Yet once you get the idea it's unnecessary to look at it and the length of the piece substantiates the idea that it's beyond entertainment (getting screwed by this "art" thing) in suggesting the total life situation of the illusion of an occasional clear configuration emerging from an equally illusory chaotic tumble (the milling around of the performers in between their positioning). The constant order and confusion of our improvised orderly and confused lives. I could go on with this: the adroit use of the rock (the cool dance, the hot jazz, etc.) but save it, there's more to come. The concert is a major achievement in the short career of a very young artist.

State of the Field

MARTHA GRAHAM & CO.

Village Voice, June 1, 1960

On my way to Town X, I met an old acquaintance of mine called K, who was on his way out but stopped long enough to tell me that his experience in the town had been singularly frustrating. He had been employed to go there as a land surveyor, but throughout his long stay he was unable to contact the authorities in charge of putting him to work.

I expressed my sympathy and hurried on, since my time was limited, but I was depressed by K's story, which seemed incredible and cast doubt on his state of mind. Upon entering the Town I asked directions to the Inn where I was to stay and from where I could make arrangements for my job. The innkeeper and his wife seemed anxious to make me comfortable; it was a pleasure, they told me, to board anyone who came to report on the forthcoming concerts by Martha Graham, who was a Very Important Personage in the Community, a kind of high priestess of the arts. They had never seen her in person, no . . . she lived in a tower on top of the mountain where she practiced her art in solemn seclusion, and her affairs were conducted through an elaborate machinery of press agents, sub-managers, and sub-sub-managers. The innkeeper showed me to my room, talking on about the dweller in the

Tower who descended every two years or so with her extraordinary troupe of dancers to enlighten the Community through her ritual dance-dramas. This year she was scheduled to present a new dance in her cycle of Greek myths, the story of Alcestis; another new one called "Acrobats of God"; to bring back "Night Journey," the dance about Oedipus and Jocasta; the full-evening-length "Clytemnestra"; and "Seraphic Dialogue," on St. Joan.

As soon as I was settled I went to the phone and dialed the number of the press agent in charge of tickets for reviewers. After a long wait because of strange signals I heard a voice which sounded like that of a full-throated woman; yet it seemed far away, almost an echo. I no sooner started my business than a blast of static interrupted our connection. Between intermittent blasts, I strained to hear that I had reached the wrong press agent, that the press agent I was speaking to was the press agent only for those rare performances given by Miss Graham inside the Tower, to which the elite were invited. For performances on the "outside" I must contact so-and-so, and she gave me another number. My new contact informed me that the paper I represented was not on the Tower list, but that possibly something could be done to admit me to one or two performances. She would, of course, have to consult the manager, who was ultimately responsible to the producer, both of whom were terribly busy, as was she . . . would I please call back in several days. . . .

You might gather from the above that I did not see Martha Graham's recent two-weeks' season of concerts at the 5th Street Theatre under the best or the happiest conditions. In fact, I saw one performance through the courtesy of the Graham management, one performance in the legitimate paid manner, and three performances in the clandestine manner. Thus, I finally saw "Night Journey" (for the first time) in a remote corner of the theatre after playing hide-and-seek with certain persons and flashlights in search of vagabond visitors.

But even from my oblique angle I saw enough to be moved by Miss Graham's duet with Bertram Ross in the roles of Jocasta and Oedipus, and Jocasta's last moments of agony and death. I was surprised to be moved because I had observed Miss Graham's agonies in "Clytemnestra" and "Alcestis" with an almost cynical detachment.

"Alcestis" had a lot of intriguing furniture that is juggled around to provide different supports and locations-of-action—mainly a huge pistol structure stage right, a sloping board for a bed just below, and a large thick disc stage-left with a hole through the center through which Hercules occasionally thrusts a flower. Somehow Miss Graham, wearing a bare-back gown in the part of Alcestis, who is supposed to be, I presume, a reasonably young wife to Admetus, does not rouse the compassion which the myth suggests she should, on the basis of selflessly offering her life in the stead of her fated husband. This block in the way of sympathizing with the heroine makes a further difficulty in finding cause for rejoicing when the heroine is brought back from the underworld through the efforts of Hercules. Even so, the ending is the nicest part of the dance because the stage is suddenly lit up with the unexpected happenings: Alcestis and her husband happily reunited over on the pistol; the pink-clad chorus girls in a line across the back; the four men gaily gamboling on the edge of the disc (now reclining to make a platform); and Paul Taylor as Hercules, cavorting like a satyr behind the defeated Mr. Ross as Thanatos.

Martha Graham's "Clytemnestra" engaged all my puzzle-solving faculties, trying to identify characters, scenes, and symbols. The dance commands respect for sheer persistence. Miss Graham and her dancers toil and trudge on the same ponderous level of action for so long that one is relieved, rather than happy or convinced, when she finally lopes off in the moment of her rebirth (which the two singers don't let you forget as they chant the word over and over). It is difficult to see how an audience can become, or remain, enthralled by a deep dark tale which includes such extended passages of the same soul-shaking movements and encounters as "The Chorus Summons the Characters" near the end of the long Prologue, followed closely in the first act by similar tears and confrontations in the lengthy mediations of Clytemnestra. The dance unquestionably adds up to a colossal bore. Yet, of course, there are spasmodic interludes of interest and excitement. One such passage occurs in the first act, when long after you've seen all you care to see of the meditations, Iphigenia breaks away from her father, tries to go here and there for a way of escape, then shakes up the whole sequence by running over to Clytemnestra, who has been huddled in isolation over on her seat in a purple veil, and is now surprisingly thrust into the action. Miss Graham acts surprised herself (she *has* been meditating), and recovers with a start to caress her distraught daughter.

You are expected to become involved in the dramatic issue of the dances through the "significant" gestures of her own or other leading characters—the movements of the chorus, which parallels the tone of the action; and all other "theatrical" agents, chief among them being the decor, which offers supports for many different pictorial images, images closely bound up with the gestures in conveying the dramatic intent. In "Night Journey" for example: the image of Miss Graham and Mr. Ross straining against each other and the rope (which is twined around them) as they stand on the decor. Indeed, in "Night Journey" Miss Graham reels out the fate of her protagonists through tightly bound images and gestures which serve the tragic outcome instant by instant. The final moment, as Jocasta strangles herself, is truly tragic because it reverberates with all the compelling intensity of each preceding sign of intimacy and doom.

The gestures are the bloodstream of Martha Graham's "message" to the world. It is possible that she fails only when the choreographed movement passages, which are heavy and static without relief, intrude on the spell she is trying to keep intact. In these three dances, "Night Journey," "Alcestis," and "Clytemnestra," I was amazed to see the great variety of gestures all signifying grief. Not only the many hand-to-mouth or hand-to-head motions, and the fingers forming tears, or vibrating at the cheeks, and the mouth opening as though to omit a wail or a scream—her body sucked in at the middle while she does them—but the larger movements as well: the sinking and swooning, and the whole vocabulary of suffering, which are part of the "Graham technique," and are used over and over in all her dances.

THE BOLSHOI

Village Voice, September 27, 1962

Went to the Bolshoi on September 7. The Hurok organization is quite spiffy, as you know, so we got tickets to one performance only: "Swan Lake." I think I might have preferred "Spartacus," but I'm not complaining, because it was worth it to see Maya Plisetskaya. In fact, I got to thinking afterwards that a dancer like Maya Plisetskaya is the only good reason for all that excitement anyway.

Not that I didn't like other things as well (i.e., Nikolai Fadeyechev's grand solo—when he finally got the chance—as Prince Siegfried; the zingy Spanish dance in the third act), nor that I minded sitting in the orchestra with all those rich people; but I'm not a great lover of traditions (unless it's British and has a Queen in it), so the Grand Manner just looks phony to me, and I can't understand why Feudalism is so applauded, even if it is just the stage. Also, as my eyes traveled upward past those dizzy tiers of gilt boxes and balconies, I couldn't help thinking that a fraction of that sea of people could set a fine choreographer, of the struggling unknown type, on his financial feet. Or just wondering what the hell they were all doing there. I suspect the Americans of looking for rockets concealed in the scenery.

PLISETSKAYA

Anyway, there was Maya Plisetskaya. Like any other great dancer, she makes it plain that a craft is only as good as its practitioner. The classical ballet is a museum art in many ways, but the dancing itself is always beautiful when a great lady does it. I think an artist like Maya Plisetskaya would do the same for any craft—Danish gymnastics, for instance—but it really is impossible to think of her without the crazy format she works within: as though an artist of her gorgeousness (how many could sway at the Met for three hours?) could not have developed and thrived without the silly pretensions to magnificence that the ballet inherits from its snobbish origins.

And in what other setting in the world could a prima donna make such endless bows (each one preceded by the most incredible preparations of the arms) before an enthralled audience of several thousand. That's something for the girls to think about. As somebody just said on this television movie: "If country boys didn't fall in love with beautiful circus riders, there wouldn't be any circuses."

Embedded Writing

INSIDE "ORIGINALE"

Village Voice, October 1, 1964

There was Allan Kaprow at one of those Avant-Garde Festival performances at Judson Hall co-produced by Charlotte Moorman and Norman Seaman and he was carrying a big sheaf of script or score which he said was the score for Stockhausen's "Originale," so somehow in a conversation during one number it was agreed that I might be an Actor (one of five) since one of the Actors was reluctant or out of town or indisposed. Next day Allan called me and said the actor was well or anxious or back in town and that therefore I might like to be a conductor. Next call I became an Actor again. But after Allan talked to Mary Baumeister, closely associated with the composer, he proposed as they agreed that I should be a free agent which later I discovered was what might have been called a "guest" since a personage called a "guest" was included in the score as an optional possibility by invitation of the director. As it developed there were several guests during the week of performances. Friday night the chimpanzee was ill and Mrs. X's daughter, who brought her two German Shepherds to the first performance, was out on 57th Street requesting the pleasure of an appearance of an elderly lady with her shaggy white dog to replace the chimp. The fourth night three unexpected guests made a rush on Nam June Paik, handcuffing him to a metal bar of the scaffolding. The three intruders were disposed of on the fire escape and locked out there. One of them was later found to be stuck head down in an apparatus on the roof. As a free agent I went to the last rehearsal just before the first performance to size up the situation. I looked at the score and asked a few questions about who was doing what when, etc. Stockhausen's score is that curious hybrid of control and indeterminacy common to works by many artists in the contemporary tradition of providing the possibility of unforeseen situations within a framework of instructions and temporal limitations. The framework for "Originale" consisted of strict time units for each action or performer. Thus an actor, according to specifications in the score, might have to appear at 30 minutes and depart at 39 minutes (within the total time of 90 minutes). A further specification for an actor was that he choose selections from classical or modern drama to read or memorize for the performance. That left a wide margin of determination by the performer. Moreover, he could deliver his passages in whatever manner he desired. And I judged from the outfits, which changed night to night, that costume was similarly a matter of personal taste. Also, each actor had a bit of free time to do anything at all.

Along with the time structure, the sound score of the piece seemed absolutely determined. Stockhausen is best known in this country and abroad as an outstanding exponent of the new electronic music, produced on tape by a sinus generator. This technique was developed in the studio for electronic music of the West German Radio under the direction of Herbert Eimert; and Stockhausen was one of five composers represented in the first performance of such compositions (1954). The electronic score for "Originale," notwithstanding the included score for live piano and percussion ensemble, was the single dominant and pervasive element of the work. Considering the hodgepodge of properties, animals, and assorted activities in the piece, the time structure was not a unifying factor but a method of insuring a change of pace throughout a lengthy composition.

My own idea when I went to the rehearsal was to assess the pace with a view to doing something when it seemed dynamically appropriate. As for what I would do exactly, I tried to be empty-headed about it in the spirit of improvisation, but I pondered the shape and footing of the scaffolding as one accessible instrument because I like to climb and hang on things. My only other thought was to interfere or make some relationship with the "painter" (time was allotted to a painter, who could do what he pleased), who made a big scene in a white outer-space gear standing on a ladder on the stage dropping raw eggs on the floor, shaking red pigment over the eggs, lying on a cot, laying a steamy stink bomb in a large can. I notified the painter of my intentions and he said to just be careful because he couldn't see very well through his cellophane visor; but if I had made some realistic account of the painter as the same fellow who walked around in regular clothes during the rehearsal flipping about the German Shepherds not being caged or leashed, I might have taken a quiet powder during his theatrical debut. The outcome, of course, after I had a good time crawling behind him into the recess under the stage, sitting on the floor pouring a little salt over his red pigment, adjusting a pair of white heels that happened to be there, and flailing the steam from the can with my hat, was that painter and wife, the following evening before the second performance, bore down on me with hot denouncements in the name of serious intentions and such jazz, which prompted Allan Kaprow to bear down on them in the name of grace and so on, while Allen Ginsberg, who had also been a subject of my happy interference the night before, sitting begoggled in gentle Buddhist indifference fingering some Eastern stringed instruments, remarked inaudibly that I could do whatever I liked with him, Jill. Well, what I decided about all this was that the psychology involved in indeterminacy is a complicated business. I recall somebody once asking John Cage, in a panel after a performance of new music, if he expected people to laugh at his piece, and Cage replied that he preferred laughter to tears. According to Mary Baumeister there was a fair amount of interplay or interference at the first performance of "Originale" in Cologne in 1961. Actually, I think more often than not in these compositions the performers are isolated in their respective activities. Indeterminacy in music has meant primarily the interpenetration of sound resulting from simultaneous juxtapositions of material from independent sources. In a typical indeterminate score by John Cage, each performer constructs his own program of action from the graphic notation accompanied by instructions. Such was his "Theatre Piece" (1960), an obvious precedent for "Originale." As a piece of "theatrical music" the performers are expected "to be who they are (musician, dancer, signer, etc.) but the performer's decisions as to what he is to do will often be determined by whether he makes a sound." Until recently Cage's indeterminacy consisted of an unforeseen situation made possible by the simultaneous presentation of actions and sounds produced by performers who brought their own scheme to the performance after determining that scheme by submitting their choices to certain chance operations. Lately Cage has relaxed these controls to push indeterminacy into the realm of improvisation (on-the-spot decisions) more familiar to dancers and jazz musicians. In 1962 I performed as the “dancer” with Cage and Tudor in the former’s “Music Walk.” I chose about 45 actions mostly involving a load of household equipment, determining the sequence and time span for each action by the chance procedure indicated in the score. Armed with my 45 cards I went to the rehearsal, but when I saw the lovely graphic designs on the cards of my colleagues and my own fell to the floor, dropped in the water, or some damn thing, I gave up on them and decided to move around from one coke bottle or frying pan to another during the performance. At that time such a course was not kosher in Cage’s lexicon of behavior for the performer, who would do best to deliver himself from his own conventions (habitual preferences) by yielding to the external device of a chance procedure. However, it should be clear that habits are not so easily divested. One can force the issue by externally imposed strictures on time and sequence, but one is still left with that constant factor of the particular shape and volume of each body and the motion peculiar to that body. Cage looks like Cage to me no matter what he did beforehand to eliminate certain natural preferences in time and sequence. Moreover, the choice of equipment, determined by personal history, partially constitutes a “style,” by which the composer is eventually identified. To be absurdly elementary about it, consider the fact that Cage goes on habitually making music. Life, in any case, is always a new mixture of habit and improvisation, and Cage is an inventor in a medium that he has made his habit. The “set” performances for a work like “Theatre Piece” make a set composition in a way as set as any traditional work. Cage’s unique departure, of course, aside from the importance of extending music into a theatre of action, was to make the performer a composer in what amounts to a collective composition. Stockhausen’s “Originale” is the same kind of work except that there is more freedom in certain respects and less in others. As mentioned above, the performer had no choice in the matter of time, a choice essential to Cage’s position since Cage doesn’t mind (philosophically) if the audience is bored, although he could conceivably depend on the law of averages to provide the pace that he refuses to set himself. In comparing “Theatre Piece” and “Originale,” I am struck by one overwhelming difference in the two works. Cage’s score is absolutely consistent in that its simple instructions apply to all performers alike and there is no extraneous material obtruded by the composer. Stockhausen’s electronic score and other determined factors are hardly extraneous in the sense that they are commanding elements in the work; yet the obvious desire for “free” action is countered everywhere by controls and restraints which make even much of what is free look like a set-up, which indeed it is, as in the case of Nam June Paik, whose performance was a solo specialty act and whose plunge into a tub of water, following a breathless silence during which the Korean composer stood in a spotlight saturating his face, neck, and collar with shaving cream and rice, was accompanied by a Wagnerian burst of electronic thunder. I agree with Earle Brown, who described Paik as a "kind of Oriental Kammerkrieg" (in a letter called "Planned Panichood"). Paik's specialty is much more than an act. But I'm talking about context and disposition in a collective work. I think Stockhausen's idea was to make a great theatrical "combine" of sound, movement, lights, colors, properties, and players, and he figured it out like a playscript with parts for friends and acquaintances, with sections providing a simultaneous overlap of activities, other sections providing a focus for a single activity, with the constant presence of plant and animal decor, electronic equipment and technicians. Some people said it was a terrible mess. They also said, as the *Times* critic did, that there was much to admire. I know that it was an exciting occasion in Germany in 1961 as the first German happening. To some sophisticated New Yorkers, who have been through what Richard Bellamy refers to high-mindedly as the "classical" period of the happenings, "Originale" looked like a soup of ingredients from any number of familiar events. Sherman Drexler, for one, thinks that nobody should want to see another happening and that a sign at the exit should have read "This Way to the Egress," alluding to such a sign at the end of a Barnum and Bailey show of fake freaks. But "Originale" is not in the tradition of happenings as we know them by the painters (Dine, Oldenburg, Kaprow, Whitman, etc.). It is possible to make clean separations between one kind of event and another in a movement of international proportions deriving from one or two common sources (e.g., Cage); yet Stockhausen's work belongs essentially to the new tradition of "theatrical music" realized on a more modest scale by certain American composers following Cage's suggestion. If "Originale" was a soup it was because Stockhausen mixed up three sizable components in his calculations. First, he wanted a Merz combine in which the Milky Way would have figured had it been feasible. Second, he is a composer, and his background as a composer is in a European deterministic tradition. The new electronic music offers a range of sound possibilities before unknown, but the composers in this medium have subjected their experiments to serial permutations traced back to the 12-tone and serial techniques of Schoenberg and Webern. Third, Stockhausen has been exposed to the attitudes and methods of Cagean indeterminacy and he wanted, as he has demonstrated in earlier compositions, some measure of free action by the performers. Thus the result was a weird triple exposure of chunks of set pieces (often having the mytho-poetic quality of events in painterly happenings), a muddle of indeterminate confusion, and a pressure from clock and director to keep within the bounds of a meticulous score. I don't know why the Fluxus people were picketing the concert (somebody told me Fluxus committed suicide recently), but it might have been interesting if the director had invited the picket line to participate as "guests." From one guest to another (real or optional): I felt superfluous enough to guarantee that any intrusion could be welcome and horrible at the same time. Beyond that, as Duchamp once remarked and I have quoted before, perhaps the proceedings were "insufficiently lighthearted."

OVER HIS DEAD BODY

Village Voice, March 28, 1968

I was privileged to be present Friday night, March 21, at Judson Church, at the most unusual manifestation of a performer-audience situation I have witnessed in a decade of attending a theatre in which the performer-audience relationship has been pushed in every conceivable direction. Unusual is a mild word for it. It was a kind of psychological trauma involving two principals and the rest of us in a spontaneous drama expressing the agony and the comedy of the condition called human. The occasion was the Destruction in Art Symposium preceded by Destruction events in Judson's backyard.

The atmosphere in the yard was a bit like a bazaar—the spectators milling around passing from one set-up to another: an excerpt from Hermann Nitsch's Orgy-Mystery theatre; Lil Picard with plastic bags full of feathers set to flaming on a charcoal burner; Steve Rose standing by a frying pan on a hot plate cooking an orange and a banana; Bici Hendricks handing out ice picks to anyone wishing to hack at a large vertical hunk of ice surrounded by raw eggs; and preparations for Ralph Ortiz's chicken-killing event was the first presentiment of a rumble nobody expected. The two live chickens were strung up from trees several yards apart. John Wilcock calmly cut the chickens down and, assisted by Michael Kirby, made off with them to an adjoining yard to release them over a high fence. Ortiz later said he was delighted the chickens were rescued. He accepted the frustration of his plans as a worthwhile event in itself and re-programmed himself by subsequently attacking the two trees (he climbed one, Jon Hendricks the other), sawing a limb off each one after a preparation (pouring) of the cow's blood originally to have been part of the chicken scene. The attitude Ortiz assumed about the interference in his thing became relevant to the amazing drama that ensued inside at a scheduled panel of the artists involved. A soap-box orator from the yard, whose hysterical blather was punctuated with a few brilliant remarks, threatened to dominate proceedings in the lecture-room. Hendricks, Ortiz, and Hansen accepted him without relinquishing their own purpose and somehow finally integrated him in the total situation.

Hendricks announced a performance by Charlotte Moorman of Nam June Paik's "One for Violin," a piece dating from 1961. I know the piece from Paik's performance of it in '64 at a Fluxus concert. In a rather disorderly atmosphere Miss Moorman assumed the appropriate concentration and a courteous hush fell over the room. The piece entails the destruction of a violin after a long preliminary passage in which the performer raises the instrument in slow motion from a position at right angles to the waist to a position over the head in readiness to smash the thing on impact with the table. Miss Moorman got maybe one minute into the act when a man from the back tried to stop her. She dispatched him with a push and resumed the performance. And her more determined spectator approached the table and the war was on. Charlotte was angry. She demanded to know who he was (translated: who the hell do you think you are?). He said he didn't want her to break the violin. "By breaking a violin," he said, "you're doing the same thing as killing people." And something about giving it to a poor kid who could use it. Attempting to go on with the piece she said "this is not a vaudeville routine" and "this is not an audience-participation piece." But he persisted and I think Charlotte slapped his face and suddenly there was a tragedy in the making and shockwaves in the air and terrific agitation all around. Someone suggested he give her his coat in exchange for the violin. He removed his coat but she wouldn't have any of it. I was inspired by this suggestion and found myself hollering in the din: GIVE IT TO HIM. Charlotte accused her intruder of being as bad as the New York police. He announced that "we are sitting down and refusing to allow this violin to be broken." He forthwith stretched himself out on his back on the table in front of her. As Ortiz said later—she had to over his dead body. It happened very fast and there are probably as many versions of the climax as the number of people who were there. As I saw it, Charlotte's tormenter sat up and was sitting on the edge of the table and at some moment turned to face her at which point with malice aforethought she bashed him on the head with the violin and the blood was spilled. My description can't do justice to this extraordinary situation. The ramifications are extensive. It wasn't so much a question who was right or wrong (I thought, if pressed, both were right and both wrong), but what might have been done to avert the inevitable. That seems the ultimate political question so brilliantly posed by this little war right in the ranks of those so violently opposed to the war at the top.

The victim introduced himself as Saul Gottlieb. Charlotte was contrite and ministered to his wound. She explained the point of the piece is to show that we think nothing of killing people in Vietnam and we place a higher value on a violin. She said she didn't mean to hit him but he was in her performance area. Speaking of the therapeutic value of such actions Ortiz said Charlotte was trying to displace her hostility onto an inanimate object and Gottlieb wouldn't let her do that. Our soapbox man said that if "we the people want to come into the government" (represented here as artists) "we should be able to." He also told Gottlieb he was sick because he stood there and let her hit him with his back turned. Gottlieb said that Charlotte was determined to break the violin regardless of what happened and was unable to de-program herself. The adjustment Ortiz made in his chicken event became instructive. What were Charlotte's alternatives in the face of being robbed of her artist thing? Blowing her cool she was left with a literal destruction. The irony of a symbol converted into a reality. Yet why didn't Gottlieb honor her appeal for attention? "I request the honor of your presence at . . . " etc. At what? At the daily level, let's say, how we take turns in a conversation piece. Many more things were said at the Judson gathering. The last thing I saw was a touching demonstration by Steve Rose of a simple exchange based on respect. He requested the indulgence of his audience in a piece he wished to perform. He said it would begin when he finished talking and it would end when he sat down. He stood as he was and looked round slowly at the people there gathered with some slight perplexity I thought. And that was the piece. And the audience expressed their appreciation at a point well taken.

BASH IN THE SCULLS

Village Voice, August 13, 1970

EAST HAMPTON—One acre of love sun and sound at the Sculls. Drive along a Georgica road where the rich inherited the earth of East Hampton. An open sesame table at the head of the gravel driveway. Smiling women for equality. They say well look at least five other people called in to come for *The Voice*. Barbara Guest parries all checkshuns and leads me dancing and singing by the hand down the yellow brick road to the Crossbones. No she didn't but she was just charming and also flatterfull of good will too. This party I think

Tom Wolfe would identifry it as Radical Chick for Women Striking for Equality later on this month after receiving the necessary funds from such parties as these that Bob and Ethel Scull sponstered at 25 grubs a poison to see their premises. That's not true but it's the way Bob himself now striding tord me cross his greeny lawn in his ducky white pants and candy striped shirt open at a mossy chest and his new Commander Whitehead beard under a rich smile did put it that people would be paying to see the place. He's happy to see me and so am I. Nice little bungalow you've got here Bob. Mmmm. I can't give you the style number and we're not allowed in, it's a lawn party, but it's a right angulated one story black and white and windowy modern minimal everybody's building/Some are building monuments/Others are jotting down notes. All my colleagues in the crime of reporting I never meant. Charlotte Curtis. *Time. Newsday. Swiss Television. United Press International Syndicated News Service.* Once I mingled in a group of five of which four of us were taking notes. My editor (there too perchance) said it's the ultimate sort of party where nobody shows up except the people who write about it. I tried interviewing Charlotte Curtis who was interviewing two men who might've been interviewing her while a lady was interrupting to interview me about whatever went wrong between Betty Friedan and me. What went wrong between Betty Friedan and me was a lapse of sexual interest. I liked her below the chin and was ready to talk at that level but she got super huffy when I arsked if there shouldn't be a pub(l)ic conjunction between Women's Liberation and the Gay Liberation Front. Her eyes went big 'n bulgy and her lipstick leered crimson and she said crisply enunciating each word that "it" is not an issue. What? She repeated. *And,* there's no relationship between the movements. Well, and she softened a moment. I *am* against all oppression. Good, but don't you think . . .—and she waved me off, excuse me I have other important things to do as she spun on her maxi and I called out after her you mean "it" is embarrassing. And Scull standing there looking at his feet his hands folded at the duck white pants behind over the coccyx. He wanders me a tour of the lawn garden fountain sculpture layout. Here's a tomato red tube fabricated Alexander Liberman. It matches your napkin Bob. Mmmm. A stainless steel Walter De Maria cage. A neon number. A gray minimal Morris he called a donut, it has a square hole. A wood beam di Suvero faded weathering beautifully into driftwood. A fountain of three di Suvero caste bronze hands, and the story to go with it about how the one hand where the water sprouts out of its palm was supposed to cost 400 and Mark demanded 4 thou and got it and Scull says to me you know that Mark insults me, calls me a robber baron and the worst names—and I love him. He's beaming. Unhhuh, . . . you've changed

Bob. *Yeah* I feel *great*, just great. He looks yachtsman cocktails. Tanned and supersuccessful. His wife Ethel is standing near the mikes by the pool in a quilted maxi looking slim and Betsy Rossish. He turns and smiles and says fondly you know we've been married 26 years. By the pool. The pool! Don't Go Near the Water! The pool is the centerpieces here the perfect aqua rectangle undisturbed by its peripheral human slow motion of cameras cocktails interviews. Back in the bushes by a road bordering the lawn sits a barefoot guerrilla. Why donchu come in I called out. Because I don't have $25. I was near him and I turned and scanned my sister and fellow guests and when I saw the host of the Philistines I was afraid and my heart greatly trembled. No it didn't. But *lo* a voice from heaven, saying, This is my beloved Daughter in whom I am (not) so well pleased. It was time. Something had to happen here. A new historical folks pass. In a flash I turned into a One Eyed One Horned Flying Purple People Eater. No I didn't. I continued interviewing and being interviewed. I talk to Edith De Rham who wrote *her* book one year after (in '64) Betty Friedan did and who saw that women didn't have the freedom she had in being able to pay for a maid. I say then you must've had an experience that wasn't so pleasant to make you that sympathetic. Yes, she was married before her present marriage and with*out* the money for a maid and she wanted to jump off a bridge from it. Right. It had eluded me that the movement had so much to do with maids. We need a better distribution of maids. Maids for everybody. I decided to test her on the gay issue which Betty Friedan said is not an issue. She isn't hysterical like Betty but torrentially defensive. You see we don't hate men and so forth. And a story about a "queer" designer who was always describing his fabulous mother. I register that she's had gay men figured out for some time. Mother will never be duplicated. I remind her of a related notion, the high regard gay men have for women. And a notion she might not be familiar with: the same good feeling toward men from gay women. And throw out my theory that the women who hate men the most (and vice versa) are those who go to bed with them. She doesn't like any of it anyway and gives the old one-two about being normal or natural in preferring her opposite. "I'm not narcissistic you see." St. John of the Cross where are you:/There is in every perfect love/A law to be accomplished too:/That the lover should resemble/The belov'd: and be the same/And the greater is the likeness/Brighter will the rapture flame—Narcissime: qui consiste a se choisir soi-meme comme objet erotique.—Our interview was being interrupted by another. Edith's book by the way was "The Love Fraud" and I'm sorry I don't know what it's about a fraud I guess. She said she's happily married now. Who can I seduce here. Betty wears lipstick. Ethel is busy being hostess. Barbara disappeared. Charlotte is taking notes. My editor is here with her boyfriend. So I'm talking to Scull again over a manicured hedge. Admiring his Commander Whitehead beard, just the right dash of distinguished gray-white in a black brush as clipped as the hedge. Schwebbers Electronics has that kind of beard now too. Scull is expansive suddenly: I can't *wait* to see my depressions in Nevada. You're *What?*—My depressions.—Oh. My sculpture in the desert in Nevada, by Mike Heizer. Oh. Say Bob who's that? I've spied my quarry across the pool. Pale blue cycle shades. That's Gloria Steinem. Gloria! Terrific. I made haste round the pool through the cameras cocktails interviews. She's in a bareback and just as pretty at eyeball distance. Our past and future is settled immediately. Midwest-Smith-India-*New York Magazine*. And I disclose my unscheduled pool event. Return in peace to the ocean, my love; I too am part of that ocean, . . . we are not so much separated . . . —We are instantly by an introduction from Betty Friedan who's been giving a pep talk at the mikes about Women for Equality. She introduces Gloria. I wander back to the other side of the pool, the hedge side. I was coming into that abnormal condition known as elation. I would cast my swine before pearls and give that which is unholy to the daubs. I would return my body to the water (Gene before he died said he was returning the earth to the land as he threw his flower pots from fifth story to sidewalk). And I lectured my brethren: the proper posture is to listen and to learn from lunatics as in former times. No I didn't. I sat down to organize the explosion. Removal of pants shoes socks hardware. I had to leave my notes behind. Too bad. I walk quickly to the center of the shallow end. Almost fall skidding on the slippery edge. Last Chance Balloon. Tarzana from the trees at cocktails. I didn't cross myself. I didn't yell geronimo. I dove in and did my lengths. I hoped my colleague reporters would be noting my 10 point Australian crawl. I did a little exhibition breast stroke as well. The second time round I got rid of the faded blue railroad shirt with a hole in the sleeve (Yes it was a calculated costume). She's terrible, she's beautiful. She isn't beautiful, she isn't terrible enough. Anyway I was alone in the aquarium. Water lovely. No rubber ducky (in the tubby). I emerge. Slippery edge. Jill tombe pour la seconde fois. Scull is waiting eagerly with big yellow towel and so happily I think he's my trainer and I just won the race. I go beyond the hedge into the trees. A maxi lady is lurking in the bushes. WHY DID YOU DO THAT? I mean but extremely furious. I'm wiping the chlorine out of my eyes. It isn't self-evident. Well . . . I was . . . uh . . . hot–and drunk. HOT. And DRUNK.—God, where's my notebook. The other notebooks are coming tord me fast now. They're saying you were hot and drunk. *Were* you hot and drunk? Yes. Were you protesting? Yes. Are you a woman . . . ? Yes.

Were you part of a red Stocking Plot to Sabotage this Party? Yes. Were you showing off? Yes. Are you a radical lesbian? Yes. Do you like the Sculls? Sure. Did Mr. Scull put you up to it? No. He neither endorsed nor discouraged the exhibition but I did get permission from my editor. *WHY* did you do it? Well... I think one should be serious in one's purposes but not necessarily solemn. Well... Have gun, will travel. See pool, will swim. Well.... It was a Conceptual Swim. Well you see I have this resportsibility to make my life interesting to my readers each week. And then I stormed the mikes and lectured my brethren again: Except ye become as little children ye can in no vice exit the killdom of haven. No I didn't. I went behind a tree to write up my swim. Scull appeared. They're saying I put you up to it. Well just say I was hot and drunk. And offer me a dry shirt please. He gets another blue workshirt. Where's Gloria? They're not even thanking me for the awful time I gave them. No, it's getting all changed around. You were great. Terrific. Sensational. Verweile doch, du bist so schon. But Gloria won't dance. Betty is still put out. Ethel and Edith and Charlotte disappeared along with Barbara. A voice on the mikes is saying Ladies and gentlemen the party is over. Radical Chick is over. One acre of love sun and sound. Was there any perfecting of spirits here this afternoon? I'd like to leave my clothes impaled on a souvenir spear. Tell it all, brother and sisters. Dinner at the Silver Sea Horse. The Wheel of Wandering On.

Profiles

ON A WHITE CAMEL, INVESTIGATING EVERYTHING

Village Voice, January 11, 1968

"This is my year you know, the year of the gorilla in the Chinese zodiac." That's James Lee Byars, standing there in a big white woolly coat. I checked his pants. Blue corduroy. January 1, 1968, noon, I approach the CBS plaza on 53rd Street. There's Byars in a more familiar outfit: black felt derby hat (rim down), large blue shades, black leather suit, black silk shirt, black bow tie. A CBS reporter called him a hippie artist. He's just a conscientious maverick, enchanted by projects for disarming any bystander. He's standing in the middle of the street in the middle of a small clump of people surrounding a little roped-off area where a man is pumping helium into a tan heavy-duty weather balloon. It's capable of being inflated to ten feet in diameter.

Byars holds a spool with a mile of gold thread wrapped around it. The balloon will take off carrying first some yards of white cotton string (a tether to carry the balloon above the heights of the buildings), then the gold thread. It goes up at only 100 feet a minute. It's been calculated to rise at 1,000 feet a minute. Rising, hovering, rising again, buffeted north and south by strong winds, it gets stuck on a building someplace dead ahead, probably around

Park Avenue. The second balloon explodes on the street. "Accepting variables." The next two are red and capable of being inflated to four or five feet in diameter. They rise beautifully at the calculated speed, clearing the buildings, veering off to the northeast, but carrying only part of the mile of gold thread. The thread breaks and decorates trees on the street. A couple of scavengers make off with it. It was purchased by the Craft Museum at $100. "Accepting the notion of celebration." The street was closed for the event, classified by the city police as a "street fair." The helium man launching the balloons is an expert from the New York weather bureau at Kennedy Airport. The balloons were passed by the Federal Aviation Bureau as "aircraft." Eight hours before the release of the balloons the Craft Museum had to notify the bureau about the launching and the anticipated heights (i.e., at 12:05 p.m. the first balloon would be at 5,000 feet) so that all pilots could be warned that a mile of gold thread at the end of a balloon would be flying in the area. The permit to launch the balloons was obtained only because there are no rules about sending up something that weighs less than six pounds.

Byars said he enjoyed watching the sky and speculating on the gold thread falling down anyplace at someone's door. He also says it may be on some air wave and moving to England. "It may be there when I get there." He's going to be the "extraordinary student at Oxford in philosophy for a week." He'll advise them to take him on when he arrives. Thus finishing up his formal education, having completed elementary school at the Edgar Allan Poe School in Detroit.

But right now in his white fur coat he's off to Chinatown to confer with a seamstress about a piece of pink silk, 12 by 100 feet. This "dress" will have a number of holes in it. Byars will have his head in a hole at one end of the silk, Dick Bellamy at the other end. Byars is going to be Bellamy's "consciousness ornament" for about 100 hours, echoing everything he does. He'll try seducing other people into the holes to be additional ornaments. "What is a dress?" "How do you negotiate a door in a 100 foot dress?" "How do you sit down?" "What does plural clothing mean?" "Why shouldn't a man and a woman wear the same dress?" "What is a group?" "It's a pleasure to see pink in midwinter." "Pink is such an abused color in the U.S." "I looked all day for a pink pencil." "Imagine the pleasure of just suddenly seeing 100 feet of pink." "I want to take this dress to Oxford and get the dons into it." "Supposing a million four-hole dresses 16 feet in diameter, white and cool appearing (phosphorescent algae), were available on every walking street corner on a summer day for free, popping out of boxes. People might throw off their hot stuff in the gutter and jump under these dresses. We could dress up the whole city in an hour."

Last month Byars dressed up an Ailanthus tree (tree of heaven: symbol of the unkillable infants of the extremely poor) on 84th Street and Madison Avenue. As a tribute to this tree he wrapped all its circumferences in thousands of little pieces of red paper (hand-painted vermilion) and red string. Then he unwrapped it and the operation took a whole day.

"The best dances are by the people in the streets." One day he saw a waitress in a donut shop who had fantastic coordination and attitudes of surrender to a lowly duty. He asked her if she'd had any dance or drama training. No she hadn't. "Do you have any philosophical presuppositions that influence your daily patterns of attention-giving in submitting to your task?" No, she said, she was a part-timer. Byars asked the Jewish Pantomime Theatre if they'd send 100 white-dressed mimes to come and admire her. They thought it was out of sight. "So I flew to San Francisco and wrote on white paper 100 feet by 6 inches. 'One hundred white-dressed mimes came at once to see you,' sent it to a friend in New York and asked her to deliver it to the donut girl, which she did."

Simultaneously generous, offering himself, and demanding, probing, and pressing people for things. Underway now: a consciousness sample—ask one million people to put one minute of attention on a piece of paper and send it to the Museum (Goldovsky-Bellamy) at 1078 Madison. Next, after Oxford perhaps, a walking tour around the world to pay tribute to things like Abebe of Ethiopia, the world's Olympic champion long-distance runner, and to the insect hospital in Ahmedabad, India. Also to white camels, wherever they are, and to the Golden Temple of Pattan in Nepal.

"My mission is to investigate everything."

"I think of myself as a kind of cosmological cavalier."

"I'm interested in the interconnectedness of imaginative affairs."

"I'm interested in numerical manifestations. My favorite number is zero."

"I don't think we can persuade accident in our direction. Had I made some appeal to the unknown in trying to get the gold thread up I might have been too disappointed to try to get the next balloon up."

"By the way, would you ask *The Village Voice* if they'd like the remaining gold thread to inset a piece in every copy of this issue?"

FOR AMERICA

Village Voice, June 25, 1970

LOS ANGELES, or San Francisco—back and forth. Present psychology being to love them and leave them, and return and love and leave again and return and keep loving and leaving until I imagine I have it all under control and can return to New York. That's as personal as I think I want to be. But I don't know. Sitting in Pasadena with Mark astride one of his steel beams I looked up as he spoke of his fear in doing the work required at the heights of a 40-foot sculpture and said I think of my column also as a dangerous activity. One moment I want to be intensely personal. The next I'm cancelling the impulse as though stopping a jump to suicide. Then I'm carefully selecting a particular suicide. Then arranging a resurrection by the artifice of style. And so forthright, or wrong. Once in a while I visit a potter's place in Stony Point (New York) and always sigh there after the life of a potter. Or Mark for that matter and his dangerous sculpture. But then I'd be unable to say how difficult it is to be personal and how much pleasure there is in arranging various ways of saying it. It's a way of postponing being personal, if writing about it is actually avoiding it, I doubt it. I was trying to postpone an analysis of a character function I've been discovering about myself and I'm going to (postpone it) because I talked it all out and decided it's too complicated with variable components, other people, places, to be very clear for the moment's being I did exclaim to Mark there sitting on the steel beams that this was the sort of thing in any normal week I'd be volleying about in my head as a dead ball a weak lob a smash serve or a backhanded curve out of the head and on and off a piece of yellow paper. Just don't write about me, Mark said. About you? I mean my sculpture. Oh shit. The man. The sculptor. The life. The people. Places. He's still thinking there's a thing called art criticism and something else called the man. I do my speech about how I don't ever see a work any more unless I see the man the maker the work the place the people the everything and myself as well in a total entanglement. Hey Mark there's pieces of you I was babbling as we drove up to the site in the parking lot after one more eating or sleeping excursion. All the pieces, I was thinking. Like the pattern of this trip. My loving and leaving in San Francisco and finding Mark and returning and leaving to find Mark again and returning and loving and leaving and Mark and leaving Mark the third time the other day in Pasadena to be back in San Francisco. All the additional pieces of Mark. After two years. His mother in Inverness. His brother in Sausalito. His brother's wife. And two kids. His girl friend. His two dealers. His impossibilities. His incredible hugeness and generosities. Picking up as many hitchhikers as the truck would hold and tending them all along the way like a mother goose; bags of cherries and boxes of strawberries and enquiries after their comfort and destinations. Mark an Atlas striding the globe. Driving along. Ten minutes silence. Then urgently: "I don't know how to stop the war." Silence again. Then impatiently: "I'm getting tired thinking about it." All the pieces. Sitting at dinner in L.A. with Barbara his love and the two dealers. Stretching his arms out palms up encompassing the table, the globe. The big joke, but still imploring: "Whadyou guys want from me?" And I see the artist as a Tantalus. Better a Sisyphus. Doing penance in eternity. But he digs it. The torch for cutting and the torch for welding and the crane for lifting and his legs for climbing. And even sitting slumped all tension and a stiff neck on the wall-to-wall in the Museum wanting for the dealers in his head a caged animal prowling bar to bar waiting the money he needs to buy the next steel for the next piece in somebody else's yard or lot, the money he can't wait to give away as soon as he gets it he'd better move on to where he's going and buy the steel too before he absolves his bad conscience by unloading the grubs he needs to continue to be a suffering artist. The pieces. His mother writes him and addresses the envelope Sculptor Mark di Suvero. His mother. Dinner at Inverness. European manners. Graciousness. Musty smell of antiques and old portraits. Sherry consommé Sitting below a portrait of herself as a much younger and still striking woman looking the image of Hank as well—the third brother, I've known, the brother who gets people out of jail as Mark says. The other brother moves money around. He was going to be a poet. He's Victor in Sausalito. He's the oldest. Handsome rugged and high spirited like the rest. Yet cool and controlled. A sudden extravagance reminding of Mark. A patriarchal stance toward his brother. Indulgent. Concerned. Admiring. Advising. A touch of Theo and Vincent in their relationship. All of them sea captains. Adventurers. Conrads and Drakes and Vasco da Gamas and Marco Polos. And fallen aristocrats. Exiles from Italy and China. The three brothers carving out a piece of America. Renaissance realities and aspirations. Captains and architects and mathematicians and lawyers and businessmen and artists. Victor on the surface of it a straight life: old redwood house up high a fabulous view of the bay. A Luncheon for people like Jessica Mitford on the deck. A pitcher of bloody marys and polite conversation. Namedropping. A story about Kay Boyle who sold a Joyce letter for lots of cash. A story by a British professor who looks like Andy about trying to buy a library in Europe. His American wife I ask if she went to Spence or Chapin. Oh, how did you know? Like that. Airs of Bloomsbury. And Mark behaving himself. Except for spilling coffee all over my pants. That was paying me back I suppose for spilling olive juice all over his dashboard as he careened around a corner downtown just as I spotted a London taxi and yelled about it and he screamed bloody murder over the olive juice while still careening around corners and swearing and swopping it up with the other hand. His fury immediately expended. His violence in the work. Trudging up at 6 a.m. from his studio to parking lot, his truck left at the lot the night before, in his crippled magnificence, what's left of his legs (after his accident 10 years ago he wasn't supposed to walk again ever) holding up a fine big torso making a flopping simian gait inordinately outrageously beautiful totally Mark could be recognized at great distances, to cut and weld off some early energy and conflict into the sculpture after a bad night's scene at a restaurant I was flamboyantly waving a knife and fork emphasizing an unpopular program for peace and causing Barbara to strand us there and an $8 taxi back to Pasadena. Work. Penance. Tears. Apologies. I cried twice that day. The first time after driving Barbara's car out to Watts to at least see Simon Rodia's towers. Flat wastelands of Watts. Shanties and railroad tracks and black middle class. Two blocks away I sight the towers. Unimpressive looking. Drab. Delicate. Not nearly as high as I imagined. Park and pay 75 cents at the entrance and walk in and almost instantly overcome with great emotion. What can I say. The place is breathing the color and care and love of this man they said was a simple man who lived a vision for the 33 years he worked and dwelled there. A total act of love—Mark had said. Not for fame or profit. An Italian immigrant, tile-setter, he bought this little triangular chunk of land and wanted to build something for America (". . . there are nice people in this country") and then America wanted to tear it down. Now it's called a historical monument and there must be a constant struggle to preserve it. You have to see this place to believe it. I wish the revolution would come to Watts to see Simon Rodia's towers. The fuzz, the students, the hardhats, the politicians. Everybody. America doesn't want this. It's too fabulous. Too free. Too private. Too religious. Too personal. Too handmade. Too dedicated. Too beautiful. Too grand and too simple. All those shells and pieces of crockery and fragments of 7-Up bottles embedded in the gothic tracery of skeletal intricacies rising up in diminishing concentricities to their apexes. The last time I cried over an erection was in England at Coventry where the people of Coventry, which was leveled by the war, put up a monster new cathedral adjoined by the porch to its predecessor preserved in ruins—the old 12th century cathedral. I thought of that and Simon and Mark as I returned to the Museum. Rifled through the library there looking for the '65 issue of *Art Forum* featuring the towers on its cover. Right after he died. Why do they do that when they're dead or dying. Does it matter. I don't know. Anyhow I say to Mark sprawled on the wall-to-wall: terrific coincidence, this is the issue in which the only article I wrote for *Art Forum* was printed. No, he says, it's Fate. It led you to the towers. And by the way in the same issue is a photo of one of Mark's old wood beam structures. All the pieces. Late one night at Inverness in a cabin behind his mother's house making excited diagrams looking for the Oedipal correlates for my nonexistent family. It seemed as though the delusion was about to become a reality again or to merge as to seem indistinguishable in his acceptance understanding of our mythological necessities. Mark as a huge human. Eight years of changes. He's still impossible too. He bearhugged me goodnight, "as brothers" he said. No more grabbing at parts as a potential screw. We tried that once anyhow. I think we love each other now. I see him as a model for a new America. He'll be mad at me for writing all this.

STEIN: AFFECTIONATELY OBSCENE POETRY

Village Voice, May 4, 1972

In history one does not mention dahlias mushrooms or hortensias. Letter from Carol saying it is pleasing to see that G.S. interests you and invades the dreams of your friend Jane. G.S. is indeed someone in whom to be interested as is Natalie Barney (L'Amazone) who was at one time the lover of Romaine Brooks who painted a portrait of Lady Una Troubridge who was the lover of Radclyffe Hall who depicted a good number of these people in "The Well of Loneliness." They are all of these people extremely interesting but only one was a genius and that of course was Gertrude who is most truly "the mother of us all." I was drunk the other night (Carol goes on) and someone began to talk about Rilke's "Duino Elegies" and I in my drunken state heard it as do we know Elegies and I thought this was a rather schoolmarmish thing for Rilke to write and then I began to think that it sounded quite Gertrude Steiny. . . . Do we know "Elegies" and if we do know "Elegies" how well do we know "Elegies" do we. And that's the end of that story. G.S. was for a while very much opposed to commas. At the most she said a comma is a poor period that it lets you stop and take a breath but if you want to take a breath. Endeth the quote know yourself that you want to take a breath. Endeth the quote from C's letter. I have thought a good deal about commas myself. I have not thought a good deal about commas. Knowing myself whether I want to take a breath I'll use the comma and if not not. Gertrude Stein has always interested me but never so much as recently. Two years ago it occurred to me that there must be some intimate connection between her stylistic obscurities and her domestic lesbian arrangement. Unknown to me Edmund Wilson made a similar speculation in the '30s. The origin of the speculation might've been the same for him as for me and that was the sudden availability of Q.E.D. or "Things as They Are" published posthumously in a limited edition of 500. I saw one of these in san diego winter of '70 and was amazed to read a perfectly coherent Stein, more conventional even than the autobiography of ABT in which by the way there is an embarrassed reference to the early Q.E.D., meaning quod erat demonstrandum or what has been proved. I think it was her first formal literary enterprise. The story of an emotional entanglement between three young american women who travelled abroad in the summers. The lesbian nature of the involvement was made quite explicit. Conventional as it is except for its content it has a completely unorthodox conclusion. It doesn't conclude. Thus the early title what has been proved. There is no real linear progression of the story either. The characters do go from one place to another in historical time but they never solve anything, they keep encountering each other in variations of the same problem. I think it concerns a period in Stein's life before she settled in Paris as a young woman in Baltimore in love with another young woman in a possibly unrequited romance. Stein never deviated from her sexual identity as lesbian but she did opt to establish herself exclusively through the formal aspect of her medium as an innovator. In "Portraits and Repetition" she said I said in Lucy Church Amiably that women and children change, I said if men have not changed women and children have. But it really is of no importance even if this is true. The thing that is important is the way that portraits of men and women and children are written, by written I mean made. And by made I mean felt. So she said. Her brother Leo once complained of one of her portraits that her description and the portrait failed to correspond at all. Her brother incidentally became such an impediment to her progress and confidence, offering nothing but discouragement, that she never saw him again but once after he left the house in Paris, having been replaced by the steadfast support of her friend and lover Alice Toklas. The brother represented naturally the male establishment, and as a floundering male he had extra good reason for discouraging his sister. "Nothing could solve his problem of being an intricate engine racing at top speed, but producing nothing." Thinking of Leo as maledom these two statements by Richard Bridgman ("Gertrude Stein in Pieces") makes perfect personal/political and literary sense to me: "She had now cast her lot with values that were not necessarily capable of being rationally communicated."

And "Because this position was the basis of her independence she could not afford to have him undermine it." I mean I believe these values and this position were both personal and literary and it was essential to protect both from the threat of male disapproval. The dissociation between literary expression and personal life and something called objective observation could be viewed as a political necessity which was the occasion of genius. In other words the necessity of obscurity was the mother of invention. She recalled her excitement when she discovered that the words she used were not descriptive and indeed often had nothing whatever to do with the thing being represented. As Bridgman writes, "Her prose was irritating because it communicated too little too clearly, or it said too much too obscurely." And, "She created several unreadable styles." Although her obscurity grew out of the suppression of lesbian subject matter, she did become at the same time explicit about her sexuality in the context of her obscurities, contradictory as that may sound. Every so often she comes perilously close to saying something. Really though in the poem "Lifting Belly" and the long prose/poem "Sonatina Followed by Another" she makes obvious references to her intimate life with Alice. "Pussy said I was to wake her in an hour and a half if it didn't rain. It is still raining what should I do." Somehow she found a way. She was unable ultimately to dissemble. Considering this direct autobiographical nature of so much of her writing it is clear she is the only upfront lesbian writer of quality and reputation prior to our time. Stein constantly undermined the content of her work while reasserting it in the same devious guise of her innovative practices. Bridgman says that after 20 years of enigmatic utterances, Gertrude Stein at last chose to speak in a voice of singular clarity. She was 58 years old. He refers to the autobiography of Alice Toklas. I don't agree entirely with his judgment of Edmund Wilson's precocious observation linking her obscurities with her sexuality. He says "Both of Wilson's opinions seem to me to have been correct" (he means a later amendment Wilson made that I don't understand). Lesbian sentiments contributed to Gertrude Stein's stylistic impenetrability, although Wilson did initially exaggerate their importance as an influence. I think their importance can't be exaggerated enough. If you were not impenetrable you had to write novels, and practically nobody did that either. In any case it was Stein's ultimate inability to lie that distinguishes her from those who did write in the novel form. It isn't fair to Stein to mention a writer of her quality in the same breath with Radclyffe Hall, but the comparison is worth considering from the point of view of lesbian identity. Hall's book for all its fame is still a piece of sentimental embarrassing realism. But quality aside, who was Radclyffe Hall.

If she wasn't Radclyffe Hall she was a third unknown identity behind the pen name behind the fictional character of Stephen Gordon. I don't think it matters that much. The important thing is she had to write a fiction, and a tragic one at that. I think if I'd read the "Well of Loneliness" when I should have I might never've fallen into bed with my first woman. It's a dreary discouraging role-playing story. The Sheik was no better. But what was there. The only available Stein was what we continue to have in such recent selections as this penguin book edited by one Patricia Meyerowitz who was the woman last fall contesting Virgil Thomson's outspoken knowledge of Gertrude Stein's sexuality in *The New York Review of Books*. I've quoted Ms. Meyerowitz's objections and Thomson's reply before. But at that time I hadn't seen or noticed the refutation to Meyerowitz in Alice Toklas herself, in Toklas's "What Is Remembered." She refers to the painful joke of Gertrude's about her being an old maid mermaid (the phrase the Meyerowitz quoted to use in part as proof that the two women were celibate in relation to each other) and goes on to indicate that that well might have been the base but that she is now happily gathering wild violets. It's a wonderful pointed if metaphorically obscure passage. Anyway it's all the Meyerowitzs who remain(ed) incredulous over lesbian identity who help to keep us from our own. The unavailability of Stein's work has been a chief factor in the conspiracy. Not only was Stein not hiding behind pseudonyms or fiction but what there was of it in her work was a celebration of lesbianism! Affectionately obscene poetry is not apologetic. Djuna Barnes's "Nightwood" is superior literature but for her too the lesbian subject besides being remote in the novel form is tragic and melancholic and bizarre. Contrast Barnes with Stein who said I like loving. I like mostly all the ways anyone can have of having loving feeling in them. Slowly it has come to be in me that any way of being a loving one is interesting and not unpleasant to me.—If she was unable to assert herself politically she was at least very grandly positive about her private life. And for all its tearjerking tragedy and stereotyped presentation of role-playing lesbianism and its embarrassment as literature "The Well of Loneliness" has a few startling rudimentary political assertions: "Stephen would again and again go over those last heartrending days with Barbara and Jamie, railing against the outrageous injustice that had led to their tragic and miserable ending. She would clench her hands in a kind of fury. How long was this persecution to continue? How long would God sit still and endure this insult offered to His creation? How long tolerate the preposterous statement that *inversion*" (my italics) "was not a part of nature? For since it existed what else could it be? All things that existed were a part of nature!" Radclyffe Hall wasn't so bad. She had a bad time of it like most lesbians and she had to do what we used to call pouring your heart out and many lesbians, if not encouraged to go on by the story, have identified with it. Hall herself was not totally discouraged, like Stein she never deviated from her sexual identity as lesbian, and like Stein and Romaine Brooks and Ida Rubinstein and a number of others she made a long satisfying relationship with one other woman, the one Carol mentioned—Lady Una Troubridge. Speaking of the conspiracy against identity, as regards the painter Romaine Brooks, a number of us last year picked up the *Times* one Sunday to read with great astonishment that this woman most of us had never heard of had just died at the age of 96 and we could now go and see some of her paintings in a small retrospective at the Whitney. In that posthumous article she was identified as a lesbian, and her paintings many of them described as lesbian portraits. Brooks belongs to some fugitive continental elite society of lesbians that flourished particularly in the '20s.

HURRICANE BELLA SWEEPS COUNTRY

November 2, 1972, *Village Voice*

> my staff doesn't understand that i can't permit myself to be beaten over the head by everybody. my schedule beats me, my staff beats me, my constituents beat me my friends beat me—telling me i'm beating everyone else. if things go on like this, i won't make it.

Nevertheless, Iwantedtosee bella, and bella's staff didn't want bella to see me, and bella herself probably didn't care, and finally I interviewed her by telling her about myself over a side order of gefilte fish at fine & schapiro's on 71st street near broadway. I don't like to interview people. It's very embarrassing. It feels like an improper inquisition. It feels as if I don't believe anything in advance of my questions, or rather as if I already know the answers so it's a silly game to ask what I know already, or at the least that it's dumb to ask questions unless it's for gossip or information in the course of a dialogue with a friend. Nevertheless I asked bella some questions, I suppose because we were surrounded by her aides and cohorts and they might've wondered what all the fuss was about if it wasn't to ask the candidate some questions. I asked her some questions and I don't remember what they were or what she said if anything, I know it didn't matter since I agree with her about everything, and I didn't want to arouse her wrath or alarm her constituents by asking a few things that I'd *really* like to know, like have you ever considered having a lesbian experience or how would you feel if your daughter made a lesbian marriage or how far do you think women can actually progress within the male established government and legal processes or how many bellas would it take all at once to make more than a mere dent in that system, since traditionally a strong woman emerges and is hailed and honored and promptly forgotten, but I did ask something along these lines and that was did she think the national legalization of abortion would terminate the current feminist movement the way the vote did in 1920 and she said decisively absolutely not, that we have too much going for us now and she was referring to the national women's political caucus through which she and many women see the ultimate full representation of women in the political power structure. So I did ask something. I think basically I just wanted to spend some time with her and my only excuse was posing as a reporter. I did feel really concerned last June however, and at that time I put myself out to act like a real reporter and as it turned out I was too late and the candidate herself wasted no time or words in telling me so. I was very angry at the albany dudes cutting our woman out of her district, then I was just as angry at all the other dudes for acting as if she *deserved* to be cut out of her district, I mean that mindless collusion of powerless people in the judgment of any authority, as though the fate that befalls anybody constitutes its own justification, that a conviction or an indictment from above automatically confirms the guilt of the victim, and I was almost as angry as the feminists who it seemed to me were deserting their big woman in her most difficult hour, and naturally I was angry at myself for not getting out there and saving the woman single-handed. A weird pall hung over that whole primary. It seemed as if the people who liked bella were afraid to say so and the people who didn't would stop at nothing to silence her forever. This paper for example was involved in the most outlandish incriminations, making a big deal over such items as the use bella's office made of an article that *the voice* printed by bella's "friend and associate" mim kelber, claiming that the omission of the identification *the voice* had made at the end of the article of kelber as abzug's associate in its reprint as a campaign leaflet was a sign of bella's horrible character, even though kelber had in fact identified herself within the article proper and there is in any case no moral issue at stake in the use that anybody makes through selection and omission of already printed material, as though it isn't a standard universal practice to select and omit portions of statements by people for political persuasive purposes. Considering that mim kelber's article was the only substantial literature that this paper printed on bella's behalf it isn't surprising that the paper objected so strenuously to any impression, such as they thought might be created by that omission, of the paper per se being in support of bella abzug. The same objection was made to the selection bella's office made of something positive that hentoff had said. These were trivial and irrelevant arguments against a woman of bella's stature. The smear campaign of a paper like *the post* is something else but I really think all of it from whatever angle was designed to shut up a particularly vocal woman and to step on the face of a victim as I suggested above and to save a sick candidate with an honorable record from the humiliation of a political defeat in his final moments. I don't mean that anybody actually knew that ryan was about to die, I think in fact that many believed he was medically fit, a few doctors in any case had so testified, certainly his illness was a rumor that neither side wished to see embroidered, but I'm convinced that people really do know what is happening at whatever substratum or superstructure of consciousness and that the overwhelming psychic forces at work in that particular event were those of sympathy and support and respect for the choice of a dying fellow in his private decision to leave this world a victor in his own field. I don't know, I do know there was a wet blanket over the whole business and it seemed impossible to get out from under it and do anything decisive or constructive. I called up brenda and gloria and I wrote to them too and said can't you do something or get somebody else to do something and I kept saying I was going to do something myself and then in the end when I actually did do something it was too late. I see from my record book it was wednesday june 15 when I called bella's office to do something and was informed that the election was the following tuesday, the day before *the voice* would come out. That's how much I care about elections in general, I never did know when they were happening. Anyway I thought I could at least say something post factum and I arranged to follow her around the next day, fully aware that everybody should be overjoyed to have an outstanding lesbian endorse an unpopular candidate at the last minute including of course the candidate, who was already predisposed to love the paper she must have thought I represented. Anyway I really wanted to meet her. I'd seen her on a tv documentary yelling and puffing and saying all smart things and I thought she was the hottest thing since gertrude stein whom I'd never be able to see live and in living color; or some incredible composite of powerful females for whom she has no historical precedent. She's not like anybody I know about. And I was convinced she was our leader, even if she did want to send some jets to israel. I wanted her for president, at the very least for mayor, and I knew she was far and away the best candidate for the congress since she stands for all woman's things and we desperately need a return to woman's things as she says in her book we (women) don't have any freudian obsession with missiles. Society doesn't require us to prove our superiority or to accomplish in some superhuman manner. We have very, very little to prove. That's why, in terms of political power, I feel we'd end up being a lot more sensible. And more peaceful. And another passage: This moment in history requires women to lead the movement for radical change, first because we have the potential of becoming the largest individual movement; two, because our major interests are in common with other oppressed groups; and three, because we've never had a chance to make mistakes in government and so we have no mistakes to defend. Men have made the world the way it is.—I hadn't read the book last june but I knew how smart she was and I was very angry and upset about her situation and about not being able to do anything about it. So I appeared at el diario the spanish newspaper where they said she was going to talk to the editors and discussed "the situation" with bonnie lobel while we waited bonnie told me she thought women would get a lot more timid if bella was put down and that men would take courage and that if all feminists stood together bella wouldn't be able to lose and people never cared about bill ryan before, it was all their male egos, they hate this kind of woman, they want us to run only against bad men, bad men are in districts that are so conservative that we can't win, what they're really saying is they want us to lose, and that there's been more psychoanalyzing in this race than in any other and like that until bella emerged from the elevator with a bunch of people and we shook hands and she levelled at me civilly enough and told me that before the campaign she'd turned down as a matter of principle an invitation to be interviewed by hentoff who'd been offered a lucrative sum for it by playboy and then she disappeared into an office. An hour or two later when she came out she was pointedly ignoring me but I refused to think she was. I walked down the seven flights and waited for the entourage leaning a little too casually against a wall near the door. The elevator opened and bella stood squarely facing me glowering at the world, I thought I just happened to be in the way. I sprang to attention and said timidly with great expectations well where are you going now, what are you going to do, just to consolidate bonnie's proposal that I go with them wherever they were going in the car. It was a brief moment of social illusion. The reply from my leader was the end of me. She said without a second's hesitation: Frankly jill, you're a little late. Just like that. I hadn't felt so bad since a lover of mine flew away to spain in 1969. The line was even a little like that last one that rhett butler threw out at scarlett o'hara about not giving a damn. I went into instant devastation and turned round to face the door and while I paused momentarily my exit became blocked by bella and the others standing there looking at the rain wondering what they were going to do. I knew what *I* was going to do if I could just get by. I found an opening in the bodies and slid outside to my parked van, I still had my van, hearing the bellow of abslug's voice behind me "get that woman . . . get that woman" but I really had to split. I was a little late. Of course I was late. I was furious. I hated to be told what I already knew. I went someplace to brood over my wounds and think it all over. I thought a lot of different things at once. I thought it was because I was a lesbian. No I was just being parannoyed and besides the first thing I ever heard about this woman was she was speaking out for gay rights. I thought it was because she thought I represented *the voice*. I thought she must be mistaking me for hentoff or nichols. I thought I was too tall or had too many freckles or altogether I was just too goy looking. I thought she was merely angry at the world and I could dig that and people told me she said things like that to everybody so I decided to transcend my injury and try again. Anyway I was feeling less guilty and more sanctimonious. If the bella people were so upset about *the voice* in all these weeks why the hell didn't they contact the only feminist on the paper. It was clear why they didn't contact the only feminist, because the only feminist was a lesbian. Or, as their press man howard brock said of nichols, she doesn't count for much, and I added, you mean because she's a woman. No answer. No answer in general. Beginning october 4 I called bella's office repeatedly and was repeatedly discouraged from doing anything, not by any negative directive, only by the more insidious discouragement of the indifference in vague responses. I think I'm going to renew my idea of running for mayor on a lesbian ticket. And I won't have any boys around working for me. I think if bella has trouble with her staff it's because she has a lot of boys around. October 20 I was riding in her car leaving her office on seventh avenue and a boy was driving and her woman was sitting in the back with me, I just can't imagine it for myself, I mean if I was going to be out there talking up all women's things the way bella does I'm not going to be having a *boy* driving my car, much less running my office and I don't care what they say the way *both* offices, in washington and new york, look to me is that the women are doing the same old shit work and the boys are running the show, the big cheese in washington is this very bright exceptional looking kid with curly hair and a vest, he's her legislative assistant, and the worst vibe in the place is emanating from this "older woman" in a sort of a blonde bouffant sitting efficiently at the typewriter. I know bella had two women as her legislative assistants who didn't work out for some reason and they may be harder to find than boys but anyplace you go there's always at least one hard-working highly capable intelligent girl who can do it too if not better so I can't see the advantage in having a boy, especially the big tough type she has for her press secretary, unless the boy is strictly a servant and *no* boy these days in any sort of administrative job in a roomful of women at typewriters and telephones is less than somehow in charge, bella herself has said women control everything in politics but the power. She said we wouldn't even have effective political parties without women . . . filing, typing, mailing, telephoning and fund raising. There are no campaigns where women are not the mainstay. That's very close to what jerry rubin said about the women in the back room doing the crucial work for chicago while the boys were out in the defense box getting their media massage, but nobody seriously expects rubin to do anything about it, my quarrel with the abzug arrangement is an old saw of mine about heavy feminists out there saying all right things and doing them too and not particularly noticing or correcting the inconsistencies of their daily personal lives but if I pursued this it would bring me smack down to the feminist/lesbian political line of living and action and I really had decided to suspend my stringent solutions for the cause of bella who needs me like a hole in the head. I still think she's dynamite. I like all her hats and her dresses and I don't even mind her makeup. I like her solid imposing body and I don't care if she never does diet the way she says she keeps trying to: Oh, I'm always starting diets, but I can't stick to them. Something happens, like I get agitated on the House Floor, so I go into the cloakroom at the back of the Floor and stuff myself with things I shouldn't be eating. One of these days tho' I'm going to get on a serious diet. Ha, it would really be too much for these fellows if I was svelte. They'd bust a gut.—See, that's what's so terrific about this woman, she says it all straight out, she just doesn't give a damn, she says what she thinks about the war and the big shots and how she feels about anybody and herself and the price of baloney in the bronx all with the same hutzpah and humanity like she says "I'm a very spontaneous and excitable and emotional person and I do have a way of expressing myself pretty strong sometimes. Big deal." And she says "Oh, I don't know, I guess it's my cross to bear, these things. I mean, how am I to do anything if I don't scream and carry on? How else do you get action out of these people?" She says politicians are human beings and we think politicians are plastic people and people don't expect any blemishes of people who rise in the hierarchies and that people criticize her style but her style is human and people're not used to it. She also refers to her style as a certain vigor. Whatever it is the difference between her and a guy like ryan is that between a national leader and a local outstanding liberal. The big difference of course is that one is a woman and the other a male and this is the difference that a growing number of women and some men are beginning to see as the difference that makes *all* the difference. The "woman issue" was underplayed by both sides in the primary. I remember a *time magazine* article about both candidates in which incredibly it wasn't even mentioned. Apparently people looked away from the woman issue because that was one issue the bella camp was dead right on and otherwise what was the real difference between the two if it wasn't that ryan was running on his good record and bella was an interloper and according to the insinuations of ryan's literature bella had a big mouth and we know how the media played up this difference and made bella out to be the great white witch of the west; there was, however, apart from sex, a significant difference which bella's people put forward as their leading campaign pitch and that was that bella is an activist, that she not only votes for the right things but she goes out and mobilizes people, she does things like organizing people to go to washington to demonstrate in support of her issues and bills. I'm not in the business here of itemizing her accomplishments, people presumably know what they are. I am saying that apart from the central issue of sex, or I should say apart from and related to, here is a political leader who is actually doing something about the things that so many people are talking about, although what I still want to say chiefly is that sex is the overwhelming issue of bella's candidacy as she said herself she's the only woman who ever successfully ran for national office on an essentially women's rights social change program and as a reporter noted after the primary her defeat demonstrated that america's women voters are still not ready to put the issue of women's rights above all else and as all the venom against bella indicates the country is terrified of an outspoken woman, let alone one with real power, for bella may be making waves and introducing important legislation and even pushing a little of it through, but she has no real power and if she did as she says you can be sure that they wouldn't let her talk, as long as she's not a threat to them they're prepared to see her as interesting and dynamic, and, most of all, not boring, yet for the first time in amerikan political history we have a woman in the congress who is absolutely clear on the priorities of women's issues which include not only the pivotal question of abortion but all those concerns which involve the hopes and fears of simple people, matters of wages and child care and welfare, that consistently rate low on the scale of values to the ruling white male elite whose expensive fantasies in elaborate deadly toys and adventure vehicles continue to take all precedence over the basic needs of the people which I think we can rightly call a woman's priorities since it is the women in modern civilization who have been unfettered with the major burden of caring and the women in turn who've suffered the most when their boys grow up to care more about their toys and adventures than the daily rounds of survival business out of which they originated. The women are the warriors of peace and socialism and bella grasps the significance of her role as a leader in the movement to bring the mothers out of the political closet. A key revelation of feminism is that if women don't speak for themselves they're not going to get what they want. That seems so fundamental as to be unmentionable. Yet hordes of women still respect the assumption of their fathers and brothers and even sons to speak for them, in that spirit certainly the women are out there in battalions cheering for mcgovern because he's the nicer daddy and for the duration things would be nicer, like ryan was good enough on women's issues and he wasn't attacked for his position on women but the whole point is that women don't need the surrogate daddies any more. I asked bella about mcgovern. She says he isn't "right" on abortion, but he's the best candidate that the living generations of amerikans have even seen and she excuses shirley maclaine from her sellout on abortion for her dedication to a good man. I don't see it that way but I wasn't into arguing as I said I didn't want to arouse her wrath or alarm her constituents and basically I just wanted to spend some time with her. I even drove down to washington and back and went to a session of congress all as it turned out to spend a grand total of two minutes with the woman. Anyway I thought I should begin my political education in earnest by visiting the capitol. Essentially I sent jill to washington to watch jill watching bella. The press section wouldn't let me in (*the village voice* is a weekly they said) and the visitor's gallery wouldn't let me write anything and although I went as a marine I wasn't offered any particular military dispensation either. In fact as I approached section seven or eight with my tag and gained admittance I was assailed by three guards one of whom lunged at my pendant period piece, grabbing all the metal and icons at once in his white chubby paw and demanding some explanation. I told him I was a jewelry designer for alexander's in the bronx. Then I sat down to watch our great government in operation. I heard the roll call. I watched the little man with a gavel in a high chair. I looked for bella. I listened to these speeches congratulating somebody who was retiring, one fellow saying how nice he'd been all these years and another fellow "wholeheartedly and unequivocally and enthusiastically endorsing the compliments of so & so about so & so who was retiring." I listened to an elderly upstanding type denounce dr. spock as a man who is not a "gentleman," apparently because he doesn't "deserve" the secret service protection he's receiving as a presidential candidate. I listened to lots of figures, the ones I remember being $65,000 for indian affairs and $2 million for the j.f. kennedy performing arts center. I heard the roll call again for a vote. I heard a debate in which one man said we were going down the primrose path and another said we were paying people to be patriotic and another said they were being hired to serve and not paid to kill and another called it an enlistment incentive, it was all about bonuses for reserves and bonuses for reenlistment.

I wasn't looking for bella when I saw her and I leaned over the railing and a guard swooped down to tell me to sit back. I'd never seen her without a hat. I remembered that line in her book "I must admit I was so angry that I made a very shocking speech before the vote" and hoped she would do it but she was leaning on a chair in the aisle talking to the congresswoman from massachusetts and she looked ready to split as soon as she voted no for something. I ran downstairs to catch her at the door to be informed there were seven doors and I'd better leave my name for the man to announce me on the Floor so I left my name Miss or Mrs. Ms I said Miss, he repeated, and turned to enter the Floor to announce me. I'll tell you one thing I'm beginning to realize which might shock you: It's not the reactionaries in congress who feel threatened by me. It's the liberals. Isn't that regrettable? See, I'm more freewheeling and I'm less bound to tradition than most of these liberals are.—I says what's on my mind.—"Well jill," she said, or asked. She was wearing her hat. I was wearing my aviator shades. I wished I was jewish suddenly. I wished I shopped at alexander's. I wished I'd gone to hunter college. I wished I knew something about politics. What could I say? That I'd schlepped myself down to washington to ask her if she'd ever considered having a lesbian experience? I shifted my weight and said weakly "well, I thought we might try again," thinking of our first and last disaster and of how eager bella's people were for bella to see me and how our meeting would advance the cause of the revolution. I know I was identified in her mind with *the village voice* the way red and matador are to a bull but either she liked me as a marine or she appreciated my schlepping all the way to washington for nothing so she controlled herself during our entire two minute walk to an exit and let me interview her by telling her about myself. I said I couldn't get into the press section and that congress was a boys club and I didn't like it and I wondered if a tall woman could be the speaker since they had such a short man doing it and I was driving back to new york and when could we get together. She said she was on her way to a new york delegation luncheon and she couldn't invite me and she didn't think it was particularly worth my while to return to the congress session either. We squared off at the top of some marble stairs. She tilted her head and hat and smiled winningly. I had to smile back. I felt suddenly quite chummy in fact and slapped the top of her arm lightly with my record book. So much for washington. I went and looked at some statues and listened to some more congressional bullshit and made it back in three hours 15 minutes. I was impressed by bella's schedule. She said she got up at 5 a.m. and flew to new york at 7 for a press conference and flew back on a 12 noon plane for the session. She was huffing and complaining just the way she does in her book. She complains all the time I guess. There's a yiddish word for that I can't remember what it is. I did learn a nice one from mim kelber however and that was tumler, a tumler is a person who creates a lot of excitement. Some people call that a big mouth. It's very clear to me now. We have one woman down there saying all smart things and that one woman is making up in sheer volume and determination for all the women who don't yet have a voice. As she says of the others some of the women in congress are no better than men because they're all products of the male power structure. They come in, replace the men, act the same way as men, and do their bidding. They don't come out of a movement for social change.—A big problem facing the national women's political caucus emerges in the debate over numbers and feminism. On the one hand it could be said that the more women we get into office the more likely we'll be able to get our ideas across as brenda hyphenated explained, on the other as bella has asked do we want the kind of women who are going to vote for missiles and vietnam wars or do we want the kind of women who are going to put our tax money into housing and health and child care centers and abortion clinics and things like that. I agree with both since I think in the end the psychology of women is not fundamentally destructive, and I don't agree with any of it from the point of view of imagining that any great progress can be made within the male system proper but as I said I was suspending my stringent solutions for the cause of the rear guard. We want them out there covering for us. I want them for president. I want these dynamite women who say they've always felt that a nation can be judged by the quality of care it provides for its children and not by its airplanes and its missiles. I want these women whose voice is so big they can make one feminist quip into a national joke which sums up the whole schmiel: manny celler: "Why, women weren't even at the Last Supper." Bella: Listen, manny, I want you to understand one thing: we may not have been at the last one, but we sure as hell will be at the next one." I mentioned the joke at fine & schapiro's over my side order of gefilte fish. She said it was too obvious to say the women were out in the back cooking it. I agreed and I complimented her and I complimented her on her pink hat and I think I kept complimenting her. I rarely do that. I must've been very happy to be sitting down to supper with her and her aides in a jewish restaurant. I was glad our initial interview was over too. I got into that car I mentioned a while back and was really uncomfortable and didn't have anything to say. She was sitting in the front with the driver and I didn't know where we were going. I knew I was supposed to be firing questions. I *know* questions are foolish. So I was riding along in a strange car with strange people. Then she said without turning around from out of a huge fur coat collar: "Well, jill." Then she said "So whatdya write for that paper for" and I said "So whatdya work for that male government for." No I didn't, I made some lame excuse and said when I was president I'd put a stop to the freedom of the press and she replied that that was interesting but later on in the lobby of a teleprompter place she said freedom of the press was a precious thing. I added by the way that *the voice* prides itself on its multitude of voices and I don't remember what she replied if anything. I asked her about shirley and miami and betty & such and she kind of sighed and said she heard betty was up at this place (maybe the catskills) trashing her and gloria again. I said what's wrong with her. She said I dunno why don't you ask her. I said she doesn't speak to me. She said oh that's right she doesn't like you. I thought wow she must be an encyclopedia of that kind of information. I forgot to compliment her. I almost didn't make it to supper. I was standing on the corner of 86th and broadway in the rush hour while she did her "subway stop" really grokking on the whole thing and she began to pointedly ignore me again. A new york legislator was holding her elbow and piloting her into the subway people coming out of the ground saying "Meet Mrs. Abzug" or "Come and Shake Hands with Congresswoman Abzug" I was absolutely amazed at this sort of street theatre. A barker at a side show. Bigger than life on a street corner. Smiling and chatting and handing out buttons and not appearing to mind the sore heads or the obvious ones. I guessed the "subway stop" is a whole amerikan institution. Her aide told me people like to see that their politicians are real. Yeah, I could appreciate that. I was completing my political education. I was cold and her aides were pressing me to ask some questions, right on the street corner, I couldn't interrupt those little chats with her middleaged jewish women admirers, but I knew they planned to cut me out of supper so I sort of tried but she was miffed at me again, that was clear, and besides she was enjoying her subway stop, so I tried to think what I could do by analyzing what maybe was wrong. What was wrong was that four of her constituents came out of the ground and recognized *me*. Oy vay.

And I thought she would appreciate the joke, after all, so I was talking to one and hailed bella on the side "hey bella" something or other and I guess I couldn't've done worse than if I'd asked her if her mother was on welfare so I waited and waited while she pointedly ignored me and then I made my move I blurted out oh I want one of your buttons too as though it was a crime nobody gave me one in the first place and she smiled and handed it over and things were mildly okay again, it's really touch and go with a great politician. I struggled to get the button into a suede jacket and then we went to supper where I was supposed to get down to the serious business of asking questions, finally. I ordered my gefilte and told her what I thought of the gay male homosexual movement and the revolutionary effeminists and how lesbians are not homosexuals but feminists I suppose she knew already. I suppose she knows everything. So I added as a sort of rhetorical question so whatta we want a medal for being in the vanguard? And she got it. She gets everything, she isn't any particular age, she could be my daughter or my grandmother (if only I'd come from the bronx). She isn't even a person, she's a phenomenon. That isn't true, she's a real person, a real person person, a real woman person who thinks and feels lots of things in succession and all at once, a typhoon of a woman actually who blows hot and cold and forms into funnels that suck things up and carry them for miles and drop them in unlikely places and move on silently over the gloaming gory political landscape. One minute in her office behind closed doors yelling stamping pounding the tables "I'm very unhappy about . . . It's outrageous that . . . " and the next in a solemn quiescence in the car preparing to meet the broadcasters for a completely lucid and low key speech about her credentials as a congressional candidate. I want these women in office who're in touch with their feelings and who know perfectly well when they're bullshitting and who don't have to displace their concealed feelings by dropping bombs on people who live thousands of miles away because they (the bellas) *know* when they're concealing their feelings because they're right up front with them *most* of the time. Forsleuth I wasn't disappointed in the real woman. I wished I could spend more time with her. I know she wished she was with martin, she kept saying so. She was very upset she couldn't reach martin in the pay phone at the "subway stop" to meet her for dinner. I wished I could be solely responsible for her belated victory at the polls this week. Would she think I was crazy, for wanting to feel "like one woman risking her life going up in a heliocopter to save the world when the world's obviously not going to be saved by one woman. Not even the country. Not even the state." Even so, she knows where she's going.

our time has come. we will no longer content ourselves with leavings and bits and pieces of the rights enjoyed by men. we will no longer be satisfied to remain on the outside of power looking in. we want our equal rights. nothing more, but nothing less. we want an equal share of political and economic power.—bella abzug, june 9, 1972.

AGNES MARTIN (1): SURRENDER & SOLITUDE

Village Voice, September 13, 1973

going to see agnes martin in the desert came to seem to me like a pilgrimage and i don't see why not. a pilgrimage is a long, weary journey, as to a shrine. a shrine is a tomb of a saint or other sacred person. none of these words may apply to any contemporary venture. at best perhaps they have exotic unreal connotations, but agnes martin is a spiritual woman and she isn't easy to find. unless you happen to be in los angeles when she's speaking at the pasadena museum, which was just my luck last month while passing down the coast. i was mildly disappointed since i wanted her to be as hard to find as i'd been told she was and i guess the last place i expected to see her first since she disappeared from civilization was in the civilization of a museum. yet i was relieved in a way, just to see that she was alive for one thing, and to have the opportunity to see how she felt about me before i made so bold as to trek into her wilderness with only a one-way advance telegram to recommend my arrival. i was disappointed in general to hear that agnes had been emerging at all. she has in fact made six museum appearances this past year, and she told me she flew to germany recently to negotiate the sale of some prints, it seemed therefore that i'd be visiting somebody who was just very inaccessible and not a recluse from civilization, nonetheless she is basically a recluse and she always has been thus it doesn't matter now any more than before how far you got to see her unless you like to travel and see deserted places. i used to see agnes in her loft on the battery and i don't know if she's any different now than she was then and she left new york in 1967. i think if anybody's different it's me and although i thought she was very special then i doubt that i heard what she had to tell me. i was just awed to be in her presence. i knew she was one of the great women. it was a pleasure finding a great woman in new york city during the terrible times of the '60s during every terrible decade it's a pleasure finding a great woman. a great woman may be a woman more interested in herself than in anything else. one way you knew agnes martin was great was because she lived decisively alone and that this was an active irrevocable choice and because she put very little stock in people at all and another way you knew she was great was because her paintings were. i know agnes would say the work is completely apart from the person and i have no quarrel with that myself but i see the work and the person as indissoluble too. my earliest memory of agnes is of her work alone but then a little later on i saw agnes and her work together and in fact i rarely saw them apart since whenever i went to her loft almost always as i remember she showed me her paintings and sometimes her drawings too and so for me agnes was agnes the painter although i understand her detachment. her paintings are not about the world and i suppose her paintings paint themselves and in this sense she has nothing to do with it. i think it was 1964 when i stopped in at the elkon gallery and saw all these six by six foot paintings washed out whites and tans crossed by close vertical and horizontal lines muted and irregularly perfect and i called up dick bellamy and said do you know this woman agnes martin why aren't you showing her i thought at that time that if anybody good was around he was supposed to be showing them but of course he knew her work and he wasn't showing her elkon was anyway that was my introduction to the work of agnes martin. a little later on either by design or accident i was knocking on her door to review her most recent show for art news and that was how i met her. already i thought her paintings were beautiful and i wanted to meet the artist. i wasn't the least bit disappointed but socially possibly i was more awkward than she was so i wonder how we impressed each other. her hair was long then and she had lots of it and when i came in it was all loose and she was busying herself putting it back or up and sort of apologizing for being in some disarray. i know we had tea and i looked at her paintings but i don't know what else. looking at agnes's paintings with agnes was a quiet concentrated ceremonious ritual. there was a very certain distance she traversed from the point in her loft where the paintings were stashed to the spot right next to the door where she showed them. one by one without any hurry or hesitation she would carry them from one place to another, back and forth, and when she reached the showing place next to the door there would be a certain gesture of hiking the work with her foot under the canvas up into position on the nails sticking out of the wall. then she would sit down next to you and contemplate the work with you and wait as i imagined for you to speak your thoughts. i can't imagine what i ever said if anything. i know we discussed the titles. i think very often she wanted to know if some particular title or other was appropriate but i'm not sure. i liked them all myself. desert. islands. mountain. blue flower. hill.

starlight. ocean water. leaf. untitled. i liked them all. i thought i could see what they were even though everything was a graph. i used to say to people there was this painter painting mystical geometries as though nobody else had thought of that. nature paintings ruled by the horizontal line or was it vertical. when she was young she painted the mountains as they were or as we suppose we see them or anyway the way you see them at the washington square outdoor art show. in the desert agnes told me she could see in nature there weren't any *real* verticals or real horizontals and right then she gave up on nature. in the desert there weren't any paintings at all. there was a rectangular pit maybe six feet deep and 15 feet from corner to corner next to her little adobe that she said was the foundation for a studio. she abandoned new york and painting both when she left in '67 and now she is beginning to begin again. it isn't altogether clear why she left new york and why she stopped painting but if you heard the story it's the sort of story you accept and understand without any explanations. leaving new york has become as much a ritual exodus as going to new york is a ritual initiation. people said oh agnes martin left in a dodge pickup, and nobody knows where she went, or you'd hear vague reports that she ended up in the new mexican desert. i asked agnes how she ended up there, why she chose cuba, and she said she saw these mountains on this road leading northward into cuba in her minds eye in new york and that was how come. i was amazed to find the place. i sent a telegram as i said but i never made the 6 a.m. bus out of albuquerque that i declared i would. the reason being that jane was flying in from new york and arriving 11 a.m. and i didn't know that till after i sent the telegram and i didn't send another because i didn't want to make any more declarations. Anyway about 3 p.m. three women of albuquerque drove us north toward cuba where i enquired in the postoffice if they knew where agnes lived. they said no but a man down the road did. down the road the man's daughter explained carefully and i thought it sounded pretty clear. basically she said there was a gate a dry river bed and a little forest. i don't see gates dry river beds or little forests very often so i heard it all in the singular. i'm still certain she said it that way too. well there were lots of gates and dry river beds and little forests. first you had to drive some few miles out of cuba way off the main drag if you could call the road through cuba that. the gate the man's daughter mentioned was obvious enough. an impressive barbed wire gate the sort you have to get out and unhinge and swing away for the car to pass and then rehinge again. then we were on a soft red clay road. then we crossed the dry river bed. then there was a little forest, midget gnarled trees of some sort. then i expected to see agnes's adobe. but what there was was another gate. i didn't think we should go through it but we did because there wasn't any other place to go in order to reach a dwelling unless you went careening off into the sage and the arroyas, those dry river beds in the form of drastic looking jagged ditches that snake around all over the place through those parts. so we went on and everything began to look like a dry river bed and a forest. i asked one of the albuquerque women what we were driving through actually. she said it was a short grass prairie with incursion of sonoran desert species running into pinon-juniper forest. that sounded good. i liked being there and all too, but the apprehension was mounting, especially when there was not only a third gate but a fork or a choice of going off or on the same road unimpeded by a gate. moreover we had passed the half eaten carcass of a cow right long the side of the road and that seemed to create an adage in my mind that when you see a dead cow you should turn back. besides i had the feeling we were within a clods throw of agnes's adobe but some part of my head said we were going to die in the desert. anyway we were all neurotically consuming a bag of nectarines and i was about to die laughing. i thought i'd never be able to travel in the desert with lucia since we were both particularly dying laughing. i said we should turn back. it was quite a few miles inching back over the soft clay bumpy road and reopening the gates and closing them behind us and wondering where the hell agnes was. back on the macadam we went a half a mile up to a little ranch farm to ask this man and his wife if we'd been on the right series of gates river beds and forests of agnes martin and the man said yes and his wife drew diagrams in the dirt and the man gestured out across the plain and said that's her mesa, right there, as though i should be able to see it and there was a curl of smoke out of a chimney that i was missing. it was clear anyway that we had to go through that third gate where the fork was where we'd turned back so we did it again and we came to a real little sage and juniper forest and there it was a small complex of vehicles and structures that had to be agnes. agnes the classicist. classicism she says is not about people and this work is not about the world. classicists are people that look out with their back to the world. it represents something that isn't possible in the world. it's as unsubjective as possible. the classic is cool. it is cool because it is impersonal and detached. if a person goes walking in the mountains that is not detached and impersonal she's just looking back. to a detached person the complication of the involved life is like chaos. if you don't like the chaos you're a classicist. if you like it you're a romanticist. painting is not about ideas or personal emotion. painting the desert in her head. the horizontal line. there's very few verticals in nature. and there she was as vertical as i remembered her which was only a week ago at the pasadena museum sitting on a chair in the middle of the stage surrounded by an overflow audience her hair short to the ears and still brown and wearing sort of tangerine velveteen skirt to the floor with a white starched blouse slightly femme flared at the elbows and twisting a white handkerchief in her lap as though it was worry beads and my friend with me said she looked a dead ringer for gertrude stein. picasso said he was impressed by gertrude stein's physical personality and anyone might say the same of agnes martin. she's extremely handsome and she has the most brilliant twinkling blue eyes and her body is full and she's very solidly there yet shy and a little retreating at the same time. she giggles and jokes a lot and laughs at herself and i'd never seen her so solemn and formal. and i'd never seen her in a skirt or any sort of a "blouse." i could see she was on her best behavior. even as though it was sunday school or something. the audience too was reverent and expectant. it was a new aspect of agnes to me. although not one i wouldn't have envisioned. as i said she was for me a spiritual woman and i was awed to be in her presence and i believed whatever she said i knew she was a right person a natural woman a presence of the universe. she made pronouncements and spoke in aphorisms and she was known to go into trances and she proclaimed the future and she had no pretensions about herself except perhaps as a painter which may possibly be the subject of her intimate and abstracted speech that she's given lately in several of these museums. it's called the underlying perfection of life and almost the first thing she says is we are blinded by pride and that living the prideful life we are frustrated and lost that we cannot overcome pride because we ourselves are pride but we can witness the defeat of pride because pride is not real and cannot last, when pride is overcome we feel a sudden joy in living, the best place to witness the defeat of pride is in our work . . . all the time we are working and in itself . . . all the time in your working your self is expressed in your work in everyone's work in the work of the world we eliminate expressions of pride. her speech is 4000 words long she told me, and she memorized the whole thing. she speaks of pride, and pride, and perfection and solitude and fear and helplessness and defeat and disappointment and surrender and discipline and the necessity of all these and the necessity of the defeat of pride. besides knowing why she left new york i wanted to know why she left new york but i had no way of asking. she was glad to see me by the way. she baked an apple pie for the occasion and then when i wasn't on the 6 a.m. bus from albuquerque she was disappointed and ate some of it. i was glad she was glad to see me and i was glad we drove past the dead cow again and found her. i left jane and the three women of albuquerque in the car a discreet distance from her adobe and walked over there and hailed her and she emerged from the door beaming in dark blue work clothes very tanned or desert weathered i thought and that makes her eyes bluer and more sparkly. she was pleased i didn't bring everybody to the door at once because she wanted to change her clothes. she put on a clean shirt and pants and i explained that the three women of albuquerque were going home in case she wondered. but first we all had the apple pie and a french fish soup bouillabaisse with salmon okra and tomatoes. i was very nervous. or very high and nervously attuned to her emanations and expectations. later jane and me agreed we were afraid of her. i couldn't remember being afraid of her before so i decided i'd changed a lot. i must've been more presumptuous about myself before or not so aware of the extraordinary presence i was in. or we were both crazy and i thought she was my peer. i don't know. i *was* in awe, but less conscious perhaps. there was the most incredible evening in '66 i think it was when i brought five or six people over to her loft and we sat around in a vague circle in a sort of a trance as though it was a seance although nobody mentioned it and there was at one point this great overhead crash i don't know what it was it wasn't thunder and lightning it might've been a skylight on the roof or even her skylight but whatever it was she didn't bat a lash she went right on talking and asking us all what sort of a wall or body of water we imagined in our minds eyes and when we saw the wall or the body of water would we cross it or could we and if so how would we do it she went right on with this exercise testing us i imagined for correct answers anyway as though nothing had happened which is her basic approach to life. nothing happens. no verticals. everything the same. a quiet existence. not much time for other people's problems. lots of time to herself. solitude and loneliness and contentment with one self. the union of opposites without trying to do so. the friend who went with me to the pasadena talk wrote and told me the whole thing seemed much stronger now than it did at the time but what she absolutely remembers about it is that everything she said she also negated completely, and she doesn't know how she did it. she does contradict herself all the time with the most bewildering confidence. she'll say all conventional people spend 90 per cent of their time wondering is it right or wrong. what you do is right, that's it. then she'll be cato and censor and tell you how absolutely wrong you are. she'll tell me one moment that associative thinking is the basis of all our distraction and the next that i'm exceptionally lucid when i'm at the typewriter. she'll tell me i'm very prudish and priggish (and she *knows* i'm a snob), and later on she'll say i shouldn't use four letter words. she'll say she wanted to ask me something although she wasn't into winning anything and then suddenly there's an argument and it seems as though somebody has to win something if we're to proceed to the next. i think she's delighted to see people but her fear of being disappointed by people is intense. she says she talks all the time when people come in order not to know more than she wants to know. she said you mean you realized how mean we all are? she said about people who come to see her believe you me, i run em off if i don't like them, if they're inconsiderate. she said it with a little chuckle. and told about a couple who came and lived off her for two days and the woman ate a peach from their car right in front of her and didn't offer her one. she doesn't know really why people come to see her. i wasn't sure myself, being such a pilgrimage and all. i just know she's important to me. and i was very curious to see how she was living in the desert. and i still wondered why she left new york even though i knew. i didn't know how to ask but she offered a number of hints gratuitously. she said i don't blame people for not being able to see the paintings, goodness knows, i have no idea why i did them myself. she said i had 10 one-man shows and i was discovered in every one of them. finally when i left town i was discovered again—discovered to be missing. she said she didn't know if she had left the world behind or the world had left her. she said she left new york because of remorse. she said that out at the edge of the canyon after we walked out through the sage to see the sunset. i didn't say anything at all. i guess it isn't necessary to clarify everything or anything. the canyon and the sunset were what seemed to matter and that didn't matter either. a glow was on us though and agnes extended what i thought must be the rarest compliment for her. she said everybody who comes is very conventional except me. it was after that that we were walking back to her adobe and she said she wanted to ask me something although she wasn't into winning anything. it was certainly a difficult moment.

AGNES MARTIN (2): OF DESERTS AND SHORES

Village Voice, September 20, 1973

it was certainly a difficult moment i was saying i was saying that was when we walked back from the canyon and the sunset and agnes said she wanted to ask me something although she wasn't into winning anything and i knew it would be some sort of political question which would mean she would stop liking me having just said out at the canyon that everybody who comes is very conventional except me. i have no idea what she meant by the question all i can say is it concerned domination and i think whether i hadn't experienced domination or being dominating, i thought possibly she was alluding to women as role players, i had no intention of mentioning the despairing word feminism, agnes was born in 1912 and it doesn't take much ingenuity to see that she's better off in the desert throwing mud at her adobe and polishing her green truck than i am going around meeting hundreds of strange women who might have nothing more in common than electricians and philosophers but who in the name of feminism take issue with your four syllable words so that we can all be the same that is to say feminists, thus i believe i was appropriately evasive and the only remark i remember is agnes saying her sister says she believes in men women children and dogs and we left it at that although that wasn't the end of it. the thing is in any case one remains modest and gives honor to the sage who stands outside the affairs of the world. out around her adobe she pointed out the loco weed, which drives horses crazy she said. she explained how you make adobe mud bricks by filling up four rectangular sections of these open wooden frames with the mud stuff and then leaving them out to dry or bake in the sun. she talked about animals having thoughts and how she doesn't keep domestic ones any more, she doesn't want them around any more than people. what she keeps exactly is five vehicles in perfect working order and a beebee gun and a regular .22. not counting the small adobe in which she cooks and eats and possibly reads and undoubtedly muses, an open tall shedlike garage where she was parking her new shiny blue vw sports model, an outhouse, a tiny cave log room guest dwelling and a compost affair and she still sleeps in the dodge pickup or the pickup detached from the truck in which she lived for a couple of years riding all round the u.s. and canada till she found the proper mesa. when we drove away i said it didn't seem as if we were driving off a mesa, she said that's because we drove off the back end. anyway she keeps all her machines in good shape. before we woke up she polished her green truck, a '48 chevie, she said. the jeep we didn't see because she keeps it in town in case the roads've been more washed out than usual. i didn't see how we made it in in her white dodge truck returning from taos there must've been some rain and the dodge had zilch traction so i kept ditching off to the side to a standstill and somehow retreating backtracking and then racing forward as though to hit your mark meaning staying on the road as in archery if there's a wind you shoot or aim way off target in order to hit it or even boomerang yourself. after the first night there she gave us a vacation and we went to taos. i was relieved in a way since the telepathy is pretty heavy and i had had a nightmare and the scrutiny is relentless and while she completely disarms you she then flatly contradicts you and as i've indicated i was fearful of exposing what could only be a profound political disagreement between us. i read a hilton kramer review she had there of her retrospective in philadelphia and couldn't help saying the reason she doesn't have the reputation hilton kramer says she should have is because she's a woman. but agnes knows exactly who or what she is or isn't. she shot back i'm not a woman and i don't care about reputations. i said well i wouldn't come to see you if you weren't a woman. she concluded the argument saying i'm not a woman, i'm a doorknob, leading a quiet existence. in taos jane thought of buying her an enamel doorknob we saw there but we brought back some cheese and syrup instead. also jane bought some eggs milk and apples and agnes said that was exactly what she needed so as concerned the food we were in perfect agreement. another safe thing was finding out more about agnes, i never asked her much before, i never seriously wondered why she was so different and a natural woman of the universe, or even why i felt close to her while knowing she had her life a lot more together. i never knew she was scottish for instance, but i didn't know how scottish i am until recently either. i think the first thing i asked her over the apple pie and french soup bouillabaisse was where did she come from. then i asked her if she likes the bagpipes and she replied oh yes, a half a mile away, she doesn't come from scotland herself actually. she was born and grew up in saskatchewan, somehow i always thought it was vancouver. i thought vancouver was a wild uncharted territory, but i happen to be in vancouver right now and i can see how agnes couldn't possibly have come from vancouver, i never inquired what saskatchewan is but it sounds northern and wild and right for where agnes would have to come from. she's a mountaineering camping pioneering frontier type of woman whose unnatural habitats for reasons of turning out to be a painter were vertical claustrophobic cities like new york. she's climbed big mountains alone for years so i can only imagine how she felt going three hours upstate new york with me and thalia poons one summer for a little two day cook and sleep-out next to a crick river and 20 yards in from the macadam but she never mentioned what an elementary tourist trip it was. the crick was deep enough to submerge and swim a few strokes around where we camped and she seemed happy tearing off her clothes yelling at last at one with nature and doing so. it was there that she divined my future and said i would go insane again which i did. another fairly safe thing to talk about is insanity since i suppose we would both agree that nobody knows anything about it except the insane. i think it was at the very end of that summer that i did go out again and agnes and thalia were the ones who rescued me up in brewster where i abandoned my car and called them and waited for them to drive up in somebody's vw bug and didn't take the whole bottle of thorazine that agnes suggested i should but rather about 400 mcs or mgs or whatever they are. possibly agnes asked me what was wrong with me and i said i was afraid to die. yet in her wall and body of water game in which she asks people what sort of a wall you imagine or body of water and when you imagine it if you could cross it or go over it and if so how you would do it i was the one apparently who had the correct answer, at least to the wall question, and that was that the wall was transparent so naturally i could walk through it and whatever was on the other side was the same as on this, so it doesn't seem reasonable that i was afraid to die unless the game we played occurred later on and i was by that time dead or dead on the one hand and alive on the other so it didn't matter. on her mesa in the desert agnes told us the women in her family live a long time although her mother died young, at 75. she told us all about how she died, how it took two years and how happy she was when it happened, i mean how happy her mother was, and agnes's final pronouncement on death was that you go out either in terror or in ecstasy and clearly her mother was ecstatic. she said her mother was one of the little people. agnes isn't very tall herself but partly because of being full and solid of body she appears a medium height. she says at 60 your body begins to fall apart, whether she is or not it doesn't seem to cramp her style, when we emerged that first morning from the log cave guest dwelling she was standing on a ladder hurling handfuls of mud at the wall of her adobe. by little people i believe she was alluding to the fairies of old celtic scotland. the rest of what i found out about who she is or where she comes from was that an ancestor was the scottish poet who was the author of flanders fields and her father was an essayist and there weren't any painters in the family. she thinks everything happens according to destiny and i objected on grounds of social oppression which was one more instance of my political tactlessness. i was saying that my mother painted lobster pots and boats in the harbor at sunset and that her potential for being an artist or an artist's artist or an artist to herself and nothing else was undeveloped for social reasons but i was saying altogether too much. someone has to be absolutely quiet when the other holds forth agnes remarked. and she talks all the time when people come in order not to know more than she wants to know. but i was thinking some of the time how to get agnes's attention. jane had the idea that sometimes she must feel awfully heavy to herself and then i thought she hasn't had enough people respond to her humor and jane said yeah they're probably too busy at her feet. were we supposed to ask her the meaning of life questions. do people go in order to ask her the meaning of life questions. i guess they would. but she doesn't have any answers, for nobody can tell anybody something they don't already know. she says what she knows for what she knows is what she is and what that is is perfect for her and she is still on the path herself. she says one thing she has a good grip on is remorse. and that suffering is necessary for freedom from suffering. and that the wriggle of a worm is as important as the assassination of a president. and that our work is very important but that we are not important. and that what you want to do is your work and what you want to want to do is your work. and that people ask her whats going to happen in art, where is art going and she says gosh, i hope it's going to go in all directions. and that a sense of disappointment and defeat are an essential state of mind for creative work. a working through disappointment to further disappointment to defeat. what does it mean to be defeated. it means we cannot move . . . but still we go on, without hope, without desire, and without dreams, then it is not i, then it is not us, then it is not conditioned response . . . without hope there is hope, we go on because there is no way to stop, going on without hope and desire is discipline, going on without scheming or planning is discipline and without striving or caring is discipline . . . defeated you rise to your feet like dry bones, these bones will rise again . . . undefeated you will only say what has already been said . . . defeated having no place to go you will await and perhaps be overtaken . . . defeated, exhausted, and helpless you will perhaps go a little bit further. helplessness is very hard to bear, helplessness is blindness, in helplessness we feel as though some terrible mistake has been made, we feel cast into outer darkness as though some fatal error has been made . . . feelings of loss and catastrophe cover everything and we tremble with fear and dread but when fear and dread have passed as all passions do we realize that helplessness is the most important state of mind . . . lack of independence and helplessness is our most serious weakness as artists. and that's the way agnes goes on in her 4000 word speech that i heard at the pasadena museum and a few of those things she said to me too and i think her critical attitude her relentless scrutiny her voices of perfection her examination of your words and deeds is all in the spirit of improving your character for otherwise why would you go such a distance to see a woman who is herself on the path of perfection which is to say to becoming most totally who she is. she said sitting in the adobe or someplace if only i could get non resistance. she understands remorse but she needs non resistance, that's clear isn't it. yet while walking seems to cover time and space in reality we are always just where we started. i went for a little walk along the rocky edge of the canyon behind her adobe and was amazed to see a tremendously long procession of small black ants in an orderly line up and down this rock facing down into the canyon some going up and some going down with a few stray dissenters or were they the lost ones. i picked up a sandstone to take back to the world. i returned to eat supper. i didn't do much else there. i did take a shot out her door with her beebee gun at a can she placed for my aim after a quick lesson in how to hold the thing i hit the can and quit while i was ahead. also i thought there was a sudden rainbow just to commemorate our visit and i said i'll bet you rarely have a rainbow here and agnes replied yes we do, all the time, it's forever raining when the sun is shining. but the last perfect double rainbow i saw was a couple of years ago in mendocino so i was in and out of her adobe ooing and ahing catching it out in the open or through one window or another watching its aspects and fading disappearing act. about 6 p.m. the wind was blowing in the canyon. by nightfall we were in bed, there isn't any electricity, and i had another nightmare. there was of course just a little bedtime story, of multiple rapes in cuba, a most dangerous part of the country apparently. but agnes had a nightmare too, she was quite indignant about it, she said she knew those nightmares weren't hers, and that's why she can't be around people, because she takes on their... she picks up their... and jane told her i needed to live among people and agnes said then i must have more pain. i could of course consider exchanging the pain for the nightmares in the desert. yet i could say like her that pain is necessary for freedom from pain. anyway if we are always just where we started there isn't anyplace to go and we might's well be where we are. i was reading recently about merlin who retreated from the world into his forest hermitage. it was said that at the sight of a crowd of people his madness breaks out anew. it was said also that his laugh was especially well known, the result of his more profound knowledge of invisible connections. agnes has this laugh or this cosmic giggle, but i wish to say she isn't any magician. she disavows magic adamantly. she hates magic and fetishes and superstition and the i ching, she says superstition is a belief in power, that there've been whole ages where art was only fetishes and that superstition is the enemy of art. she is also as a classicist as a cool artist a woman who looks out with her back to the world a painter who paints not about ideas or personal emotion but who paints the desert in her head as a classicist she is also eloquently opposed to romance and romanticism. she said she never met anybody who wasn't searching for love. she thinks this is a great mistake. she described a time of her own enslavement in this respect and how she became definitively done with it. the voices of perfection. of being alone with your self. of everything being the same. of not having any verticals. of lots of time to herself. of not much time for other peoples problems. of solitude and loneliness and contentment with one self. the union of opposites without trying to do so. a zen sort of person who never studied zen. a woman perhaps who's endured many insults, and who forgives everybody—and nobody. a woman who doesn't believe in influence unless it's you yourself following your own track. a woman it seems to me absolutely fearless of saying what she thinks. after all she doesn't depend on people. the work is what counts and the work is so fine and the people like the work so much that they pay her to live without any people. once she took a freighter around the world and someplace in india they took her off the boat and confined her in a hatch because she'd gone into a trance. no doubt the people on the boat were altogether too much. the boat in the desert is a beebee gun a .22 and five vehicles in perfect working order and i'm not without a little remorse that i went to see her myself. do we have to give honor in person to our sages standing outside the affairs of the world. or bother them with ideas of themselves that they don't have themselves and be bothered ourselves by ideas of ourselves they may have that we don't or bother at all. i don't know. in albuquerque after she drove us out and we were having lunch in la placita i asked her if she didn't think she was leading an exemplary life and once again she knocked the whole thing, oh my no, i'm a murderer, i'm a this and a that, i'm working out the hairy ape in myself, i'm just beginning, and so on, and i remembered how she leaned forward intensely in the adobe and said somewhat incredulously and you realized how mean we all are and i nodded yes, so how could i exempt her from her own conclusions about life. the work is the thing. the grid is still because the whole can be grasped by the eye and mind at once. the value she places on the known rather than the seen suggests innate ideas which she sometimes calls a memory of perfection. agnes martin: a study in the memories of perfection. "the ocean is deathless/ the islands rise and die/ quietly come, quietly go/ a silent swaying breath/ i wish the idea of time would drain/out of my cells and leave me/quiet even on this shore."

Travel Writing

TELL ME THE WEATHER

Village Voice, January 2, 1969

I read somewhere about a man dying of being snowed on while he lies with his head stuck in a dog door. Possibly that's an apt metaphor to describe the general condition. Often I wonder how it's possible to keep moving without going anyplace. That seems the ideal position. Yet I'm hearing all the time about people actually going places. David Bradshaw goes hunting for deer in Vermont. Jasper Johns leaving for the Carolinas to spend time around some Bucky Fuller domes. Rosalyn Drexler off to London or Edinburgh to see about her daughter and one of her plays. Peter Hujar just back from Little Rock, Arkansas, having taken some photos of a football game for *Sports Illustrated*. Ann Wilson also back, from the Virgin Islands having baby hauled a small boy to his grandma altogether a 30 hour trip. Henry Martin just in from Italy for a week to see about a book about art on somebody. Steve Paxton out on the coast right now having no trouble showing his pornie movie although that's where they banned "The Beard." And Ralph Ortiz with the scariest story about Vancouver where he short-circuited some head fuse by smashing a Beethoven symphony cum record player and also a grand piano stuffed with mice and getting the whole place wherever it happened bloody absolutely messed up read bad from being so destructive. Then, Ralph says, on the plane trip back he saw a Canadian newspaper with a big photo of himself looking fiendish wielding overhead the axe the weapon he got everybody so upset with. I asked him if anyone on the plane recognized him. He said no he was cowering under his lapel. But also on top of all that the Canadian Parliament in Ottawa was discussing him because they wanted to know how it happened that the Canadian Government would be donating the money to a gallery in Vancouver for this sort of unfortunate event. No doubt Ralph doesn't need Canada for awhile. If he did he might be asking how to get back into the palace this time without attracting attention. It's curious, by the way, that some American tv people think the only clear approach to the problem is to cut down the sheer number of killings, beatings, burnings, and flesh wounds per show. But did you know that the scientists detonating the first atom bomb in the desert had no idea the extent of damage to occur when the thing went off, that the calculations were all on paper? What I think sometimes about a guy like Ralph is that he's one of our socially concerned artists who likes to stagger, snort, and swing one leg over the top of a house to clean the air of invisible spirits. A man on stilts, they say, can cover more ground faster than a man on foot. I have a friend about 40 years old who still shakes her legs when she gets excited. What do they mean by that expression shake a leg? I'm not going to feel badly until after I have my coffee. Are we really brought up to keep on the move? Recently Hannah Weiner was talking about paying the rent when I suggested a poet act to tour the colleges, like putting a package deal together. She said yes she'd been considering that. "Have package, will travel." Whereas Barbara Stacy told me she was thinking of leaving New York (forever) but she wasn't financially prepared to do so. Feeling confused about it she consulted the I Ching and threw the number which led her to the text on waiting and it said when there's an obstruction and you can't move or make any immediate changes make the inner trip, concentrate your attention inward. That's precisely what an 8th Street Bookstore salesman was telling me one day when I asked them for a book by a turn-of-the-century French psychologist on the interplanetary travels of a Helen someone and I said wow that's a pretty expensive book, for which I was rewarded by a twinkle and a suggestion that I could probably take the trip for much less money. I thanked him and left feeling I'd accompanied this Helen someone for several interplanetary trips the cosmos over.

Driving through a snowstorm to New Hampshire last week we got a buzz on the radio which friend Polly said was the sign of a UFO in the vicinity when you heard this buzzing in a snowstorm in New Hampshire and friend Gene said I wish they'd come and take us away. And all Ann could say was that she wished she could see a neon sign of a cock in various stages of erection. We didn't see any of those unidentified flying cupcakes. But the snowstorm was a scene and a half. They were talking on the radio about the astronauts going around the moon. Don't tell me the news, tell me the weather. I had that sexy feeling of being taken someplace on a weather report. Meredith Monk told me about some college kids at a college where she performed where most of the kids were like you'd expect but some of them looked like they wanted to be taken someplace. Which reminds me of a perfect story about a David who used to look very all right working here at *Harper's Bazaar* when one unsuspecting trip he was hitchhiking to San Francisco and happened to be picked up by the Grateful Dead on their way to the same place. They were traveling in their hearse as always and everything was a-1 okay until a fuzz car seemed to be trailing them and the leader, who was driving, commanded his whole car to swallow all the stuff they had. And thus beganneth the story of a David, whom I saw in London leading life of happy ne'er-do-well wearing longish hair and rough looking outfits. So whattya gonna do. Thousands of people are now looking for what only a few of us once looked for. The only thing disappointed me about this last New Hampshire trip was drawing a blank on a possible gondola ride up and down a mountain. I went to a ski slope without any skis. They said on the weekends they wouldn't permit gondola trips for tourists minus their skis. I talked up a storm about getting a whole piece out of such a trip, but they pretended not to understand. I tried the same lady at two windows with different stories without realizing it was the same lady. They must be short on ladies. That's what the fuss is over the gondolas. However, it's an expensive looking slope. And I made plenty of discoveries there. For instance, the worst skiers dress the most ostentatiously. The good skiers can look like ordinary bums walking around in the coffee lodge. Skiing is just like dancing. Either you can do it or you can't. Over cups and cups of coffee I watched all these stick figures spilling or zigging down the last run of the slope. I guess each sport is all about using mostly one part of the body and the rest of the body falling in line. No doubt skiing is the big knee sport. Badminton is the big elbow and wrist sport. Dancing is supposed to be an all over sport. I imagine whatever you do though you'll have a similar style. I noticed how fancy some of those ski bunnies are. Like in the parallel action how the torso will swing gracefully but much more exaggerated than necessary when it goes in opposition to the knee movement. They'd probably look the same in a discotheque. I told an elderly skier I could feel the slope even if I wasn't doing it. He said could I know about sex just reading on it in a book. I replied he had a point there. But I have a theory about how we have archetypal knowledge understanding feeling of our former lives as fishes and birds and so on. Skiing is a big flying sport. I'm a high flier. I fly in my dreams a lot too. How much do you have to know to fly properly? What's the proper method for flying down a mountain? Why couldn't I be flying in my coffee as I space out my eyes up the slope through a picture window lightly? One of my most beautiful flying dreams was up against a ceiling in the breast stroke. Anyhow a little eight-year-old girl skier, probably an expert, told me the proper method for flying down a slope. According to her there's only one way to do it. You have to take lessons. I asked her why. She said otherwise you won't know how to do it. Oh I see. For example, she explained, it's wrong to come down doing the snowplow. Why? Because it isn't right. I see. You mean you have to do something else besides the snowplow I said. Yes, that's right. And you have to take lessons. Otherwise it's wrong. Her father thought I was raising philosophical questions, but we continued the conversation. I asked her if you have to learn how to fall. Naturally. And what's the object in learning how to fall? She didn't know. She was just certain there was a correct way to fall and someone had to show you how. One time I fell out of bed and split a cartilage in my knee. Maybe she's right. But I dunno, I just don't fall out of bed any more. And I don't recall taking a lesson to fall off my first roof into a deep snow just for the helluvit.

LIKE A BOY IN A BOAT

Village Voice, September 11, 1969

You might want to get off here and join the world again. No I didn't. But you do. And I take it all back. When she makes a mistake a little girl aged four says she's been foolish and deluded. How do you define a mistake? A mistake is anything you decide to regret. Therefore there are no mistakes. A regret is a fantasy about the past accounting for a terrible present. A mistake is an accident of birth you imagine as a gift to grow up on. If there's a mistake and surely you could've done otherwise, what might have been done? If there's a regret and you might be mistaken what should be done next? Or thought? How do you report a death without sounding sorry? I could write a classical obituary but Gene isn't a proper subject. Gene Swenson is dead. I thought it would be from flying off a rooftop but it happened in Kansas in a car with his mother. The next to last time I saw Gene was before leaving for Europe in June he was yelling at me behind an extended arm and a pointed finger. I don't know the content of his fury because I was making just as much noise in my own distress while cowering toward the exit. Before London a young pregnant near stranger read me an I Ching reading which I interpreted as having succumbed to an inferior element and having relinquished my inside power since in any case according to this hexagram the principle of darkness had become ascendant at the summer solstice. The real true story of Europe was Patrick whom I never mentioned. When you crash land in a foreign territory you need a priest if you don't meet an undertaker. I never look for anything. Patrick appeared as a cloud taking shape of an angel the way the others back home were rising up in steam out of the man hole covers. One of them was trying to get his teeth fixed in order to land in London to be an Orestes to rescue the Electra from the clutches of the Clytemnestra who would somehow have to "pay" for a murder in the family. Since my teeth were in good shape I had nothing to worry about except a London looney bin if an assault on the fortress by a couple of mythomaniacs from the colonies was misunderstood. One of our own kind right now is planning a land mass translocation to move England south off the coast of Spain or North Africa or the Canaries, for a better climate and/or because the Island is tipping upward and eventually London will slide into the water. That's George Brecht, whom I saw last on his way to obtain admiralty maps of the depths in the North Atlantic. About that time James Byars was at Oxford as a self-appointed extraordinary student in philosophy for a week going about to the 28 departments or colleges, asking everybody what questions they were asking themselves. Curious activities by Americans abroad. As it turned out I did nothing outstanding myself. I joined the world again after a year in orbit. I paid eight shillings for my birth certificate. I felt sorry for myself. I thought I should go in storage for a while until things blew over. I was traveling because the I Ching said it was a good idea. I had no notion of where I was going. I didn't care. I felt alarmingly normal. I had nothing much to say for a change. I didn't even think anyone was after me. My head was turning into a cemetery of deluded proclamations. My pace was changing from hare to snail to stone and stucco. Not being in control of all these alterations it seems I had only to accept them. Along the way Patrick said there was nothing to worry about. At 18 Patrick is a natural saint. He doesn't mean to be much of anything but gentle. Very tall and skinny and blond, the hair straggling to shoulders and covering part of a baby face, the unironed shirt dripping at the unbuttoned cuffs below the knuckles, the soft refined British accent, the posture angled over appearing to wish for invisibility, the recurring story of "the big trip" to

India, the peace inside around him that isn't a political issue, the respect for nothing but a presence, he's too young to project any formulas for grace and he practiced no discipline that I could see. Such was the real true story of Europe if I don't take it all back tomorrow. Driving to London airport I said I had a vague sense of mission accomplished. Jonathan thought it was selling a car to someone in Spain. Why not. I complained about returning to write my memoirs. I'm too young to write my memoirs. Besides, it'll be damaging and incriminating. But Charlotte said never mind you haven't been to jail, you don't so far as we know carry communicable syphilis, you're certainly acceptable in polite society. Great send-off. But I was crash landing into Kennedy and there aren't any Patricks in America and naturally a week later I'm doing the comic or tragic routine of walking along a *Vogue* thing about myself under arm only two hours after my car and brief and all my clothes are stolen and I open a certain door to pick up some mail and hear a voice at the top of the stairs saying that Gene is dead. The next to next to last time I saw Gene was the day he was released from Bellevue in June and I drove him across a bridge into some trees and he hung a hand out the window like a boy in a boat having never felt the drag of the water before. I didn't know Gene well until over a year ago when the art world was deploring his rage on the steps at the doors of the various establishments. First time I saw him in '63 or so I thought the spastic mannerisms and erratic speech and exploding blue eyes didn't go with the charcoal suit and ivy league good looks. Sometime in '68 I wrote a thing called "Pieces of Gene." I had this image of Gene all splat in pieces outside the UN after applying for international citizenship. A better story might be how he appeared at a MOMA opening in bare feet holding a lantern aloft and replied when asked what he was doing that he was looking for one honest man. According to Basil, a friend, Gene was sent out of Kansas to be a genius. He went through Yale. He became an art critic and historian. He lived for 11 years in the same tenement. He had no money. His sexual interests were inclusive. He was politically obsessed. "People who aren't interested in politics aren't interested in anything." He had a Pan Am reservation to the moon. He upset everybody. Mostly he was upset himself. "My finger nails grow long and still I don't have a job."—"If only I had been allowed to put my pants back on after my performance and come back down to my apartment."—"The harvest is past, the summer is ended, and we are not yet saved."—The last time I saw him he was Gene the Gentle, walking down the Bowery slow motion, fragile, transparent, not really there. And scared shitless. Trapped. Didn't know what to do. Leave New York and don't go back to Kansas, that was all I ever said, I dunno what the others said. Not that anyone could keep up with his roles. The Village Priest, Poet, and Philosopher. The hippie revolutionary. The scholar and art historian. The home town boy from Kansas. And at last the reports would come in how he was barefoot on the streets with a bible and getting the number messages off the radio and he was becoming his Crazy Gene self and he was beautiful but it wouldn't be long before they'd come to get him because he'd wreck his place or something considered unsociable and thus for the third time in June he was going into the recovery phase of a cycle that included being a prisoner of state and so forth the garbage everybody knows about. Maybe he's lucky now. I have no opinion really. I'm just recording a few impressions. I'm thinking how to end it. Excessive in all things, Gene wasn't much of a humorist, but here's a line he wrote I'd prefer to ponder over the endless political ravings I always claimed was nothing more nor less than his father. "Special to *the N.Y. Times*: The President of the U.S. clad only in a scanty tribal costume, announced the resignation of the American Government last night."

THREE AMERICAN PENNIES

Village Voice, November 13, 1969

What does it mean, I'm wailing the phrase into the hallway down the steps under an armful into another journey, what does it mean, I know it means something if a glass container and a plastic container go flying out of a cellophane bag into their glassy and plasticky fragments in pools of goo on the landings below my wailing complaining questioning what in the name of any great god goo is the present design in the total scheme. There is a design and I am not a free agent and I will to mine own self be true by not knowing and not pretending that I know whatever it is at the moment which is not to be known. Later. For now for what happened before I've unscrambled one image as an indicator which was registering its message at the time only as a strain on my resources to locate a friend in a scary altitude in a foreign terrain. It was Valleraugue in the south of France. I've bent quite a few ears over Patrick but I didn't see Patrick myself as the perfect standout until the night before that drugstore junk went into pieces and pools down the stairwell and the night after a big container of hot 'n' sour Chinese soup filled up the floor of my car from lurching off the front seat as I jammed on the brakes at a light, and right after watching Cousteau and his pals on the tellie rescue a baby whale marooned on a sandbar and thinking how great to be all beardy and salt washed and sun bleached cruising about making friends with whales and then I got the right image of Patrick, Patrick who wouldn't understand some of these scenes in the cement desert, like his tall American writer friend on stage at the New School sousing up on gin and vermouth out of a paper bag next to a chair where she was sitting playing monopoly with three other writer pals all appearing at the request of Buddy W. to talk about words or something for his Intermedia class; or at the Met opening doing an old routine looking around before leaving how to make a spectacle of herself and finding a reliable soul-mate our American Michaelangelo Mark di Suvero the lion head welded into a turtle neck red sweater which he removed and roared and pitched up on his spindly legs under a massive torso and wielded a new looking metal cane which was a live property in the ultimate tumble the floor spectacle the sprawl under all that verticalypso cocktail clinkerchief kertails kerchoo kerfooey she wanted to rip it all apart so she walked off with a trophy a piece of a dirty undershirt of di Suvero's stuck in the opening of a metal neck piece. No, Patrick wouldn't get it. Patrick Cardwell Derham. Whattaname. Two days out of Dover near Rouens happens the first image. This bloody black British Ford doesn't respond to its ignition equipment. Early morning just out of a roadside hotel. Patrick and two French boys hitching to Scandinavia heave ho on the tail for a push-start as I sit at the wheel. No soap. Rest. Again. Nada. Rest. Third time and lots of panting, I'm sitting at a dead wheel, I look up and around, the French boys gone, where's Patrick, Uh oh, alarm, Patrick makes a beautiful anemic sight slumped against a tree trunk, the exhausted long blond haired Buddha, I'm traveling with a Buddha but I don't know it yet. Alarm. Are you okay? Yes I'll be all right, weakly. I walk back to the hotel to phone for *mecanique*. Returning I find Patrick in the car bending intently over a pale blue tin box crammed with vials of pills. Holy Batman boy, whas that? Homeopathic medicines.—Ummm, one of those. Clearly he's looking for *the* pill to cure exhaustion from push-starting British Fords on early mornings in French countrysides. I never saw the tin box again. But I hear the story how four good catholic children grew up to abandon Catholicism and to be sold on Homeopathy. Even so, I tell Patrick, you're going to be a priest, I don't know what kind, but a priest neverthechurch-less. And you'll go to India again. And... And he asks me about Cage and the like and I'm imagining he thinks I'm older wiser I'll tell him what's whats, but I dump it right back on him, this somewhat unconscious 18 yr. old Buddha who doesn't say much (no, he isn't withdrawn, he says, he's "inward"—of course), I hand him the credentials I hope he'll never have, for in his innocence and angel smiles and earnest but relaxed good nature he knows the way that I've recently lost and I never find the indicator on a credential card. At Pont St.

Esprit we split cuz I want to go east toward Nice and he's hitching due west to a cottage in Valleraugue belongs to two English friends. He gives me instructions how to get there on the way back if I want to. I do. But it's an indeterminate altitude once you hit the town. Straight up to Cloud X. There's a road, Patrick said, across from the gendarmerie round back of a camping ground. Don't drive up the road. But I've got no gut for walking up a foreign mountain. The friendly gendarme says yes yes you can drive, and yes there's some weird looking kids up there somewhere. Good. I drive. I shouldn't. Right off I see what he meant. The road is no wider than the car which is narrow. Pronto the drop on the left is precipitous. And the turns are bobby pins. And the pavement becomes dirt littered with small boulders. So I'm roaring up in second not looking right or left and thinking there's no turning back and where the hell is this "cottage"—I'm really in a lather—and there isn't a living soul, etc. Then I cross a black hose, then the steepiest incline in the middle of which my horse stops balks fumes refuses, so we roll back down to the hose. Life, maybe. I get out. I see where I am. It's not real. I'm at the top of the world. I'll fly away and never be heard of again. I can't look. Endless chasms of light struck valleys. Really giddy from this. Scared out of my skull. Start yelling. HALLO HALLO HALLO. That hose does connect to something. Up a high embankment, up up to a dilapidated looking stone structure. H A A A A A LLOOOOOO. And I'm desperate, struggling up the embankment my voice echo bouncing off the goddam mountains. Then it happens. The image. First there's another human voice. It yells JILL. Fantastic. Somebody up here knows me. Then a white thing is floating down the slope. It's got a flying blond mane. The rest of it is all white. It's Patrick in his Indian cottons. It's Himself. Then we're sitting where the water is coming down the rest of the mountain in another black hose and I'm drinking all of it. All up. Never so happy. Relieved I should say. And Patrick is the Buddha, but I still don't know it. Later I notice what's around his neck. I recall the morning leaving a hotel someplace between Orleans and Pont St. Esprit he mentioned a charm he's been wearing for some time from India, from an Indian who meant something, and it was gone. I said let's go back for it. No, it was all right. I was impressed. I'd go back, and forth also, for my metal thing. Now I'm remarking on his new necklace. The feature is a tiny blue denim bag with a draw-string. He opens it and produces three American pennies. Too much. I really like it. They're the pennies I hadn't retrieved after he used them one night in some hotel, crouched over the I Ching to find out why he was traveling with me. And one day on top of the mountain at Valleraugue he says let's look at it, the I Ching, just as I'm thinking the same thing on my way to the chemical toilet, and he gives me the reading for the darkness changing to light at the winter solstice and I know later on it'll all come together.

THE MAKING OF A LESBIAN CHAUVINIST

Village Voice, June 17, 1971

Lesbians who are not chauvinists are monogamous. The new liberation front is the lesbian chauvinist movement. A lesbian chauvinist is a woman who enjoys a variety of affectionate and sexual experiences with different members of her own sex. If she marries another woman she no longer qualifies as a chauvinist. Gregory Battcock is the only pure male homosexual chauvinist I know. He says he doesn't try to mess up his boyfriends' minds with love, security, false promises, fidelity, and the like. I asked him what does he do if a lover develops more interest in his person than his attitudes can tolerate. He says then he makes himself as obnoxious as possible, even developing bad breath if necessary. Revolutions are all about language, inventing and distorting your terms to suit the new strategies of survival. Male chauvinism is now a dead phrase. The new lesbian is co-opting it to define her positive attitudes of polygamous independence united with an exclusive interest in her own sex. Such an absurd but real position might more accurately be described by the term chauvinism than the attitudes of the heterosexual male who won the term in its pejorative sense in our time through its revival by the feminists in their proper instinct for a word just obscure enough to express an educated disdain for the cause of their social and private distress. I stopped using the word when I heard the musical "machismo" on the Coast. Now I'm bored with machismo too. I'm bored, in fact, with the problem or the concept. I'm very interested in this new idea of lesbian chauvinism. Derived from Nicolas Chauvin, a soldier of the First Republic and Empire, whose demonstrative patriotism and attachment to Napoleon came to be ridiculed by his comrades, the word has as much relevance to the polygamous lesbian as it did to the American male of choice in the ongoing battleground of language. I wish I had thought it up myself. I'll be satisfied if I demonstrate its usefulness to define a situation already long in existence but not socially comprehensible until truly invented by the whimsical dislocation of language to express reversal of value attending the same phrase. It isn't easy to be a lesbian chauvinist. Lots of people still think you're as wicked as the male of that description who owns and runs the world through the elaboration of his sexual preference into the various patterns of subjugation and captivity much noted by the polemical feminists who have realized at last the intimate connection between power, economy, property, and sex. I don't own or run anything except a deteriorating '66 vw van. The most difficult aspect, however, of being a lesbian chauvinist is the problem of maintaining the life style appropriate to our new definition by warding off the temptations of monogamy in a society in which the prime unit of its functioning as a warring nation is its embattled family. Next week I'll redefine my position as a lesbian monogamist. This week the revolution is the liberation of the lesbian chauvinist. The grand edifices of theory and speculation are elegant smokescreens for personal tactics of destruction survival and renewal. I've been a happy chauvinist in spirit since the summer of '68. A lapse or two since then into the exquisite agonies of feudalism or monogamy is not an aspect of my journey I go around boasting about. Not that it matters to anybody. People are learning to ignore the exaggerated claims and denials of their friends and various exhibitionists. People are learning to despite all problems and solutions that aren't their own. People are learning to be severely disappointed by the slightest deviation from any problem or solution that sounded good the week before. As people myself I feel the same way naturally. All we want to do is to dictate our own thrilling letters. All I'd like to do actually is write the feminist version of "My Secret Life." I've been postponing an account of my amorous adventures in London '68 because they seem, at this date, embarrassingly harmless and meagre, and/or because I needed the revolutionary context of the new lesbian chauvinism to make the experiences pertinent to current or ancient issues. In connection with Lois Lane I mentioned that my momentous visit prompted my return to America as "a roaring lesbian." I meant that I discovered I could sleep with a woman and not feel like it was the beginning or the end of the world. Meaning that it was possible to just go to bed and have a good time and get up and share a cup of coffee or not even do that and say goodbye and thank you quite amicably like any self respecting male chauvinist for whom the pleasures of the body are not necessarily complicated and constrained by the emotions of greed envy fear guilt anger jealousy etcetera all the defensive-aggressive equipment attending the onset of romantic love. The British taught me this lesson. They were very hard on me. I arrived a gaping tourist and left a hardened sexist. Not really. I cried all the way home. I don't remember why. But I remained as mushy as I ever was which was pretty mushy. Possibly I hadn't grasped yet that it wasn't a crime to fall in love with every British princess who seemed as interested as I was in the mere pleasures of the body. Actually, there were only three, I think. That was enough. For a three week visit the average was outstanding. For a pure innocent virginal American it was lurid and licentious. For a victim of lesbian monogamy it was a revelation. Having dutifully tramped through Westminster and St. Paul's and Charing Cross and the National Museum and Trafalgar Square and Picadilly Circus and the subway system and Soho and the Tower and around the Palace & so forth one day I decided impulsively I had to visit a gay bar. I had never done this in my life before. Except once as a very young lesbian naturally not connecting my thinking with my activities, therefore imagining I was a nice normal person, I went slumming with a friend to a Village place, meaning a low down dive, to watch the freaks and get excitedly aghast at *members of the same sex dancing together!* By the summer of '68 if you can believe it I guess you can I was still disconnected in this way my thinking or my attitudes or prejudices and my attitudes or prejudices and my true nature were distinctly and neurotically separate from each other. I was a walking contradiction in turns. I just couldn't see myself as a freak. It was bad enough I was too tall for my age and wore my freckles when the sun came out. I was even strolling around in those fashionable gabardine culottes or leather mini skirts, I must have looked ridiculous. A lesbian still pretending she was available for invasion. Anyway, I went all out for some inexplicable reason and learned about a place called the Gates or Gateways Club. George Brecht located it for me. Very reluctantly. He said he was disappointed in me. I guess he thought he had an exclusive patent on chauvinism, not that I knew at the time that's what he was. I assumed all men had the right to drink a lot and insult womankind and drag as many as possible off by the hair into their caves. So naturally he was not enthusiastic about being an accomplice to my initiation as a rival chauvinist of the lesbian variety. Not that either of us knew the ultimate significance of his innocent investigation. The Gates, by the way, is the bar that figured as the freak joint in "The Killing of Sister George," which I saw a few months later in New York. The entrance had a speakeasy feeling about it. You'd never see it if you didn't know where it was exactly. The door opened directly on a flight of stairs leading down to I imagined a dark den of sin. It was just a smallish well lit rather cheery basement room with comfortable round booths, a bar, a jukebox. The woman at the bottom of the stairs was a hardened something or other. Dressed high femme lipstick earrings stocking heels etc. with an incongruously low dark voice and garish features. The bartenders were handsome heavy set butch, a type that has always repelled bewildered and frightened me. I sat down and waited. Eventually the only other customer addressed me sort of look over her shoulder from her position turned three quarters away from me I could appreciate her bleached blond straight short hair and middling cockney accent. Hearing my own American she warmed up and even not too much later turned round to face me. She introduced herself as Maureen. She got so warm in fact she was inviting me to her place to meet her roommate who "likes American girls" and her own lover who was an ex-patriot American. I said I'd like to do that but later on if possible after I found out what this bar was all about. Soon I found out. It seemed the entire gay woman population of London must have decided this was the place to be that night. I had no idea there were so many gay people. I was very embarrassed. I didn't know what to do. I suppose I just sat there transfixed with horrified curiosity. I had a very snobbish attitude. I'm sure I didn't think I was a lesbian too. Yet I was rigged out to conform to one of the two stereotyped roles obtaining in conventional gay society until recently. Excepting my long hair. But they overlooked the hair because of my tie. The tie seemed to guarantee my role as a female who would play the part of a male. In my three lesbian marriages I had never played any part whatsoever unless it was all parts, so I regarded the attitude with amused toleration, thankful to be attractive to one half of the jam-packed room for inadvertently wearing the right thing. A year later I returned sans tie and was so confusing apparently to everybody that I became a model wallflower. Or else I had aged considerably. Or they had caught on to me. Or some damned thing. I didn't seriously figure any of this out until recently. Some experienced friends have by now explained the customs. I don't like any of them. No self respecting lesbian likes them. Aside from the exorbitant mafia prices of drinks or minimum the bars are corroded with long centuries psychologies of self hatred addressed to everybody. And the frantic behavior of excessive monogamous thinking, quite naturally, since self hatred breeds extremely precarious relationships and the lesbian is not yet liberated into her chauvinism. I learned fast at the Gates. I asked someone the time and was threatened with murder by her girlfriend. I supposed she was desperate. It was a good thing I just asked the time. I realized right then I'd better not make a move or talk or dance or anything or they'd be flying me home as a corpse. So I waited. I didn't wait too long. I was pretty popular as I said. Thus there were a succession of sidewise or bizarre approaches. All femmes. I was a butch! The most exciting proposition was a note pressed into my hand by the femme I thought to be the most beautiful in the place; she was so expert in her treachery, passing the message on the run as it were no doubt while her "steady" was collecting their coats and momentarily out of sight. It was really dramatic. A sequence in a spy movie. I repaired to the ladies right away to read it and find her name and a telephone no. scrawled in pencil. I took the names and numbers of two others who weren't as spectacular in their looks or approach and left to go to Maureen's flat to see about her roommate who "likes American girls." I felt saturated by London lesbiana. I felt I had learned something. I didn't know what exactly. Probably my unconscious was fast at work transforming me overnight into a raging chauvinist. One thing was certain. It no longer seemed bizarre for two members of the same sex to be dancing together. One other thing was certain. There were lots of lesbians in the world. Maybe half the world were lesbians. And I suppose I left with the faint suspicion that I too might be one of them.

Coming Out

OF THIS PURE BUT IRREGULAR PASSION

Village Voice, July 2, 1970

In support of the gay movement on the occasion of the gay celebration week: I guess yes I've been saying it in this column for a year and a half now, but always fragmentarily in the context of the literary exercises. So this will be straight on. I don't recall any decision to declare my sexuality, in print, as though it should necessarily have interested anybody in any case. It happened that the column was moving at that time away from the theatre of dance and happenings toward the theatre of my life as a personal solution to among other things the Cagian philosophy—which I had until then taken seriously in the context of other people's work—of the continuity and inseparability of life and art. Gradually the life became the theatre became the column. The life being everything of course included everything. Sex was especially interesting since I was in love with a beautiful girl and we were having a very good time of it, at home and on the road. This was embarrassing. I didn't really want to make trouble for myself. Nobody ever gave me reason to believe that I would be adored and acclaimed for loving my own sex.

I was legally married once and for that good behavior I received lots of encouragement and congratulations. Not too much from the spouse himself. Whenever he was greatly angry he would imply that I was homosexual. He was right but I was also heterosexual and living out the part of my karma that had to be with a man and exercise the female function in reproduction. I wasn't thinking. Who thinks. Nor do I think now that I should have been thinking. One think is certain: I was sexually confused and didn't know who I was. My heterosexuality was a flash in the pan you might say. And bisexuality in feeling or practice is too precarious for most people in our society strictured by the absolute heterosexual structuring based on the family unit which drives the homosexual underground. The structure of the society doesn't correspond to our bisexual needs, I don't want to argue bisexuality. In my best moments, I feel trans-sexual and relate to the classical and ancient myths of the sacred character of the androgynous creature, which is rooted in our primordial biological origins. As a mortal A.D. 1970 American I believe that the early family dynamic of each individual creates a predilection for one sex or the other accompanied by a powerful cultural prejudice which favors the choice by each sex of its opposite number. It is the conflict between the culture and the *feelings* of the individual whose objects are made extremely unavailable which constitutes "the homosexual problem." As a latent heterosexual I received the greatest encouragement to express the latent, or least inclined, aspect of myself. Typically, having fulfilled the reproductive function, I was ready to match my object with my deepest feelings but the objects were much less available than a couple of pre-marriage innocent homosexual relationships had led me to believe. I can only imagine that in very favorable conditions the least inclined aspect of one's sexuality might flourish in accord with the social demand. The odds make it unlikely. The course of action then becomes hazardous. The double life of the homosexual is not a sickness he would wish for himself. The bizarre styles of a type of homosexual who has "come out" in the past, besides facilitating identification one by the other, are the witty and angry parodies conforming, by confronting, the stereotyped ideas of a confused public. The latent heterosexual whose true homosexual feelings survive the cultural prejudice is the outcast unviable position which the current gay activist movements are dedicated to making apparent. I stress that our sexuality is defined by our feelings. Freud on Leonardo: "For it is not the actual activity, but the nature of the feeling which decides for us whether we should attribute to anyone the characteristic of homosexuality." The homosexual whose feelings have been thwarted, repressed by the demands of a heterosexual society, is a confused person, out of touch with his feelings and very often acting in contradiction to his real needs. The gay movement is stressing the positive identity of the homosexual. The key phrase is COME OUT. Come out of hiding. Identify yourself: Make it clear. Celebrate your sexuality.

Notwithstanding the hostility of heterosexual men to the homosexual woman, I can say that since my personal campaign to "come out" I have never liked men better and wish they would like me as well. And I hope the heterosexual women also get it together. Just yesterday a heterosexual (-ly inclined) female friend told me she was afraid to be seen with me for what people would say. I thanked her for saying it and went on to scream about the total situation and felt paranoid and angry and revolutionary. The men intimidate the women (a man actually had told her that I was trying to make her homosexual) and divide the women against the women in their fear of losing their objects. To a lesser degree the women keep their men in tow by similar intimidations. It's so confusing I want to drop it. In the spirit of the day my friend Ann says she wants a homosexual experience and I'm doing another weird number by insisting on her heterosexuality (all agreed upon) probably so I can have one heterosexual female friend left who loves me no matter what. I wouldn't speak to her when she turned up at a gay women's dance, and on the way to the Gay-In at Sheep's Meadow I said so I suppose you think you might pass for homosexual. There is some irony but purpose in an over-reactive allegiance to a new found confirmed sexuality, parallel to the kind of reverse prejudice being shown by the new beautiful blacks toward the whites whose color they once thought to be desirable. Also an exaggerated stance is a way of repressing the latent feelings which once confused the issue by receiving cultural encouragement obscuring the deeper need. And an exaggerated stance can clarify one's availability to whom. I want friendships with men that are purged of the availability confusion. Other problems are created in relating to women whose latent homosexuality was never expressed who may be conscious or not and who can make a lot of trouble when the consciousness is low. The issue all the way around is mutual respect.

Jesse Falstein of the Gay Liberation Front says "once we take the risk of admitting that we're beautiful perhaps we have the strength to make the world believe it."

Ann says that as a homosexual and a woman and an artist I'm in a hopeless position. There is nothing to do then but to take it all on. I indicated above that I began declaring my sexuality in the column here in the context of the illustration of my life as total theatre. Truth to the life as a theatre. That's right. But I must add now that already by then (a year and a half ago) I was personally militant about my homosexuality. I had been misbehaving at the heterosexual loft artist parties for instance. Dancing with my heterosexual female friends, if they would. Things like that. Angry. I was angry. I saw nothing in the society around me to affirm a sexual choice that finally I had to make to clarify my life. Nothing except a possible stray lost girl looking for a temporary mother which I wasn't (two children notwithstanding). I never made the underworld gay bar scene. Didn't want to. I was a stray lost girl myself. I didn't know what to do. And I found out that two stray lost girls together make up a frightened team. It was all far from clear. Anyway it was a stray lost girl team that I made in '64–'65 terminating in the beautiful disaster of Bellevue which caused me to conceive the wildest schemes for personal happiness. I would destroy the psychiatric profession, for a start. I would cause an international scandal by publicly seducing Queen Elizabeth and Jackie Kennedy and Liz Taylor and such like media dishes. I would save the world which desperately needed to be saved from its wickedness in depriving me of my personal happiness. I hatched a plan a minute. And did nothing. Except to tell my friends, who already knew, that I was homosexual. But I was on the way and didn't know it. The more I said it the more familiar it sounded. The more familiar it sounded the more I began to think I really was what I said I was. The more certain I was of what I said I was the more I began to be what I was according to what I said I was in short and long, I did something about it. The more I said it and was it and did it the more confident and integrated I began to feel frankly like a person instead of a stray lost girl waiting once a decade for another stray lost girl to happen to fall into bed after a drunken heterosexual party. I was a hopeless case as it were. So by accident I gave birth to myself. One day in 1965 I lay down on a bed and had enormous labor pains for as long as it took to give birth to myself. Subsequently I went to sleep for a long time. Then I woke up and recalled my second birth. Then I went to sleep again and gradually reawakened to my new self which had some new ways of writing and dressing and talking and thinking—mostly being.

Last week at a GLF meeting as part of the gay celebration week Sidney Abbott said "lesbian women are the ones who early perceived the oppression of women." I don't know. I don't think I early perceived much of anything. There certainly wasn't a white suprematist male chauvinist capitalist pig around. Wrong. I had a white suprematist male chauvinist pig called Eddie, a second cousin who came over once a week to give me a piano lesson and eat a piece of pie and play a game of pick-up-sticks. He was very good humoured and lived quite happily with his aging mother. No, for me it's a downer and a bummer to dwell on the oppression of women. I see that women are oppressed. I hope for the alleviation of all oppression. (The movement has raised my consciousness, i.e., at a dinner in L.A. with one heterosexual girl and three heterosexual men I said I wasn't going to listen to a whole evening of male accomplishments; I heard the set in the opening remarks.) But oppression is a worldwide interfamilial interstate intercontinental interpersonal phenomenon. It is a prime fact of a political structure. I can't dwell on our oppression and remain a relatively liberate fugitive artist. Oppression is real. Our lives are illusory. Men and women are real. Our sexual differentiation is illusory. Space and time are real. There is no past present or future. We are living in the past the present and the future which is an eternal present. We appear to be becoming but in reality we are being in the everlasting now. If the now is not a beautiful present when will we be beautiful? The talk of oppression is about a beautiful future. An oppressed person becomes beautiful in the presence of a beautiful presence. At the meetings I have felt an absence of spirituality and cosmic consciousness. In San Francisco at the Family Dog Auditorium once a week a few thousand far out longhairs gather to unite in being and to gather strength to go out to infect the world with being. At the Gay-In in Sheep's Meadow the oppressed homosexuals united for an afternoon of expressing being. In celebrating my being I can't accept any program for resisting or attacking "the enemy" such as feminist Ti-Grace Atkinson advocates in the struggle for liberation of women. Ti-Grace spoke at the Daughters of Bilitis during the gay week. She says that men are the enemy and she speaks of spikes and armor and militant tactics and ideological pitfalls and the murders of feminist revolutionaries in Russia in 1919 and the vaginal orgasm as a mass hysterical survival response and frightening things like that. I like Ti-Grace and I'd like to help her by going to bed with her but I think she needs intensive bio-energetic Reichian therapy by a male chauvinist pig who wouldn't rape her or redeem her but who would be kind to her. I wasn't too kind at her lecture when I called out a proposition for bed. I only half meant it, I was putting her on—she defines feminism as a theory and lesbianism as a practice—and challenging her address to lesbian women who feel like the arch feminists. I meant the proposition in part as a gesture of affirmation of the body which looks to me on her to be disconnected from her head which thinks a great deal in the university tradition. Denying her body to men as a political tactic seems a maneuver consistent with her radical feminist position; but a body I assume to be bound up in its armor of fear and hatred of an "enemy" who never satisfied it will project and sublimate the frustration into a political rationale that sounds hysterical to me. I don't think Ti-Grace is inclined toward her own sex (either). She's a brave girl. She told the audience at some point that we had an "encounter"—which we did last January. I've known her for a few years but formerly within the art world. I saw her at a party in a Peck and Peck type outfit that I didn't believe and I knew what she was into so I made a move as a gesture instinctively toward something I wasn't sure what. At the lecture last week she posed some interesting questions. First off she countered my challenge by defining and denouncing it as behavior belonging to the male psychology. I'm glad she said that. It illustrates our stereotype ideas of role-playing passivity and aggression. Arlene Kisner of the GLF said that any time a woman asserts her own desires and needs does not mean she is showing male psychology. I'm not excusing myself. There was a fair bit of hostility in the scene I made. My program for self identity sometimes includes aggressive posturing that belies a sexually passive nature. But I don't think Ti-Grace had mere aggression in mind. Part of her feminist rationale is that the female dynamic is love and the male dynamic is sex. Translated Man-Sex-Evil. Versus: Woman-Love-Good. Further translation: superiority of mind and spirit in the Puritan box of horrors derived from every Christian medieval dualistic dogma for salvation and damnation. I tell you it blows my head out. We want to get things together and there's always the old kind of divisiveness in a new disguise. Ti-Grace also brought up the subject of whore houses which we discussed, or I belabored, a few months ago. She says there must be something wrong if . . . in the tradition of a crusading zeal for reforming prostitution. Eliminating would be the word I guess. I wanted to make it clear it isn't the whore house in actuality that interests me as a possibility for women, necessarily. It's the whore house as an arch symbol of the man's more extensive recognized sexuality. Why are there no zoos or baths or houses for women? In L.A. a haterosexual man said to me but women don't need whore houses, they can have a man any time they want. Maybe so, but they can't *pay* for the *specific* satisfactions they might want that are not available in a prosaic married or unmarried life. I don't believe anything is wrong anywhere. Whatever, it seems to me the idea is to expand our sexual potential to meet the greater freedom of the male for variety and quantity, so forth. Ann has a house rap that goes like how to begin with all the rooms have holes so she can watch everybody, especially a rape scene; a room with people in costumes with their genitals exposed; a room with cupids and roses and velvet swings; and a room with sinks with men doing the dishes being sucked off by 11 year old girls. Sometimes we have sex for tricks and sometimes for feeling, sometimes a feeling turns into a trick or a trick a feeling or a tricky feeling and when it all comes together it's fabulous, isn't it? Woe and behold! Someday I'll give it all up to contemplate my navel.

Coda for the celebration of the new gay: Read Colette's "The Pure and the Impure"–: "A woman finds pleasure in caressing a body whose secrets she knows, her own body giving her the clue to its preferences . . . And the shadow projected on the intervening space need not be that worst intruder, a man. The most ordinary irruption can mortally change the steady hothouse warmth in which two women devote themselves to the cultivation of a delusion." "In May 1778, two wellborn young girls, related to the Welsh aristocracy, ran away together and, having chosen their fate, cloistered their solitude, their reciprocal tenderness for 53 years, in Llangollen, a small town in Wales. Lady Eleanor Butler, the elder of the two, died at the age of 90 . . . At the source of their serenity, going back a half century, they at least could find, still warm in its ashes, the romantic memory of their first elopement, the wild race at night on foot through mountainous roads, their feet bleeding in fragile cloth slippers . . . they could remember two nights out in the open, sleeping in a ruined barn, Sarah shivering with cold in spite of the protective arms around her . . . nights of anxiety, of mounting fever, and then the approach of pursuers guided by the barking of Sarah's little dog . . . infatuated with romance they had leaped from a window rather than leave by way of the open door . . . they corresponded with each other by secret means, bribed servants, and at the moment of leaving, had seized firearms they did not know how to use and fled on horseback, although they had never in their lives sat a horse . . . there were complications, legal processes, tragedies, childish tears . . . but from all this a unique sentiment sprang, straight and firm and flowering like the iris nestling against its green stem. . . . What did they want? Almost nothing. Everything. They wanted to live together. When at last the two families yielded, overwhelmed, unable to make head or tail of this folly, of this pure but irregular passion, the two girls suddenly became as gentle as tame doves . . . the matter was settled. A vow of reclusion descended on this couple of young girls, separating them from the world, veiling and changing and remaking the universe in their eyes. . . . We would know nothing more of the Ladies of Llangollen, had not the elder according to the fashion of the time kept a diary only twice interrupted in 43 years. The younger, Sarah, was called Beloved and Better Half and Delight of my Heart."

From the diary: "A day of the most perfect and sweet retirement."

"Rose at seven. A sweet spring morning. Ten. My beloved and I drank a dish of tea. A day of the most delicious and exquisite retirement."

"Writing, drawing, sweet sunshine, blue sky. Soft smoke from the village ascending in spirals. Birds innumerable."

“Soft fine rain. My Beloved and I went the Home Circuit Celestial lovely day.”

“My Beloved and I gathered holly berries, primrose and strawberry plants for our Banks . . . then visited a cow, saw her suckling her son, went to the new garden, gathered gooseberries. The country in a blaze of beauty.”

THE WEDDING

Village Voice, January 14, 1971

LEUCADIA: 20 miles north of San Diego . . . because we’re sitting here splitting fields and relaxing together and Pauline Oliveros is playing me a tape of a performance of her Composition to Valerie Solanas and Marilyn Monroe in Recognition of Their Desperation. The friends of our friends are our friends. Dear Everyhead at home, this is happy gay land. Can you believe the place is a Leucadia where a Pauline who is another American and musical Gertrude Stein lives with her recently wedded wife on the Pacific near the cliff of a sunrise ceremony this July 4th performed by a minister of the Universal Life Church which makes the difference between the generations between say ours and Gertrude’s merely one of great pride in announcement. I told Pauline that the name of the World War I model-T-Ford owned by Gertrude Stein and Alice Toklas was Aunt Pauline. And that Pauline is the name whose bearers I collect on my grandmother journey toward some place far below the Northern Sea or like Persephone arriving from Hades to join her mother Demeter when the spring is timing to go through the world together but unlike Persephone not having to hear anyone say Ah my dearest you ate those pomegranate seeds and therefore must return some part of the year to sit in the dark places on the throne of yr lord and master. Nah, this is 1971 in Leucadia which is the ancient name of one of the Ionian Islands and the place Sappho is said to have ended her life by a heroic leap off the summit of a magnificent cliff. (At Lesbos she was the head of a great poetic school, for poetry in that age and place was cultivated as assiduously and apparently as successfully by women as by men). You can’t go anywhere you can’t get back from. Before and after follow each other. Picture a lesbian estate on the cliffs of California where doors open green and bodies open blue . . . Pauline married Lin Barron who she is also a music person a cellist and composer and student at the University of California at San Diego where Pauline is a professor of electronic music and composition. For the two days preceding the wedding she stayed at the Minister’s house in quiet seclusion. Till death do them unite or in life they can part as in all things only perchange when we cease to have any motives at all can we comprehend the magnitude of the event. I fell in love in Los Angeles the night of the brinking day I was planning to leave and didn't stay because of it. That's the way isn't it? You're takin a very big gamble on gettin some sorrow. So last night happy new year I made the gay rounds in San Diego by invitation a pretty opera singer who later did me in good so I felt as well treated in a strange city I'd never seen by day as I imagined one would as the recipient of an Eskimo wife offered by her old man who makes a stranger feel at home in this manner and custom I've heard it sounds fine any old way you get done.... You wiped me out I murmuranted. Happy New Year she said. So today January 1 in Leucadia I arrange drive L.A. tomorrow to meet the one I glimpsed many hours over body and loving and not even concerned to be getting it off by the light of a bottled blue candle of a Duccio Madonna captioned Our Mother of Perpetual Help. Is this the beginning of a new civilization or the symptom of a dying one. Demeter saw the chariot approaching and like a wild bird she flew to clasp her child. Sappho's painting of passion... has never since been surpassed (in antiquity her fame rivaled that of Homer). The only boy Daphne ever loved was a boy disguised as a girl. The day of the wedding Pauline went out below the cliff about 4 a.m. to hide out there with her conch shell trumpet and wearing her muslin gown toga Greek style made by the minister's wife. Pauline is impressively round and solid and good humored like Gertrude for whom she dedicated a piece in 1966 called Participle Dangling. The one I just heard, for Valerie Solanas and Marilyn Monroe, in Recognition of Their Desperation, is scored for string quartet, bass, three flutes, organ, and Buchla Electronic Music System. Many male composers think of her as the only female in their field. She wrote an article in the New York Times this summer on the subject which should be an encouragement to the other active women. In L.A. Alison Knowles was deploring the artistry of Charlotte Moorman whom I said we must cherish in all her vulgarity. Charlotte has no respect for cock in the desperation of her sex to sit on the stage of history. A magnificent woman Charlotte. Tits and teeth and all. And better latent than never. Even if she becomes more and more absorbed in some difficulty we can't fathom. Her hair was unbound as she ran down the slopes of the Mountain Ossa. Daphne saw him (Apollo) standing upon a peak with the light striking his quiver and she knew him for the most beautiful of the Olympians but when he called to her she fled from him for she had vowed that no God nor no man should possess her. Madam, your breakfast plate waits for you. The decision reached itself really. Mascula Virgo. Going against the grain of her sex. Do you think the time has come to share with a waiting world the names of the prominent people whose lives have been changed by taking LSD asked Leary who answered yes which I answer to the same question I would terminate by saying who have taken homosexuality for the news is urgent to the health of the state in which the girl on the run and her pursuer become alternate versions of the same plight. In San Francisco in a gay bar they told me it was a place that Janis Joplin frequented. Dear Kate Millett, thanks for your letter, I'm sorry too about the unpleasantness of our encounter, I meant to withdraw my challenge since everybody is working on different phases of a personal comeout program. We'll try to materialize the tellie show for March, I'll let you know. Gregory you met will be on it. We'd like Paul Goodman and Gore Vidal and Allen Ginsberg and Susan Sontag and I asked John Cage who doesn't think it's important. Pauline and Lin here will come if possible. Sappho is rising. As the sun was coming up Pauline emerged from underneath the cliff at the sound of the conch shell trumpet of her mate arriving above also garbed in the muslin gown toga they were married by the minister who rang a bell and symbolized their union by wrapping them round together in a long cloth and releasing two doves to inform the animal world. The newlyweds and company of friends descended the cliff to the beach to celebrate. Apollo wears Daphne as a laurel around his brow. For as she felt his breath upon her neck and his hands upon her shoulders she swayed; she knew herself changed, and rooted in earth, and safe from pursuit as the blood in her body flowed down to become sap and her limbs and the flesh and the flowing hair become branches and leaves and Apollo mourned for her where he stood and loved her now as a tree even as he had loved her as a maiden. The country of Lesbos is very fertile. The country of Leucadia is luscious too. You can hear as I did after driving back up to L.A. as I sd to join the one I loved by the light of Our Mother of Perpetual Help the sound of one ocean clapping. Pauline played me her record of the Songs of the Humpback Whale. I wish we could arrange transportation for all far below the Northern Sea or anyway a fantasy I'm developing of triumphal re-entries such as Pauline Oliveros in full concert returning to Houston where she came from. Gertrude arriving New York 1930 or so or when by steamship a celebrity was said to have baffled reporters by making herself clear. (Alice cackled and giggled perhaps a little maliciously). Isadora scandalized herself by flaunting the red flag of her Russian boy poet husband. Janis Joplin told Cavett and America on the tubes she'd been laughed out of her class, out of the town, out of the state, "so I'm goin' home man." I've got my eyes on a royal barge setting out from Calais to Dover. My fabled father is waiting. Ah Persephone (sd Hades), strive to feel kindliness in yr heart toward me who carried you off by violence and against your will. It's okay dad we're feasting on the guacamole and the oysters on the half shell and passing up the pomegranate seeds this trip around. The Female Freeway, a book of poems just out here by Lynn Lonidier who engineered the rituals of the wedding. Dear Lee, Pauline did a tarot reading for me. The first or basic or significator card was the four of wands—two laurel wreathed females under a laurel arch. The outcome card the knight of swords. In a dream I called a reconciliation-with-women dream I appeared as identical twins in the denim jacket laughing bent over slightly on the road under weight of a backpack. I tell Pauline not only is the coincidence of her first name a cropper but the first two syllables of her last name belong as well to my last livid maternal relative. And do what you will you will with the eros in it, and the olive, as in branch, this part of the Pacific coast between L.A. and San Diego is very Greek somehow.

LOIS LANE IS A LESBIAN (1)

Village Voice, March 4, 1971

I plotted this augmented "confession" driving out of New Orleans at 5 a.m. with a broken left shoulder feeling cosmically sorry for myself and the world. I could've been some river boat rake shot up in a gambling game and crawling off to die in a swamp, that's how bad it was. At midnight I fell down a flight of stairs in the unlit landing of a warehouse where some kids had been showing me how they manufacture water beds. At 12:10 out on the street there, after broadcasting my agony sprawled over a car hood, I heard this nice clean American male heterosexual hippie who had been my escort explain that we should sleep in my vehicle together. At 12:15 I figured I couldn't have been in worse shape if the concussion I had just sustained had been administered by the billy club of a cop who was now offering to rape me as a reward for being so attractively destroyed. At 12:20 I climbed over the frying pan into the fire where I signaled through the flames the message that we both liked the same sex. At 12:25 my ex-companion of the water bed company was in greater shock than me and I left him gaping and fuming there to go on and win a medal for driving or careening through enemy territory in critical condition to a hospital where for four hours I waited in vain for somebody to determine the extent of the damage. At 5 a.m., as I said, I was on the road. I didn't look back. New Orleans was a disaster area called Mardi Gras. At 2 p.m. when I arrived there the French Quarter I thought was the most exotic area every side of St. Mark's Place and Carnaby Street and Telegraph Avenue and Commercial Street in Provincetown. By 7 p.m. I had lost and/or been ripped off of eight bills, I hoped I would never see another peace emblem or insignia ever; I had paid $2.55 for a ginger ale in a low class strip joint, and 25 cents to pee in a normal restaurant; I had been inadvertently charged by a troupe of longhairs pouring out of a lavender bus demonstrating for more pay for their local police force; I had declined the advances of a New Yorker who recognized me in a coffee shop, and passed up the subtler advances of a girl called Jill cruising me in a headshop; the American eagle on my van had come loose and askew; and I had read in my own newspaper that I was part of a phony new industry of interpersonal technology of which my confessional gush is consecrated to the proposition that we must all abandon the privileged privacy of our most precious relationships or perish from emotional constipation and that these confessions are becoming increasingly profitable, both culturally and financially, and that I have been publicly exhorting every pretty girl in America to come out of the closet and into my bed (yeah) and that I want to look good so badly that I wind up making every else around me look bad.

If I hadn't been so upset over the new evidence that some of us are still finding it so difficult to celebrate all the things we are I would have been more astonished and flattered that a successful white American male heterosexual film critic had invested that much time and energy and rhetorical diligence to pay so much hostile attention to the meagre outpourings of the most oppressed and confused and unrecognized minority in every country of the world. It is as much your privilege to think I'm exaggerating as it is mine to believe I'm stating the case to fit the facts. Each of us is a barometer of social conditions which we observe through the perceptual screen of our needs. Reviewing and re-reviewing my experience of growing up and sort of surviving in a male dominated heterosexual world I am now prepared to say that a female who is a lesbian in this society is about as well off as a Sabine woman trapped in a camp of black corporals. I am, by the way, more in sympathy with the black cause than ever before, and in fact with all causes, for it has recently occurred to me that all causes are the same cause (as my critic said, we are all in the same boat) and that what we're doing here then is educating all the members of ourselves to certain needs which have gone unheeded or unrecognized or worse damned and vilified and thrust underground so that we can all coexist more happily together. My initial reaction to the women's movement was a classic. The line was "What's the matter with *them, I've* been doing it all these years." You can hear this same line from accomplished females all over the place. It's an elitist capitalistic attitude which blesses the fortunate and condemns the ignorant. My initial reaction to the black movement was hey wait a minute I didn't *choose* to be born white, and let me tell *you* about the problems of a white homosexual female in a . . . et cetera. Now I suggest you go up to a black person and say White People Have Problems Too and see what kind of response you get. I'm going on record here to notify every heterosexual male and female that every lesbian and every homosexual is all too aware of the problems of heterosexuals since they permeate every aspect of our social political economic and cultural lives. That we were in fact educated on these problems. That we were brought up and spoon fed or pitch forked on the crucible of the problems of thousands of Romeos and Juliets radiating outward from all our sublimely miserable and broken families into the movies and the funnies and the histories and the psychologies and the novels and our great Western classics. It is, in fact, the heterosexual problems which create a gay liberation movement or any movement to end the artificial social construction of sexual specialization which makes some of our members ill and confused. It is the heterosexual problem which creates this tremendous body of clinical literature to brand some aspect of sexuality perverse and abnormal. It is the heterosexual problem which creates the monstrosity of transsexualism, surely the most pitiful operation going, to "help" some gullible people *not* to be homosexual in a society far from convinced that all the equipment we are born with is perfectly beautiful. It is the heterosexual problem which creates therapies designed to "cure" people of their natural sexual interests. These therapies and those clinical studies belong to the same market of a disease called normalcy. A healthy society would enjoy and encourage all of its perversions by which in fact the society would be defined. Polymorphous perversity is the norm. There is no norm. Unless it's Mailer, who perfectly embodies the heterosexual problem. I think all of us are authorities on the heterosexual problem. Knowledge on the subject is instantly available, in case you've missed out, in every daily newspaper with their front page accounts of the Wars. We are bored with the news from the heterosexual fronts. We want to hear from the lesbians and homosexuals now. I want homosexual movies and novels and funnies and histories and songs and classics. Even problem stories. Certainly the songs. Let all those gay rock artists come out from behind their phony lyrics. But the movies! The big medium. I don't expect the next batch of gay ones to show us nothing but the doomed clandestine affair of Therese and Isabelle in boarding school, and the wrecked life of Sister George whose girlfriend leaves her for a great white witch of the west whose cold clawing sexual advanced constitute the only sexual revelation in the film, and the huge tree of D. H. Lawrence's well equipped "Fox" falling on one of his two heroines to effectively wipe out the contender to his hero's object, or the girls in "Persona" never getting to the point, or the sisters in "Silence," and the boys in anybody's band parading their stereotyped images to a public greedy for their distress and martyrdom.—Andy Warhol could give us a few straight stories. Eight hours of Nancy and Little Lulu in bed. Or Blondie and Lois Lane. I don't care much about endings one way or another but the homosexual movies could begin by making up for all the years we grew up watching Gary Cooper and Richard Greene ride gloriously into the purple sunset with Myrna Loy and Mrs. Miniver etc. to live happily ever after. This film critic a few months ago wrote in the context of some review that "although I don't belong to the happy-endings-for-homosexuals club . . ." which made me ask him when I saw him "why *don't* you belong to the happy-endings-for-homosexuals club?" Exactly. The question is why we don't all belong to the happy endings (and beginnings and middles) for everybody club. Can you imagine me saying, in any context, "although I don't belong to the happy-endings-for-heterosexuals club?" Can you imagine anybody saying "although I don't belong to the happy-endings-for-black people club?" Can you imagine any intelligent observer at this moment in history writing an article damning the blacks and their social agonies? Or suggesting that James Baldwin or Eldridge Cleaver or LeRoi Jones were something *more* or something *other* than their blackness—that they were not so much black people who happened to be fine writers as fine writers who happen to be black? We are not *any* of us something (or less) or *other* than anything that we are. We are the sum total of all we are and we are all what we are in every thought and in every action we manifest.

The Western habit of separating everything and of constantly defining our own spaces by the creation of an enemy is the habit that projected a profession called criticism by which people glibly judge and assess the complications of the lives of others. I never woke up one morning to say Ah now I am going to write something culturally and financially profitable called a confession. I don't share our film critic's obsession with careerism in the forms he describes it as Looking for An Edge. Confession isn't a luxury. It's a necessity. By any American standards none of us is rich. When any artist in this crazy pragmatic country begins to survive by doing just what he wants to do, his art, it seems to me an occasion for rejoicing. That the artists themselves should be attacking each other for arriving at this precarious position of a tenuous security seems to me the height of insanity. In New Orleans that apocalyptic afternoon I picked up the James Taylor cover pix issue of *Roll-*

ing Stone along with *The Voice.* Taylor is quoted: "It is very strange making a living out of being yourself."—and the writer goes on: "which neatly defines the personal confessional school of songwriting which promises to supplant much of the hard rock of the '60s."—Confessional literature in any form hardly needs an apology for its current expressions. One shouldn't have to refer to our honorable ancestors St. Augustine or Rousseau or de Quincey. The form is a misleading one in any case, for one might always ask what is *not* a confession? Still, there is a kind of religious consciousness, awakening, by fire and shock, which powers the necessity, an inner compulsion, to forge a confessional style. Nerval and Rimbaud and Artaud are such artists in the French tradition. The French historically have seemed especially susceptible. In any country the tradition can be related by a short mental jump to the religious ecstasies and confessions of a Teres of Avila. At the present moment in America there's an activity we might call confessional journalism which is practiced along the whole gamut of profit at one end and revelation at the other. It's interesting to me that our film critic should express his distaste and displeasure over the medium while practicing it in the same breath. If I had anything to do with stimulating his interest in himself to the point of public display I'd be pleased since I believe the entire practice of criticism is a pathetic projection of personal terrors and inadequacies and suppressed ambition. The rhetorical expertise of some of its practitioners is the best educated refusal to deal with the central problem of the world—the Self. My "confessional gush" is consecrated to no other proposition than that of collecting all of my selves that I can raise to consciousness in the shape of current experiences into some form of literary energy at the moment I sit down most every week to write that damn column. Sometimes I get a masterpiece seizure and work very hard for a structural coup. Sometimes I'm unsuccessfully trying to merge my literary ambition with my cause concerns. It's *always* a dilemma. What to say and how to say it. And you have to perpetuate the illusion that it means something to somebody besides yourself. Otherwise why the hell would you be publishing it? Why the hell am I bothering *here* to regress to an old academic style to answer a person who feels that his own myths and feelings are being ridiculed when he sees an exhibition of another way of life? Because that's the way I feel *right now.* I have straight friends whose lives I honor and respect and *they* don't feel ridiculed by the difference they discern in *me.* If it's anybody's turn to feel ridiculed, and by the massive heterosexual culture, you know who it is, and that's what the gay liberation is all about—to end this ridiculous posturing about anybody else's sexuality. My first and final line if I had only one on the subject would be that if you can't walk out of your door and down the street and into the park in any familiar embrace with the one you love the whole society is in trouble. Men will have to give up the idea that every female is their potential mate. And women will have to abandon their designs on every male. Gay people are now expecting and demanding the same sanctified regard for *their* sexual interests and unions as they have rendered for as long as they can remember to the weird forces that endowed them with life in the first place. Now there is only one way for this social change to take place. And that is for all gay people, those who know it and accept it, to stand up and speak for themselves. There is no other way. The laws and discriminatory practices will alter according as the attitude does, and the attitude continues absurd as long as the society tolerates its aberrations by successfully pretending that it doesn't know what it already suspects. Ask any gay person about their traumatic confrontations with their families. Everybody *knows* everything. That is, we are in constant telepathic communication. But society is an iceberg. Most of it is under water. Knowledge which would reveal our most ancient archetypal terrors and taboos, our collective sins and guilts, is rigorously repressed. When this unconscious material erupts and surfaces we become the animal I can only imagine we once were—an animal all of whose parts were in mutual and open-ended communication. The human animal is, perhaps, in the tragic position of having to surface all the way up in order to go all the way back down, or vice versa. Total conscious knowledge means clear traffic from the depths of the unconscious to the rational parts of the functional forebrain. If the iceberg of society surfaced completely we'd be living in a painful but compassionate utopia. I believe with Freud and Brown and Reich etc. that sexual polymorphous perversity (you *can*, by the way, reconcile Reich with the others) and all its social consequences is the paradise we most profoundly wish to recover. Specialization (sexual, technological, etc.) is the monster that civilization visited on itself to sustain its material needs. We're working now for an aerial view. We need to know what we already know. Not enough can be said to inform people of what they already know. A secret is an archaic hoarded treasure. Secrets mean borders and barriers and codes and passports and thick walls and frontiers between people. Just a year ago I permitted Rosalyn Drexler at a small dinner party to convince me I'd been a dope for revealing myself at an artists' colony where I'd been I was not being self protective as Rosalyn pointed "Oh, Jill, can't you keep a secret" and I was not yet able to reply immediately "Do you keep your marriage to Sherman a secret?"—But if you think I'm having fun being a blabber mouth lesbian you're mistaken. The field is thick with clashing swords. The ground is already drenched in blood. If you think I'm feeling sorry for myself you're right. But I'm greatly in favor of people feeling that particular emotion. It's against the grain of the fearless Protestant ethic. Yet you don't know you're a human being until you feel sorry for yourself in a very grand way. Then you look around you and see possibly for the first time how we're all in it together and then you'll feel that big cosmic emotion and that's how you discover with a certain shock that you're religious even though you've read the French existentialists on the death of God.

I know the media thrives on our petty intramural battles but we really want something bigger for ourselves don't we? Why, in any event, would a quarterback want to tackle his own center? I've got enough trouble. I'm persona non grata with every "group" in the country, just for openers. The women's lib people don't like the way I swim. The Gay Liberation Front says I wouldn't get any support from *them*. Both organizations think I'm a male chauvinist pig, probably because I take more girls to bed (or want to or pretend to) than I have a right to—as though nobody was every luring *me* to bed.—A black man once told me that LeRoi Jones and the like wanted my head on a platter. The artists were never pleased that I began to find their lives more interesting than their work. The religious groups accuse me of grubbing around on a fame and art trip. The artists coalition types begrudge my sudden minimal independence in my old age. All radicals dismiss me as an idle dreamer. Gay newspaper says I'm an exhibitionist. And I suppose the Aubudon society has it in for me too. Anyway I'm on everybody's list as number one menace to the universe. I have a case of the most exquisite paranoia. It's a wonderful feeling. For a female lesbian bastard writer mental case I'm doing awfully well. The only movement I'm dedicated to myself is finding out what anybody is calling me so I can say yeah that's me. For example: Coopting the names in the name-calling dictionaries called psychoanalytical textbooks would finish a profession which defines its existence by an occult terminology of names branding whatever it isn't—that is, the enemy. Schizophrenics, Unite!

LOIS LANE IS A LESBIAN (2)

Village Voice, March 11, 1971

I thought to open these diatribes last week with a little James Taylor story which still seems appropriate to the gist of my objections to assaults on gay consciousness and of my positioning in the gay revolution. I did quote Taylor in *Rolling Stone*: "It seems strange to be making a living out of being yourself." In June 1968, while I was still struggling out of the restraints and moral dilemmas of being a critic, and before Taylor had cut his first record, I met him in London at the Beatles recording studio and accepted his invitation to spend the night at his funky flat where he apologized for his sexual inactivity (that's quite okay man, I said, or thought), explaining he was on opium, and we had a good time rapping about Reich (he was reading) and his folks and Carolina and his trips in the funny farm and his imminent career. He told me how famous he was going to be and how he was going to relate to his fans differently than the Beatles. I thought he was mildly presumptuous but basically didn't question his matter-of-fact verdict of his impending success. My own manner at that time was self-effacing. After all, I wasn't being recorded by the Beatles. Certainly Taylor wasn't interested in whatever I was besides being a girl. Even so, I might have been more aggressive if I had felt more optimistic about myself. I was still somewhat wretched from a year of languishing in bed mulling over my apparently hopeless situation as an ex-convict of a different kind of funny farm than Taylor had been privileged to attend. Anyway, what I'm suggesting here is an interesting connection between two brooding people meeting by chance in London each unaware that the other was brinking a confessional style which had at least one common source for its motivation in the melodrama of being a prisoner of state by award of a profession which dispenses the judgements and sentences fulfilling the need of society to qualify some of our mental states as more or less valid than others. Also, when I met Taylor I was not thinking of my own fame fantasies, yet two years before, in New York, I had walked out of Bellevue and Mt. Sinai swearing on all my sacred organs that I would be more famous than Norman Mailer who had been better treated than me at the same dungeon and I hadn't even stabbed anybody. I was in a grand rage I can tell you. And I was dead certain that society was in league against itself to prevent some of its members from becoming healthy by going crazy. (And I hadn't heard of Ronald Laing yet). And don't think they weren't interested in convincing me I was a pervert, meaning a disgrace to myself and America. And don't think I wasn't convinced. I don't even like to remember that year and then another half of a year in bed staring at the ceiling which was also the floor of a loft belonging to Les Levine whose footsteps day in and night out were a constant reminder that normal well adjusted people were making their invaluable contributions to Society.

That visit to London in '68 was a winner for me. I came back a roaring lesbian. Even my best friend Sheindi thought I was putting the make on her. What had happened essentially is that I had become a *mobile* sexual being.

This was a radical shift in attitude and behavior, and we well know that the more hidden nature of the female's sexual organization is rigorously reinforced by the culture in conditioning the female to be a dead Snow White until her Prince arrives to knock her up. I was as passive as any passive female I had ever met and I'd been knocked up a fair bit too, and as regarded other females I was not unlike King Aroo of the comic strip who in Chapter LMDCXVII gets kissed by the Beautiful Princess in the kingdom next door and lives happily ever after for the rest of the afternoon. I believe absolutely that the key to a real sexual revolution, which would violently dislocate the social family organization, which would drastically affect the economic-political structures, is the *sexual mobilization of women*. And that the bourgeois issues of the women's movement, important as they may be, obscure this fundamental truth. If women by some glacial reversal of biological history and cultural conditioning were actively seeking their own sexual gratification we'd be living in a very different society. I think the women's movement will stand or fall on the issue of the sexual options the women decide they do or don't have. I think the intelligent women active in liberation groups have flashed that sudden insight of the agonizing paradox of the concept of a liberated woman still psycho-sexually dependent on the male. I think the women's liberation movement is enduring an invisible convulsion of the embarrassment caused by the realization that the lesbian, however hated or oppressed, is the purest representative of their liberated ideal. I think the women are going to fight against this realization and cause great divisiveness between themselves and that therefore it will be the responsibility of the lesbian women everywhere to rise up and assert the fundamental truth of the women's revolution. We can only offer our own experience.

Since London in June '68 I have felt like a total integrated person and I'd feel that way no matter how many flights of stairs I can't manage in the dark and no matter what catastrophes befall me. Since then I've reversed my entire history, both onto- and phylogenetically, and I think I could even survive the kiss of another Beautiful Princess. Even fighting off the hordes who don't want me to live happily ever after for a little bit longer than the rest of the afternoon. I refuse to accept any social judgment which blames the brevity of a relationship (if there's any premium on longevity) on my deficient character or sexual inadequacy or incapacity to love or predilection for the abnormal which in itself constitutes the cause of its own undoing. No. These relationships are *not* endorsed by Society and it is still a superhuman thing to defy the social order by an emotional commitment right on the premises of the enemy or even by the more successful tactic of withdrawal to the boondocks where many a lesbian and homosexual couple divide their lives between the fearful organized protection of their secret amorous existence at home and the pretense of their straight existences on the job. My two grand passions of the last six years (one before and one after London) were not advantageously arranged. Besides remaining exposed in the shark infested New York art world I had the nerve to be married to a couple of Cassandras, or Cleopatras, as well. One had the kind of eyes that drive Kings mad and cause Empires to fall. The other had the kind of somnolent seductive athletic grace and classic aristocratic features that drives *every*body mad. Both were very intelligent people too. The first was in mortal fear of her blue chip family whose house she dutifully visited once a week for dinner, an occasion that neither of us thought for a moment should include yours truly confused. She was also the object of probably the most determined and persistent courting in the history of that sort of assault (by a third party on a couple) which was launched by a macho male boy wonder artist assisted with the greatest zeal in the enterprise by his dealer who even followed us to provincial cities to continue their blandishments in a nearby house or in the same hotel!—The second was no improvement for me in these respects because she was not only a beauty and a bacchante but an heiress as well. She moved in with me and spent the money I didn't have and met my famous comrades and tried to seduce my best friend and sucked me into oblivion and threw my *Village Voices* in the fire and introduced me to her mother who consulted the psychiatrists and became ill, and angry ("I buried that long ago, dear") and called her husband in from Spain and just generally mobilized all her powerful resources to save her wayward daughter from the corruptions of real love until she wisely gave up and retreated in refined resignation to Europe to brood I suppose and to wait for the inevitable. I had an authentic princess and the royal family was furious. I believe they were better off than the Rockefellers and Kennedys combined. And don't think I didn't have designs on every bit of their bread. My plan was a modern Lesbos on the mainland. Whole cities of pleasure palaces for girls. Whole paradises of Daphnes in bunches of elegant chateaux catered by beautiful eunuchs and liveried flowers. Why the hell not. Well, alas, as you know my scheme aborted because the heroine, whom I really loved by the way, disappeared, and although I tumbled after like a good Jill by flying to Spain to rescue the princess from the big bad witch, they were waiting with the psychiatric machinery and the shut-up money and a bottle of whisky on a hot Moorish hilltop to wipe me out and of course I obliged. After all, who was I but an impoverished American female posing as an important British bastard. Anyway we weren't the proper story book couple. I returned home and began screwing around right away. I refused even to be a Snow White for another Snow White any more. I'm urging all Snow Whites to get up out of their caskets and mobilize and claim their own sexuality, whether it's another Snow White or a Prince or the self in masturbation. And yes in answer to Sarris I especially urge all females to enjoy the "mother" (oneself) with whom way back in their dim unremembered history they were once as sexually entwined as the male child. The repudiation of the mother by every female, as the culture demands her capitulation to the male, must surely be the cruelest sacrifice in the catalogue of compromise in which constitutes a civilization at war with itself in the repression of its own instinctual freedoms. And yes in answer to Sarris we lesbians and/or homosexuals quite naturally feel that our sexuality is not only equal to but superior to heterosexuality. It's like spaghetti or soy beans. If you're really into spaghetti or soy beans that'll be a personal superior food *for you*. But I quote Gregory Battcock on the subject to stimulate a broader view and provoke the exclusive heterosexual: "Of *course* the homosexual experience is more authentic, because the heterosexual goes to bed only with the other person and the homosexual goes to bed both with the other person *and* with himself." And on Sarris: "Baby, if you haven't tried it, don't knock it." And further he questions the qualification of anybody to write a whole article about an experience they haven't had. I wondered myself what motivated the sudden confession of such a virulent prejudice from one of our outstanding intellectuals and did a little research which yielded this incredible admission in the New York Times in the context of the spit-ball Simon-Sarris battle: "Most malignant of all are Simon's simperings on the subject of my manliness, beginning with an attack on my review of Topaz praising a fagged-out Hitchcock for having 'improvised to the extent of exploiting John Vernon's expressively blue eyes in a morally ambivalent situation.' Note how Simon slips in the disgusting double-edged slang of 'fagged-out' to *tar* both Hitchcock and me with the *innuendo of inversion*" (my italics).—*Jesus*! I hasten to reassure our film critic: Dear Andrew, *I* think you're a man. Don't worry, we'll vouch for you on Judgment Day. But now you know, by your own admission, why there's a gay revolution. What opening or excuse would there *be* for an innuendo when the object of these disparaging intimations has gotten it all together in pride and health. If we all liked everything we were we wouldn't even know what an innuendo was. How do you think I feel to hear Shelley Winters on the Cavett show say that in her new movie with Debbie Reynolds that she plays the part of a *paranoid schizophrenic* lesbian (my italics), and then hear Cavett play the innuendo to the hilt by the subtlest but unmistakable words and gestures. It's a drag, man. See? And in private at least I'm no longer putting up with it. (To be continued).

LOIS LANE IS A LESBIAN (3)

Village Voice, March 25, 1971

In case you've wondered why Lois Lane is a lesbian it's because she's Clark Kent's girlfriend and her real hero is God. I leave it to my male counterpart to expose old Clark. Lois and Blondie've been having an affair for years, just like the nuns in the convent. If you can get thee to a nunnery that's where it's really all happening. Some closets are big enough for lots of people to get into and have a good time. When a closet is built very big it begins to look like the world. The world closet is also Bucky's global village. But all these cosmic events take place first at home in the head, so I fail to see how automation by computer or even my Sermon on the Mouth here broadcasting this exposé of the hitherto undisclosed sex life of Lois Lane will liberate people from economic slavery or seriously affect such seemingly immovable blocks of opinion as was sadly demonstrated by *the N.Y. Times* Sunday March 7 in a front page article describing new therapies for homosexuals, including aversion techniques (electric shock) and the formation of a Homosexuals Anonymous, which is precisely the place of exile where straight society wishes the homosexual to remain or to be sent back—to secrecy. I'm getting this kind of heavy message myself. If I'm not sued by the funny book people I could be shot in the South, or someplace, they say. So I threw the Ching three times and got five readings all saying basically the same thing—that I'd better cut it out for the time being these words are having no effect. I've discovered recently that I have a surprising number of soap boxes. I guess you know what I'd like to do to the psychiatric profession. But maybe you haven't heard me on children and education and old people and animals and the retarded and the autistic and the drugs and the medical profession and architecture and religion and borders and you name it actually I can get very excited about it. My agitation on behalf of Lois Lane dates most specifically back to last November in San Francisco. That afternoon a few weeks ago in New Orleans was just the detonation of the fuse that was lit back in California where I had driven away from a melodrama dinner party and a busted affair feeling more like a Joan in armor than I know it's wise or safe to. But the incident convinced me I would no longer tolerate an innuendo which sounded like an assault on a sexual identity which is fragile enough in the present social circumstances. Moving away from a more detached Tibetany trip I had to justify my sudden militancy so I just said well you have to go along with it until it's over, you can't deny that rage you experienced, you don't even know where it's going, you just keep a watch on it and see if you can explode it where it'll hurt the most to mean as much to the peoples you imagine who share the same or similar vulnerability as it meant to you when you thought you were experiencing the entire social prejudice in hurricane form in the microcosm of a dinner party. A black person these days has a certain advantage in being clearly black. I'm not keen about walking across any threshold and announcing my sexual preference over a hello and a handshake. But we might have to alter the etiquettes to suit the new consciousness of the awakened and confirmed lesbian and homosexual who no longer wish to participate in the prejudice against her/himself by permitting any host or hostess or companion to assume a sexuality not clearly defined one way or another by look or style. I don't know how it should work. Lots of radical lesbians are currently in isolation to enjoy only their own company. One told me that the straight friends I've alluded to must be unique in transcending their programming with their humanity. Maybe so. Or else I'm kidding myself. These straight people in San Francisco were strangers to me and friends of a girl who was a quasi-romance of mine for a year, meaning in the worst sense of literary male chauvinism someone you have possessed but from whom you have remained nevertheless detached. I had arrived in November with ideas of being more involved if possible but I think she was eager to make me pay for my old detachment which she considered a cruelty. The prices of interesting sex. And I wasn't completely immune to the unexpected revenge since after all I did care you know, in some way, so I felt bad enough for a couple of days and even returned after I got my head together to see if she really meant it and she didn't after a sloppy dinner at a waterfront restaurant where I got smashed enough to pretend that the interesting bed scene we ended up in would be emotionally more substantial than the way it always was when I was partly not there.—Such a business. So the next day there I was again trying to feel more involved but clutching the same old way wanting to run from the clinging which was partly responsible for the original detachment which was clearly the mode of my involvement in this particular relationship. We then permitted, so far as I could see, this tenuous affair to be shattered by straight society in an incident that was potent enough apparently to make me feel the way LeRoi must have when the black power thing hit him. Anyway I began to understand the meaning of a true social rage. It happened on this evening about 8 p.m. over a tableau of the Mr. and Mrs. and my lover and her roommate and me uncomfortable enough trying to tolerate the barking cheesecake friendliness of the Mr. while relating to the slightly hysterical but not unnatural warmth of the Mrs. who began to insist on a therapy rap which somehow evolved into the dreadful moment when she referred to a male friend, or acquaintance, in tones of slow heavy import as an "in-cur-a-ble hom-o-sex-u-al." The place got hung purply apoplex there for a few seconds during which I flashed a number of thoughts and decisions while the Mr. who had been reclining on the couch ogling the roommate got ready to clinch the opener and close the case for straight America with a ponderous guttural back-up "We-l-l, *honey*, we don't rea-ll-y *know*"—which had the effect of turning my body inside my skin into an armored tank smoking at the joints and hanging over a precipice. I became an instant revolutionary. But I had to hold on and hang in there for the evening with my old fashioned decorum because in the few seconds between her remark and his I had flashed the awful knowledge that I was stranded between the necessity of responding to an intolerable assault and my responsibility to a lover whom I couldn't betray in her closest relation to these people who knew the truth anyway I presume and were playing on the ambivalence of their friend in the normal acceptable fashion of stressing the secret to render it socially impotent. Now I could see for the first time the full import and impact of the closet game. The whole secret-shame-sorry syndrome. I was raging like 20 titans inside my skin unable to act. I went mute but nothing was right. A slaughter was in order and the lady moved in for the kill. The victim became the roommate whom we eventually carried off to cry and scream the rest of it out at home. Now can you dig also that my girlfriend had become angry at *me* for all this? Yeah, these are the wages of sin in our cockeyed society whose collective guilt is denied by the pretense of secrecy. The reverberations of this scene must've traveled down the coast to the Los Angeles fault that made the earthquake. I arose that a.m. in a pure white fury and yelled myself blue in the eyeballs. That was the end of the relationship and the end of my own equivocation as to my sexual identity in any social circumstance and the identity of anyone else with whom I was going to be involved. We are very far from the world closet of infinite sexual modalities. We are a fucked up race of animals whose heterosexual problem is so enormous that it requires its highly compensated solution in the magnified assertion of its own self-righteousness. The norm remains the activity of sending out negative energy to reinforce your own trip. The constant (re)creation of the enemy to confirm your own spaces. The Great War. The culture is a caricature of biological differences. Our first (and last) outpost of resistance to psychic integration—the maintenance of the illusion of two separate and distinct sexes in their grossly caricatured family-political manifestations. Plastic Lady and Palooka Man are the two sexes polarized at their distorted extremes to protect their own disease. The rest of us participate in the disease by going down with the ship in resignation or protest or subversion down under in the hold. That's where the lesbians and homosexuals have been hanging out all these centuries. In the subterranean passages of the mind. The colossal irony of the enforced secrecy, and fear and persecution of the lesbian/homosexual element in every population in every time and place, is the emerging truth of the intense struggle of the exclusive heterosexual drive to protect its own disease from the possible cure of the recognition and eventual practice of its own polymorphic origins. The contemporary warden of the disease is the psychiatric profession. The aim of the gay liberation movement as I see it is the slow massive reversal of this opinion held by the lesbians and homosexuals about themselves which reinforces the straight social attitude (which created that self hate) which in turn affects the already ambivalent homosexual who feeds the confusion back to the straight population and so forth on the vicious circle of compounded prejudice. Gossip is transformed into public acceptable information whenever its object enters the room and acknowledges as an asset the quality ascribed to in the attack which formed the nature of the gossip. Reversal of opinion means the affirmation of all sexuality as intrinsic and the revelation that the illness is created by social attitudes and not by the intrinsic nature of the sexuality. The Bastille of the whole monster is the structured secrecy of social etiquette. Islands of secrecy. One type is the office of the shrink. Therapy is predicated on the premise that something is wrong with you. The proper therapy would be a single visit to anybody who would have the guts to say you were beautiful. As it is the therapist has a vested interest in sustaining the illusion of a problem and the need for a secret. Confessions to the priest were also sworn to secrecy. Confession is a way of life. We confess daily. The collective guilt is denied in the pretense of individual crime. The question gay peoples must be asking themselves now is how a best friend can be next in line after the priest and the shrink. And your other friends. And your family. And your employer. And at least the apparent stranger. Either we are all strangers or we are all intimates. We are all guilty or none of us is guilty. The *projected* guilt of the heterosexual conflict is no longer tolerable to the intrinsically healthy character of the more androgynous lesbian and homosexual. "We are all members of one body." This is the true form of (re)unification. If we are all members of one body, then in that one body there is neither male nor female; or rather there are both: It is an androgynous or hermaphroditic body, containing both sexes. The division of one man into two sexes is part of the fall. Sexes are sections. (Brown) Sexes from Secare: to divide. Reintegration is by mystical participation in the body of the god the temple the kingdom of the Self the One and Universal Mind.

THE COMINGEST WOMANIFESTO

Village Voice, December 28, 1972

(paper delivered at the Feminist Lesbian Dialogue at Columbia U., Dec. 16, here slightly altered and amplified)

first or second off i'm into thinking weird all in these difference places in fact in as many places as we are women and so i ask myself when i meet this one or that one i ask where is them politically sexually & where is one in relation to this one or me or where am i now sexually politically since i'm not the me i was yesterday or last year and where are we going or am i already ahead of myself or behind and is somebody else slightly behind or ahead of that and if not then what or what anything i mean how should we behave and where should we think or what are we permitted to assume much less concerning anybody else their total life their total past who are they who am i who am i to them to become if anything & so on like is the one i'm talking to about to sleep with a woman for the first time in which case would i cause her not to if i accused her of oppressing me by being the kind of a woman who sleeps with the man and if she does anyway will she then be terrified to think she might be thought a lesbian and if so should we condemn her for thinking what we were all brought up all these centuries to actually think altho we now think we're so smart just because a few of us now know that it not only isn't bad it's great in fact it's the best and that that when you ponder it makes us the Ultimate Feminists etc. i mean we think we're really hot shit and we are and so what is that gonna do for us when so many women are still so scared the question is do we want more of us or do we want to just go around saying what hot shit we are and how you straight women are lousing us up just to make sure they'll go on doing it and if so how long would it take before the women called lesbians reemerge as a special interest group and how long after that before you can't say the word lesbian at all any more as if there *is* such a thing as a lesbian the boggler being the more i say it the more i feel it doesn't exist since so many women now actually are lesbians and you wouldn't hear anybody anymore say well huff huff this woman must be a lesbian because she hated her father and her mother was a bitch or whatever they say along those lines or she got to be a lesbian harumph because she had a terrible first sexual experience with a man and all that you wouldn't hear that except in these clinical psychiatric journals anyway even tho from this new point of view there may be no such thing as a lesbian any more and besides which we know now that all lesbians are women i have to go on saying it to make sure anybody knows i'm defining myself politically as a woman committed woman and the word feminist to me doesn't totally convey that idea since so many feminists advocate a change in our situation in relation to the man rather than the devotion of our energies to our own kind to women i have to ask does this make us enemies when we are all potentially dedicated to ourselves and when we believe in feminist issues per se i.e., abortion reform and when we are in a sense each of us all the women we ever were including straight possibly just yesterday or last year or the last time i slept with a man two years ago or four years before that in a tenement on houston street with two kids still thinking i was straight and i was even tho i was in love with a woman i still am that woman i am all the women i ever was which is all the women of the world in transition i become more completely a lesbian or woman committed woman as the centuries pass and more of me becomes me or the me i think it's such hot shit to be which it is by which i mean a woman the more i sleep with myself and eat myself and write myself and breathe myself the more woman i become i become the woman myself i am who i sleep with it doesn't mean you're not a lesbian if you never slept with a woman before if you consider the person you sleep with the most is yourself and that's you a woman from this point of view we all are lesbians right from the start altho what we are and what we think or say we are can be altogether different things it doesn't matter even by the sights of advanced ideology you can't demand that people be where they're not yet ready to be even if you say all persuasive and important listen a woman committed to herself meaning a woman as combined image of mother daughter and sister was is absolutely at odds with society which has been in the modern western world organized around the principle of heterosexuality which in effect means the prime commitment of woman to man who is committed to himself or saying it another way if you say what i really mean when i say you're oppressing me when you sleep with the man is that you're giving something so vital to the man is the same as withholding it from me your daughter your sister or how in effect you go to bed with my brother by paying him more attention you deprive me in proportion as you do so is all very good logic possibly especially when we can say furthermore look you who have for centuries given your best services to your sons what in the end have the sons done for us if not to persuade us or coerce us to serve more sons okay and go on and say and look around you do you see any lesbians becoming straight and so on no matter what we say however i'm convinced we can't very well demand what anybody isn't ready to give who may in fact be ready to change tomorrow or next year who may know a lot more in advance of her current opportunities or her present practical situation or emotional readiness or who may be putting her life in order to make big changes we don't know about anyway who probably won't be significantly impressed by anything so much as the example of our own togetherness all of which doesn't alter it's true the social fact that the very women we wait for continue to hurt us by damning us or ignoring us or hating us or tolerating us or condescending us for loving ourselves or oppressing us by objectifying us as potential Lesbian Experiences or projecting onto us the sexism and puritanism and chauvinism of their own expectations of all they've known in relation to the man we won't stop them from doing this by accusing them of it or by objectifying them in turn by say making any woman a princess or an all purpose mommie or even necessarily by carrying on about how when you saw me at that party and said so you have breasts what you meant was so you're a woman after all like a guy saying to a faggot in a locker room you really do have balls as though a lesbian or woman committed women is less than a woman or somehow a male for liking other women the way males do supposedly and thus being less a woman not being a woman in the sisterhood of man pandering females or when you say oh i happen to love a woman now but i could as well have a relationship with a man if he were the right sort of person as tho we were not all *persons* before the *feminists* taught us we were women in the sense of being a political class in which case what you're really saying is if the right sort of *man* came along or when you say if all else fails we'll try loving our sisters as if your sister was a last resort and even if you do think you mean just sex i translate it to mean loving your sisters which means sex and *everything* i still know the truth is demonstrable only by example and the only way to proceed historically is to respect personal places places even we feel are detaining us or delaying us or deterring us we respect them nevertheless for being the places any woman is capable of being the way we respect a wasp for being a wasp we don't condemn a wasp for being the type of animal who would sting us if she could i don't want to pursue the example the example that concerns me here is the assertion of our own logic and model in this way enough women by a few centuries time will become the hot shit we think we are to make a viable amazon nation or tribe or tribes of women capable of sustaining themselves independently of the male specious we have to remind ourselves that in 1972 amerika we are a fugitive band who can't afford to isolate ourselves from the women in the middle who in any case remains a potentially total ally or the woman we are gradually becoming as we become more of ourselves as we leave more of our straight selves of ourselves behind ourselves we gradually become ourselves all the women we ever were we are ourselves still the woman in the middle it doesn't make any sense to be our own enemy and if we don't see common cause with feminists feminists are not likely to see it with us either especially when it's so easy to find reason by offense to say we'll have nothing to do with you when it's still so scary to proclaim the legitimacy of an identity so recently criminal or sick or sinful we must therefore as i see it take all the chances and risk being the ones to continue being hurt and insulted by exposing our thought as the logic of the feminist/lesbian position and exposing our selves as the models of the revolution by realizing we are each and all all the women of the world in transition and not placing ourselves thus above and beyond or ahead but directly in the center as the moving force of our collective conscience.

Personal Essay

IN HER ALTOGETHER ALSO

Village Voice, January 29, 1970

She stood up from a hot tub and passed out under the sink and broke a rib or two. I like to fall asleep myself in the middle of a story. Come again when you can't stay so long. And bring camera. My blood is thin, my heart is made of tin tonight. I didn't remember signaling with my foot my intention of dying with her and my foot isn't even stuck in the door. I'm stuck on the hi-way. Clapping my hands I am not singing joyfully in the moonlight. Frigid cold out as witches' tits. I stopped because of an interesting noise. Flapflapflapflap.... Slowing down it does flap–flap–flap. Get out inspect the rear parts. It isn't the dislodged metal thing or any other hanging thing, it's a hunk of rubber on the wheel detaching itself from the parent body, so I stand some special helpless looking slouch leaning longingly in the direction of oncoming vehicles my Havid scarf arranged at some attractive chest spread. Wish the photographer was here. Whiz whiz. Nada nobody. Whiz whiz. Bastids. If I were dead praps all the problems that bothered her would be settled. What was the great catastrophe before the drying up of the oceans? The coming of the snows. I should be pacing back and forth looking like I have an appointment at the end of the world. Last year this time according to a *Voice* office index card I was "envolved in many strange and wondrous adventures. . . ." I should be leaning on my sword describing my defeat. I'm leaning on my car watching a bright red sports number slow down a few yards in front of my hood. Two smiling muscle boys are walking toward me. I hunch into my scarf and meet them halfway and stare at the snow and mumble about a disintegrating tire. Yes-s. And as they're into the jack and spare boy scout act I'm noting their Massachusetts license plate. It reads s o s. Terrific. I've been saved. I love being saved. Maybe while she was standing up from the hot tub and passing out under the sink I was backing into a snow bank stuck solid and gaily hacking away at the white stuff with a dust pan in order to find my way back to "grandmother's house" under the nothing night no stars even and falling into the embankments leaving the vehicle to be hauled out by the various rescue operation teams. I need photos of this business. No, I'm telling her, I'm not hiding my forehead, I'm showing my bangs. So she's clicking some pix of my bangs and other parts inside and outside but the ". . . strange and wondrous adventures" are not being recorded. Like looking out this window and seeing some abominable bird tracks and this leaning tower of silo and this deadduck apple orchard and many obscure but timeless traces of the great catastrophes before and after the drying up of the oceans. At that time according to certain prominent bioanalysts I became a female because another much stronger animal *also* anxious to return to the aquatic existence of which we had been deprived managed to bore a tube into me in order to create a passage to get into the puddle which became my uterus. Amazing. And I don't even have any callosities on my forward extremities to facilitate the clasping of any other weakling who got bored into. But I'm sitting in my vest and shirt and pants and pipe at a table looking at a chess set opposite my opponent in her altogether also staring at the chess pieces about level with a pair of great knockers before the separation of creation from nothing there was probably something. Flap. I'm leaning on my elbow describing a checkmate. This was my brilliant dephallible idea to get a shot like the original Duchamp at chess with the chick in the buff a blubbler possibly detaching itself from the parent bodily situation to which the organization of the female accommodated itself apropobly. I make a move. Assault with intent to ravish. The set belonged to the master and his widow themselves. She loaned me the set. She didn't want me to make the picture. You don't play chess, she said. It doesn't matter, I play lots of games. My opponent's hair is black like the original but five inches longer and it's covering the profile. I don't care for my own. No, I'm showing my bangs. My blood is thick, my heart is made of doodlebugs tonight. If she were dead praps all the problems that didn't bother me would be unsettled. Let's shoot this one out in the snow she said. Yeah let's do it on the way to the road. Now sit in the chair. Now stand on the table. Now the hands. The bangs. The tie. The dingle dangle. Now take off your clothes. No I don't do that. "He looked at my naked body and found that it was perfect and therefore destroyed his sketches." There's no padding interposed any more between life and the word. This is not a strange and wondrous adventure. I'm not terrible enough to be beautiful and I'm not a streaming pillar of orange wax as a girl in a tangerine dress rising up out of a hot tub and melting away under the sink and I don't have an appointment at the end of the world. Either. Where's the sos car? She said she was available, she'd never leave me, she has a beautiful soul too, and she's very good with crazy people and how could I resist her. Come again when you can't stay forever. I find myself suddenly within the Unthinkable Itself. The lens is two yards away. Jesus she's foreshortening some part of my bare extremities and possibly even boring another tube into me somewhere and I don't need another puddle or any other substitution for somebody else's aquatic existence. But it's dramatically decadent. Capote on the couch. Just one frame, for her she said. Sure, one frame. Then let's do it on the way to the road. Then let's go up in that leaning tower of silo and make some abominable bird tracks and find our way back to grandmother's house under the nothing night no stars even and break a rib or two and wait for the sos boys and the cameras to each infinitely small thing is as large as large things can be isn't it grand?

TEACH YOUR ANGELS KARATE

Village Voice, September 23, 1971

Once I had a boyfriend who signed his yearbook graduation picture to me love and all the other indoor sports and we thought that was a clever joke. We were both sports crazies and we imagined the whole world was a sport which it was although we knew very little about the indoor love variety so the autograph really was more of a joke than a boast and besides what love we made I think as I remember was hardly ever indoors but outside since we attended these interesting prisons called prep schools. Guy was on the Kent crew or baseball team or both and I was on the St. Mary's everything. We were the sister school to Kent but we didn't play Kent or any other sister school whereas Kent naturally played its brother schools Choate Groton Hotchkiss Deerfield Andover etcetera and nobody wondered why they did as opposed to why we didn't or rather why we were restricted to competing amongst ourselves consisting of the two teams the Defenders and Invincibles just like camp where it was blue and white or green and purple whatever it was exclusively intramural and viciously competitive. The future wives of all the Jonathan Winters Edwards the IVth or XXIVth were no slouches on the courts and fields of the schools preparatory to becoming the better educated companions and tennis partners to their future ruling class husbands. My hero in my first year was a tall tan lean athletic curly headed junior called Marty Whitcomb. If Marty became a mother I'd swallow all the bats and balls she knocked us out with. I had another hero called Stuie short for Mary Stuart who was plumpish and maternal but she was the captain of the Defenders before Marty succeeded her I think Stuie became captain because she kicked a mean soccer ball and yelled louder than anybody for our team to win and maybe also she was just a nice allaround popular girl I think so anyway I was crazy about her and appointed myself her mascot along with the stuffed monkey that was passed on every year from captain to captain to transport from game to game when it wasn't sitting on their window silly in its bright ochre cardigan and beanie. When I came of age I acquired the monkey by election to the office of my first heroes and my blazer was just as decorated from shoulder to cuff the length of my sleeve with the bars and chevrons meaning first and second teams and tournament championships in singles and doubles of all four years. If ever you were to meet a St. Mary's schoolmate of mine she'd go on about how I was a hero of the courts and fields and that was what it was all about. Our big fall game was soccer and I played right wing. Our winter game was basketball and I played center forward. Our spring game was softball and I was fine in the field but rather lousy at bat. I played with *The Voice* last week in Sheeps Meadow and Ross assigned me third base of which there were two—two bald spots a few yards apart and I didn't care myself but Howard designated one as legitimate by putting a paperback in the center of it in case anybody could see it over and through the clumps of grass weed jungling the diamond. Nobody ever did find out where second base was exactly. We were playing against ourselves so it wasn't supposed to matter. Once I was assisting the opposition who happened to be my editor Diane find her way from second to third base instead of preparing to receive the ball from the field to put her out. Since St. Mary's I've become pretty casual about the sort of competition that makes you a winner or a loser until the next game war game. In the weird professional world of culture you can pretend you're winning even if the scorekeepers are calling you out or foul or benched or home sick or unseeded or not calling you period. My best sports truly were the racket sports and I won't do more than volley now even I know

I can win unless I'm badgered like last year at a camp my son was ping pong champ taking after his mother and he insisted on a game and I wouldn't let him win just because he's a boy or my son or anything but I don't like to play a game and he's beginning to feel that way too this year at his same camp we were into a volley ball game the kids were kind of clowning around about it but one parent was extremely gung ho and even flattering his own son every time he got the ball over the net this father is a regular fellow after all but the kids many of them now are standing back to observe our winning and losing culture and making fun of it I wish I could remember all the remarks but naturally the one I do remember is my son's which was a loud cheerful accusation across the net "you're disqualified if you win" addressed I suppose to anybody who seriously cared about it. *The Voice* softball game was an 8–8 tie although I objected saying our team actually won because the time they called me out at the plate I was safe home is a good place to be safe I was home safe I was certain of it but they only laughed at me and I said it myself just to be funny. Ross told somebody he understands more about me now that we've played softball together. I wonder what that is. Maybe it's that I don't mind falling on my face striking out. My swing carries me into a stagger toward the arms of the pitcher. Maybe it's the noise I make. My friend M. says tennis is a very quiet game and I make loud samurai grunts and other types of embarrassingly audible sounds of, say, appreciation over my own good shots. I'm cheering myself on, hell I'm not winning silver cups any more and I can't put two weeks together to play every day and get my game back. I drove Richard 10 miles away from his camp to the one I went to at his age he was appalled to see this absolutely straight square place where the daughters of our founding fathers are still wearing white shirts and blue shorts and marching in to assemblies and changing activities by the bugle and signing up for them and winning prizes for being super best at anything there was the old silver cup for tennis sitting on the table set for the banquet that very night and our guide a very proud accomplished young athlete her hair up in curlers for the banquet for the blessings they are about to receive may the lord be truly thankful concerning the fitness of women for sports there can be no question even in their curlers I urge all women not to worry about your demons but to teach your angels karate for the new future sexually politically intellectually creative woman will also be an athlete a whole person trained in body and mind and not necessarily a terrified competitor modeled on the male idea derived from the Greek contest system or zero-sum game in which someone wins only if someone else loses making a redistribution of assets without any increase in their total. I mean did we have to be motivated by the prospect of a prize at the expense of somebody else's loss. I dunno. The last time recently I played a game really seriously to win was two years ago my lover challenged me to ping pong and hardly gave me a chance to warm up before initiating the game we played was tight but somewhat casual until the score of 20–20 deuce at the end I got fierce and calm and determined and edged her out after many deuce and game points after which I said now you can fuck me which she did it was a peculiar thing to say but I think I meant it as a way of evening up the score in the sense we use fucking to mean taking somebody and doing them even when it's mutually pleasurable which it was I believe or maybe as another thought I was in reality demanding my own pleasure as an award for victory it could have been both if you feel rewarded and vanquished at once by the attentions of a lover who slays you forever in sinking white blinding blah blah beautiful orgasm works both ways especially when you get it on together in the synch sense sports and sex could be a universal and eternal tie they are because any victory is only apparent in the vanity of temporal illusion. Sex and sports. The true prize is historically the woman the princess we know that. For what purpose would I be wanting to impress a man except a man pass on his approval to a woman who then wants to save me from the futility of such exertions by loving me to death. A victory of moon over banana. At St. Mary's my careers as clown and athlete were mutually exclusive and now I put them together and fool at the parody of playing superbly at being ridiculous but stylish and excellent although absurd and foolish and relaxed and highly concentrated caricature superinpositions like swimming exquisitely in a forbidden place to please one woman who appreciates style and one woman who likes your naked body and outrage all the others who might shake your hand a year later and say they met you around a swimming pool. Renatus in novam infantiam. It matters not. A year later you might wake up in bed with an old friend who never saw you swim or kick or bat or catch or bounce or run or even dance who shudders an opulent orgasm and asks you casually if you want to go on or go back to sleep or get up for breakfast so what the hell. And the little ones could care less too. I visited B. & O. whose small daughter M. was peering at me from inside this huge raspberry then trespassing onto the cushion I was in a sunken fruit of my own she snuggled one whole side of my bod and pretended to play with my dangle is a kind of a third breast in the center like the better known third eye a half a year ago I dreamt of such a breast having two nipples and shaded the coloring of a birth mark. To run at Sheeps Meadow or tennis or just to run I wear the woman's jock strap or bra and let the third breast fly around at will. It did hit me in face once. I'm still sore from using my lapsed softball muscles. My best play was flat on my back after fielding the ball by falling on it I threw it from that position to second where it rolled right on since nobody was there except the approaching runner whom I mistook for the second-baseman. My next best play was yelling mine for a fly and then ducking at the last moment to let the rushing footsteps behind me do something about it. Almost all the men, anyway Paul and Ross and Howard and Carman and Alan and Mike consistently swatted magnificent home runs. Paul grins broadly, very annoying, while he's doing it. Howard is kind of serious and apologized to me a lot after he came directly into my territory to take a throw from the outfield. Also, when he was the pitcher he didn't want to pitch to our interloper and I thought he should but possibly he was right since the interloper wouldn't go away and he was far too talkative and enthusiastic and obnoxious and I almost used the bat on his balls when I was up and he was the catcher and he said he'd like to see me in a bikini. Our side had a wonderful catcher Pam was catching and taking photographs at the same time. It was a fine game. Diane brought a bag of beer and hit a line drive triple past first and theorized that women can't throw the way men can because of our elbows. She had a couple of us inverting our arms afterward to prove the point. It's true the sexual disparity at a mixed game is quite apparent but I insist I went to school with women whose only deficiency in relation to men would be brute strength. It's conditioning it's conditioning it's conditioning. Two or three months ago I was at a place where a black woman in her 30s (I think) was playing catch with a 10 year old Kirk Douglas or Steve McQueen who was so floored by his partner's skill he kept repeating "I never *saw* a girl could throw like that" and she engaged him in a heavy rap raising his consciousness concerning the expectations of little girls vis-à-vis little boys in places he knows best like his own schoolyard and what each sex does at recess and the attitudes of his sex to the other and vise reversa his own already are set in a superior aggressive chauvinism. Last year my daughter who runs very fast was quite furious for a week or two because a track meet at her school was arranged for the boys and not the girls. I told her she should demonstrate and cause a revolution or at least complain to the principal and she said with disgusted resignation "the principal is *superior* to the children." So much for the principal but what about the invisible forces of discrimination. A young girl is not usually hip to the culture at large. Nor is a grown woman necessarily. I have a fine lesbian chauvinist (ex) friend who says she feels discriminated against only when she sees she can't drive down the West Side Highway topless in a convertible. Well that's cool but anyhow she's an athlete too and the difference between her and the black woman I mentioned who was playing catch with the 10 year old is one of consciousness, that my (ex) friend made it as a kid across the barrier to sexsportual mobility and doesn't basically question her position as an exception. Or didn't. Or does and thinks it was all her fault. I mean it's a fault either way. What's in it for a woman to go out and play with the men and feel like a dope for being no good. Or to go out and play with the women and receive no cultural feedback mirror action in every media across the land the men can see themselves playing all their sports while the women can see only a fragment of themselves occasionally occupying a small space as a strange exception is not enough to motivate a growing girl to become an accomplished athlete or consider a sport as an option professionally since the media virtually excludes her own sex she will by the same token be unaware that there are, and there are, many organizations or women who play incredible lacrosse and field hockey and softball & such now really this has to change and the female sex has to begin doing something about her atrophied muscles. I was playing tennis a few weeks back and witnessed a classic scene of a young woman maybe 17 idling by the wire on a bike outside the courts watching her father and brother very strong welldefined proficient fellows playing up a smooth storm quite a while when the sister daughter got ready to leave and asked her father and brother if she should tell "mother" they'd be home soon and I don't need to mention her undeveloped musculature and what mother was doing at home and what she probably looked like by now and what her daughter will look like later on. A society which derogates women produces envious mothers who produce narcissistic males who derogate women in such a society female exhibitionism will be prohibited and the men must perform and must perform the prejudice I have to say at the risk of offending somebody whose four excellent photos of athletes in Central Park marked the front page of *The Voice* two weeks ago that the three men were naturally in action and the one woman was standing still at the plate talking (or yelling) at the pitcher. Yelling. Hurricane Doria. Hurricanes Edith and Irene. And Hurricane Fern was no longer a hurricane but a tropical storm said the radio. The Greek males as a group were terrified of any female who was a whole woman. The Greeks were terrified of the statuesque passionate women they portrayed so effectively—Medea, Clytemnestra, Hecuba, Alcmene. And what of the huntresses, the virgins? Many modern Dianas and Daphnes are athletes virgins lesbians and we know very little about them. I think frankly the country would freak if it had a chance to see some of its superb team sports-women display their speed and intricate skills and strategies in such sports as lacrosse and field hockey, traditionally played and developed by women in favorable school circumstances. I'd like to give a badminton demonstration myself. I was keeping an ace up my old blazer sleeve and that's badminton. People have the worst misconceptions about this light weight racket sport. They see it as some kind of feather dusting. A silly game no more demanding than jacks or croquet which are fairly demanding. Badminton is a sleek incredibly fast and space consuming game with a terrific range of strategic subtleties. It's psychologically the most satisfying game I've ever played. Unlike tennis in which your arm and your racket are very much of a piece from preparation, swing, and follow through your arm is an extension of the racket and the elbow is a vital hinge as it bends or gives somewhat and then straightens out in the completion of the swing still the arm and racket are one large simple unit and your footwork and stance and profile positioning to the net are very important in permitting arm and racket their full play on the ball whereas in badminton the arm is comparatively free of the racket in the sense that the racket becomes the tail end of a whiplash in which the arm behaves very much the way it does in throwing a ball pulling the shoulder way back and the bent elbow behind the shoulder and a cocked wrist above the elbow is the same preparation for a forehand badminton swing and the swing itself is quite the same as a throw with the difference that the follow through entails a heavier spapping wrist action as you let the racket which unlike a ball of course stays in your hand terminate the whip of the arm you get a beautiful swish of the racket through the air and a popping squsshy smash on impact with the birdie whose projectile is perhaps the key element as it is in any sport to the speed and strategic range of the game. The birdie is an amazing object. The cork of its slightly weighted bottom that connects with your racket strings sends the thing like a cannon shot (excluding of course net play in which arm and racket action is reduced to ping pong level) for perhaps two thirds of its journey until the feathers slow it down and it soars or drops just like a bird for which it's named. Naturally the higher you send it the greater the float at the other end thus affording your opponent all the better opportunity to position herself for the return, but you don't send it up like that unless you're driving your opponent into the back of the court where hopefully her return will be weak enough to permit you a smash or a drop shot or a cross court flat hit close to the net and like that it's an infinitely variable game of sudden turns and changes or great unpredictability and challenge to your control over an eccentric swing in which arm and racket behave like the segments of a crooked snake as they whip around a twisting body. I must sound as though I did nothing but compete ferociously at this swift delicate drastic game but really in the six years I played it most consistently I had the best fun just volleying with a friend while rapping endlessly over a net about our schoolgirlish affairs back and forth swish tap smash and rap all alone on a court that was also for stunts and basketball I could I spose play badminton sleep walking several lives from now at an advanced age pick up a racket and startle the inhabitants of Venus for whatever fun it might be that would still be what it was all about. Fun and heroism aside, you might remember what Oscar Wilde said of football and I change the football to badminton, it is all very well as a game for rough girls but it is hardly suitable for delicate boys.

ON THE DEATH OF A MOTHER/TWELVE-PART VARIATION ON THE DEATH OF A MOTHER

Village Voice, May 7, 1979

I

November 15 the evening news networks carried obituary film clips of Margaret Mead's life. At the end of the collage on each network she was shown in her cape waving good-bye to somebody, possibly Samoan children or friends in New York. The film was repeated on the late news, and I flipped the channel back and forth to catch the same segments over again, especially the last one showing her waving good-bye. Then I went to the phone and called a friend to say Margaret Mead had died and I felt very sad but I wasn't sure why since Margaret Mead never meant that much to me. I never read her books and someone gave me her autobiography but I only read ten pages of it. A year ago I sent her autobiography to my daughter but I don't think she read it either. The next day, November 16, at 11 a.m., the friend I called the night before called to tell me they had some "very bad news" for me, that my mother had died yesterday, November 15, at 1:15 p.m. My mother was born in 1901 and so was Margaret Mead, so the only difference between them was that Maragaret Mead was known to the world and my mother only to her family and friends.

II

November 13 I had a dream I was dying of nickel-sized red indentations all over my body. That was the day my mother went to the hospital. The last time I saw her was Sunday November 5. She said she didn't feel very well. She'd just had a perm and she looked very curly and gaunt. She gave me a faded photo of herself and her father in a surrey when she was eight or ten. She gave me her camera the time I saw her before that and the time before that she gave me her mother's opera glasses. I was living only six miles away from her, seven miles closer than I was before September, and the closer I got the further away I told her I was. I told her I was living in the next state away at the far eastern end of it. I gave her two phone numbers through which I could be reached, but she went to the hospital without trying to call them or asking anybody else to. She didn't want to bother me or she wanted to die alone or she thought I would not want to be with her or she lost consciousness before she could think of telephone numbers or she thought this was just one more trip to the hospital—possibly all the above. When two people who are intimate begin separating, each one may pretend to leave the other before the other one leaves the one who is leaving.

III

November 13 when my mother went to the hospital I was driving north to a medical center myself. I thought I had a unique disease of the left arm, and I knew a tiny little doctor in a clinic two hours north who could tell me what was wrong. As soon as I crossed the border into the next state the red emergency light in my car began flashing intermittently. Along the way I called a mechanic I used to know who worked not too far from the clinic and he said he would see my car after I saw the doctor. When I left the clinic the emergency light was flashing red continuously. The doctor prescribed X rays and codeine and said he expected a dislocation. The mechanic took me to supper and charged my battery and said he suspected I needed a new alternator. My arm was separating from my shoulder. My car was separating from its alternator. My mother was separating from her body. My mother needless to say was separating from me. And my car also was separating from me on the way back home the lights dimmed and the power failed completely. In this strange town I was rescued by the police who drove me to a motel for the night. In the morning I was rescued by a man in a garage who drove me to the gas station where I had coasted in and parked the night before. At home November 14 I was on the phone calling various automotive centers about parts. November 15 I called the hospital where my mother had just died to make an appointment for X rays of my arm. That night I mourned the death of Margaret Mead on television. November 16 I was told that the hospital had been trying to reach me the day before everywhere. They reached my mother's lawyer who called my mother's best friend in Florida who called my daughter in Tennessee who called my son in Texas who called someone I knew in Massachusetts who called me. I knew my mother was dying but my arm and my car had become the executors of my knowledge.

IV

November 17 I read Margaret Mead's obituary in *the Times*. Her father had hoped for a son and once said to his daughter it was a pity she was not a boy, that she would have gone far. In my mother's funeral instructions under Daughter she had written: Calls herself Johnston instead of Lanham which is her married name. Clearly my mother thought I had gone far enough as a married woman, or she thought I would go far if I stayed that way. Since she knew I was legally divorced long ago, this seemed like her strongest posthumous message. During a recent visit she told me her big mistake was giving me the name Johnston, presumably because it gave me a clue to my father's identity. After her memorial service her best friend agreed with me that her biggest mistake was not telling me all about it (this romantic and traditional "Affair To Remember"). In September I flew to London and met my father's only son, and I never told her I met him or even that I left the country. I know my mother had hoped for a daughter, so her regrets over my name were consistent with her deepest wish to have me for herself alone. However she gave me my father's name for practical legal and societal purposes, and she never accepted the consequences of her "correct" adjustment to patriarchal realities. Her deepest wish to have me for herself was in conflict with those realities, which ultimately obscured her original interest. Even in death she tried to be legal and correct, by indicating that one mistake should be rectified by another, the name of one strange man for the name of another strange man, the latter by now ironically long illegal through divorce. By coincidence, on November 15, the day she died, I mailed a letter to my half-brother in London. He had written saying he liked me (too) and hoped as I do that we might be friends. The only mistake my mother made was not making friends with this man's father. I'm not sure how far we can go, either as a boy or as a girl whose father thought it was a pity she was not a boy but who went pretty far anyway, without being friends. Three years ago I decided I was not going anywhere before making friends with my mother.

V

November 16 I drove to New York and stopped to see my mother's lawyer on the way. I told him her designation of me as a married woman in her papers was illegal and also that she was never a married woman herself. I transferred all my unfriendly feelings towards my mother over this terrible ancient matter between us to her lawyer, whose mask of professional kindliness and paternal endurance remained undisturbed. He told me how much he liked my mother, and that he never knew about this matter of my father, and that he was glad to meet me, and he suggested December 15 as a date for the memorial service because he would be away on vacation until then. November 17 in New York I went to a birthday party in the black suit I'd bought for my historic meeting in London. Before the party I went to a Nasherai where several women had gathered to discuss transitional problems. I told them my mother had just died but the transition they were discussing didn't include dying mothers. At the birthday party I tried to make death a subject by soliciting responses to the news that my mother had just died. I was enjoying my news for its shock value, so evidently I was looking for external reflections of an inner state that I was not yet feeling. Or perhaps I should say I was looking for external reflections of a state that would defer the onslaught of feelings which naturally attend or follow this state. But since we are not living altogether naturally, the state of shock may be all we can or want to experience when we hear the news that we fear may destroy us. In a permanent state of shock we don't have to experience any feelings at all. We may actually be living in a culture which is in a permanent state of shock. If so, many people prefer not to hear any new shocking news, which could release feelings that were buried by some original shock; while others may enjoy or need shocking news to continue to distance themselves from the same feelings. Terrible things are happening to others but not to us. Guyana was terrible enough to guarantee a temporary distraction. I read all the news about it and any other morbid news I saw that I normally ignore. November 22 an entry in my record book reads: The country is obsessed and aghast at a mass suicide of a commune in Guyana in South America. The same day I entered a few sentences from the *Times* about the violent death of English playwright Joe Orton in the '60s. A week had passed since the death of my mother and the only thing I was feeling was a lot of pain in my left arm.

VI

November 24 I drove to the hospital where my mother died to have the X rays taken that I didn't the week before when I canceled my appointment. I thought it was bizarre standing up in a white sheet under bright lights being shot by an X ray technician in the place where my mother had just died. Afterwards I walked over a couple of corridors to the intensive care unit where I visited her every day last April during Easter week. It appeared she was going to die then, but she rose again on the third day which was Good Friday. I had never seen her ill in a hospital, or anywhere else for that matter. I felt very sad for her that week. I saw her as a helpless old baby. I saw her as her mother's little girl. I knew her mother would feel very sad for her. I imagined myself her mother and how sad she would feel. Her little girl old and helpless in a stark forbidding place bleeping heart machines. I held her old baby's hand and mumbled intimate hopeful things in her ear wondering if she heard me in the region where she had disappeared. I wondered later if I kept her alive just by being there, and if so if that was a good thing. Her doctor had given her two years to live and her time was up, or she was complying with his prediction by dying "on time." She was always compliant and would not have wanted to challenge the doctor's credibility. But she had another side to her that was subversive and rebellious and might like to confound a hard judgment if she could get away with it. I met the doctor myself at her bedside, where she was propped up and surfacing momentarily from the dead, a deeply jaundiced wasted emaciated version of herself, focusing all she had left in a desperate silent plea for knowledge of her condition, first to this doctor who was waving his clipboard and talking about a by-pass Operation that my mother had refused to have which he had told her would give her five years instead of two, and then to me to beg for my approval of the doctor. I didn't approve of him at all, but under the circumstances I tried to reassure her and nodded my approval as he left the room briskly with his clipboard, not having recognized me in any way. That was last April. Now, on November 24, I stood in the same place, this time talking to a nurse with an angry face who told me my mother was not there because she died. I said I know, and looked around for someone friendlier who might tell me something of my mother's last hours. The nurse with the angry face said I should talk to the nursing supervisor, so I walked over to her office which was near the front entrance to the hospital. There, for the first time since the 15th, the feelings that I had buried in my left arm surfaced through the mediation of this nursing supervisor. I sat in her office while she went upstairs somewhere to get my mother's file. When she returned, she fingered the folder as if it was a deck of cards or coins or tea leaves, indicating that it wasn't its contents that were important but its function as her medium for transmitting compassion for my mother and me. Her left eye was congenitally droopy, a sign of special powers, I believe. I was fixed by her quiet attention and the droopy left eye. I could see there was nothing but information in the folder, which she glanced through dutifully, noting the exact time of death. The meaningful information she had was a slight remembrance of my mother as a grandmother when she entertained my children on a lake nearby in the summertime. By this she conveyed she knew my mother as a person; then, after a silent moment or two, she said, "I'm very sorry about your mother," and I knew she truly was and I mumbled I was very sorry I had not been there and thanked her and fled with my feelings to my car.

VII

November 24 I now had a car that worked and an arm that didn't and a head that was connected to my arm. I was sharing my grief with my arm, but my arm continued to know more than I did. Though I could write with it if I wanted to, its condition demanded so much energy thinking about it that writing was out of the question. That my writing arm was malfunctioning and that my mother was always suspicious of what I was writing was not a difficult connection to make. The connection I was having difficulty with was this new alignment between my arm and what was happening to me. Clearly I had transferred functions under stress, but I lagged much further behind the signals of my arm's new function than my writing ever lagged behind my thoughts. My writing arm's new function was threefold: It was forcing me to consider my novel situation by making me appear helpless because of its uselessness, and by heeding the pain I felt in it every time I was surprised or startled to connect me with my grief and anger and to notify me of important business to be done when somebody dies and it's your responsibility to do it. I was avoiding responsibility by allowing the helpless result of my arm's message to dominate its other messages to take care of business. Through helplessness I could express my new situation of life without mother. Whenever possible I had people helping me on or off with shirts, sweaters and jackets. *I* was a helpless old baby like my mother without a mother to hold her hand as she lay dying. The last two words I happened to write before I heard she died were "Mother's mother"—M.M.—Margaret Mead. When I began writing again, what I wrote was a letter every day for a week to a different friend about my mother.

VIII

December 4 I was sitting at my desk contemplating one of these letters when the sudden appearance of a man I know with long gray hair at the sliding glass doors before me caused me to jump with surprise or shock which sent that terrible spasm down through my deltoid muscle. I lurched over the door clutching my arm as if I'd been shot. I let him in and explained the problem and gave him a cup of coffee. Just after he left I tripped over a long telephone wire and crumpled up on a rug clutching the arm again in yet another imitation of having been shot. Early that morning a phone call that woke me up had had the same effect. Another phone call in the middle of the night had had the same effect. I was not safe even in bed. And suddenly I remembered a day last year when I visited my mother and she told me she was not afraid to die, at which moment her phone rang. At last I got the message. My mother was calling me, so to speak, and there must be something that she wanted. What could she want. I looked at her funeral instructions and read the paper carefully. The first time I looked at it all I saw was the note about my definition as her Daughter. This time I saw the note about a memorial service. That was it, the memorial service. I had not paid my proper respects, and over two weeks had passed since her death. But I had allowed her lawyer to set the date of December 15, when he told me he would be back from a vacation. Now I said to myself I would not wait for the lawyer, that it was improper to wait so long, and immediately I got on the phone to call her best friend in Florida and the retirement community where she had lived to make arrangements for a service. It seemed as if her best friend and the retirement community both had been awaiting my calls. The woman in charge of these things at the community said all my mother's friends had been asking when there was to be a service. Her best friend in Florida was ready to fly North at any moment, and she agreed on December 9 and also offered to contact a reverend she liked whom she said my mother would have liked, to lead the service. Other details were dispatched that day, and I was no longer so incessantly surprised or startled. Now I could go on being helpless without experiencing so much pain. The way I had become helpless was by minimizing the movements of my arm to avoid that pain. By minimizing the movement of a joint, its muscles atrophy and the joint locks or freezes. I had something called a frozen shoulder. My arm was in cold storage for this alarming transition from life with mother to life without mother.

IX

December 9 the weather man said the main feature for today was rain. I thought of the birds singing in a tree of dead leaves in New York the week before. The dead tree of new life in an old and dying metropolis, the mother city of singing birds and dead leaves on old trees. The weather in Connecticut was abysmal. The memorial service was set for two o'clock. I wanted everything to be perfect. I moved very slowly and deliberately from room to room gathering what I needed to prepare for the event. I unaccompanied myself with the "Ode for St. Cecilia's Day" bought three years ago to celebrate Easter. If I was moving slowly and deliberately to avoid hurting my arm, I could say that the arm was now rendering an extra service of making me move in a way appropriate to the preparations for a solemn occasion, for which I had no precedent. But I had also become astral and somewhat detached from the physical plane these past few days, thus every detail seemed strange and of special significance. Especially strange was a vision of a figure in black as I left the house and got in my car to drive to the service. I thought I saw a tiny woman in a black coat with white permed hair walking through some trees and disappearing behind a red barn. I got out of the car and ran a few yards to try and catch a glimpse of her but either she was gone and/or I had conjured her up. I was astral enough to be dreaming what I was seeing if it looked unfamiliar. The familiar was strange enough, therefore a vision was not so unnatural. Visions normally occur in transit from one state to another, when the physical and astral planes are blurred. The strongest dreams we have are those just before waking or those on our way to sleeping. In transit we are neither awake nor asleep, but both. I was in transit in general, but leaving the house at that moment to drive to my mother's last rites made me feel especially transparent. I had a black umbrella and was wearing the black suit I had worn in September to meet my half-brother in London, the city where my mother gave birth to me. On the vest of my suit just under my heart I had pinned my grandmother's round silver pin that my mother had given me after she recovered last April. I was going to the service as her mother and her father and her only child as well. On the way I stopped to buy some flowers and a cake. I wanted lilies but settled for a white poinsettia plant. I wanted a crumb cake because the last time I saw my mother she had asked me to bring her one. Now I would sit down after the service with her best friend and two other friends in one of their apartments at the retirement community and eat the same kind of cake. I arrived with the cake and the plant at the door of the community room under my black umbrella at precisely two o'clock. There her best friend Helen greeted me and introduced me to a cheerful old lady in charge of the event. I presented the plant, which became the subject of elaborate subtle formalities regarding its proper disposition. Finally, under Helen's guidance, it was placed between the pulpit and the piano and I said I would like to leave the plant in the community room, causing the little lady in charge to smile gleefully and clap her hands together silently. Then I folded the wrapper very slowly and carefully as if it was a ceremonial flag. Next the reverend appeared and shook my hand heartily and drew a diagram on a scrap of paper of streets and houses illustrating the spot where he thought my mother had lived one summer in the sixties. Next I became a sort of receiving line to lots of little white-haired old ladies who said they would miss my mother. My role had been cast by ancient custom, and all I had to do was respond to the cues of those who had already played these parts. I met two elderly sisters in whose house my mother had lived for seven years. Only one woman seemed indigent at my mother's death. She introduced herself as Agnes and said she was a good friend of my mother's. She said the doctors shouldn't issue death sentences, and that this weighed heavily on my mother. Then almost everyone was seated, and I very much wanted to sit unobtrusively in the back, but Helen said we should sit up front and I followed her reluctantly and self-consciously to a couple of chairs before my plant between the pulpit and the piano. My mother had often said she hated the old custom of laying out a body in a casket. By now her body was long cremated. A man I know told me that when he died he hoped everybody would have a party and stand him up in a corner to enjoy it. A woman I know told me it was important for her to see her grandmother's body. Another woman said the same of her mother. I suppose I felt the same because I tried to imagine my mother's body after she died. However, I was glad her body was not at her service. I agreed with my mother about more things than I often cared to consider. I felt her presence there anyway as soon as the ceremony commenced and the lady at the piano played "Abide with Me." I was immediately overcome by the event and expressed myself in the conventional manner. I was also extremely embarrassed and struggled as quickly as I was overcome to regain control of myself. Helen passed me a kleenex as if by sleight of hand and as soon as I blew my nose in a muffled fashion I was back in control. I had plenty left over for other times and places. I would not die bleeding to death like my mother, whose refusal to cry, I had decided, was the source of her disease, which originated in childhood with upset stomachs and culminated in hepatitis when she was eighteen at the time of the death of her father. Not long before she died she told me how much she resented her own mother crying when her father died. I pointed out that she had lived with him for quite a few years and naturally she would feel very sad when he died, but my mother was unrelenting in her judgment of her mother's expression of weakness. Her own grief apparently was absorbed by her disease, by which she changed tears to blood. Possibly it was my mother's judgment of this expression of weakness that embarrassed me at her service. Possibly it felt incongruous being womanly in a black masculine suit. Possibly I didn't want to satisfy the assembly by expressing their sadness for them. Possibly they would be as anxious about it as my mother if they were brought up in the same suppressed tradition. I recovered by concentrating on the words of the cheerful reverend as he intoned the proper prayers and eulogized my mother. He said my mother was a good conversationalist and a talented artist and a courageous person and a good grandmother. After the service someone said she held her cards close to her chest and someone else said they liked the way she laughed. I heard some things I knew about her and I learned some things about how others saw her. I liked the way she laughed too. I thought she held her cards very close to her chest indeed. I know she was courageous, but I had mixed feelings about her as a grandmother. I know also that she was a talented artist, and I wish she had had the encouragement she needed to take her art more seriously. From Helen, I learned that my mother played the piano, a new piece of information that made me realize how little of our lives we had shared together, and how alike we were in ways I had often denied. Just as the service ended, in that pause before an assembled company rises to depart as they realize that what they came for is over, a low murmur of my name rose behind me and subsided as quickly as it became audible. I stood in the world for my mother now. I was acknowledged as her daughter and heir to her place in the world. I shook hands with more of her friends, bowing slightly to receive their greetings. I would go on with my mother's life—in my own way. Being in your own way is being different from mother. Being in your own way is a way of reminding yourself you're as much the same as you are different. After the service, upstairs on a tour of the premises, Helen looked out a window and pointed to a bird on top of a tree and said the view keeps changing all the time.

x

The view is the same and different, as I am the same as my mother and different. I wanted to think I was only different for a long time. Then, at the end, as her life was ending, I was afraid I was nothing but the same. Naturally if I were nothing but the same, I would die when she did. November 18 at four in the morning I had a dream I was old and dying and crying. I had been superstitious about being the same and dying. I had seized upon any coincidence to confirm my fate. In July or August sometime her car had a flat left rear tire and so did mine. In October I hurt my left leg and she sprained her right ankle. Last April when I returned from a trip to California, I found my oval mirror broken on the floor. I pieced it together and said to a friend I wondered if my mother was all right. And in fact she wasn't, as I found out the next day. When I returned from London in September, the same mirror had cracked in those places where it had been repaired, and this time I thought she must have been ill while I was away, and in fact she had been. The mirror was a mirror I bought three years ago, right after visiting her for the first time with the intention of making friends. Later I had the idea that the reason I bought it was to see myself in the sense of seeing myself differently from the way my mother saw me. Finally the mirror behaved like my car and my arm, as if it was an extension of my mother's intelligence. But unlike my car and my arm the mirror had no reason to take me anyplace during the critical last days when it seemed essential to define myself differently, if only by being someplace else. In fact, I made a decision about the mirror that rendered it useless in this respect. I decided not to repair it again, and I left it on the floor in its oak frame in its cracked condition. I decided it was up to my mother this time, that if the mirror was associated with her magically, I would let her, i.e., the mirror, live or die without any interference on my part. If I left her there to die, the day I was speeding north to see the doctor about my arm I was escaping my mother the mirror, which had apparently failed me in its first function of providing a reflection that was different from the way my mother saw me. Or rather I should say that I had given up on its first function myself. In the end I let it be my mother, lying on the floor in my bedroom, too much the same for comfort, in as bad a state as my arm and my car. A critical issue of difference and sameness was hanging in the balance. One opinion about the condition of my arm was that it was dislocated, another that it had fused. Both friends and professionals disagreed on whether it had dislocated or fused. Finally it was apparent to me at least that it had done both. Certainly it was dislocated, if not literally, figuratively, in that it had separated its "normal" physical functioning as an arm from the rest of my body. And certainly it had fused in that its tendons and ligaments had glued or adhered such that the shoulder was frozen. When two people who are intimate begin separating, they join in one sense and differentiate in the here and now, vice versa. As soon as I was accustomed to feeling both the same and different, I had only to defrost my arm and to deal with all my regrets.

XI

December 17 I found myself standing in my mother's emptied apartment haranguing her best friend, who long ago apparently had realized that such outbursts had nothing to do with her. I was filled with remorse and anger. For her part Helen had only wistfully expressed her hope that my mother had received her last letter from Florida. In trying to sort out my feelings, I can't distinguish clearly between feelings of sheer loss and feelings of remorse for what was not accomplished before I lost her. I never told her I loved her. I didn't hug her enough. I didn't bring her enough plants and crumb cakes. I only took her out to lunch once. I lied about where I was living. I was not there when she died. I had waited much too long to make friends. I had waited so long that our friendship was a lot more formal than it was intimate. I gave up on anything more intimate for fear that an emotional breakthrough would cause her to hemorrhage and die. I found it difficult to accept her limitations and our limitations together. I found it difficult in that she never accepted the conditions of my birth. Since naturally she was guilty about this herself, she was surprised when I told her I was glad she was my mother. But I told her I was glad she was my mother because she made a very interesting story for me. The way she interpreted the compliment was that it made her a grandmother. When she nearly died last April she had asked me to think well of her when she was gone. I told her I knew she had done the best she could and that was the best I could do. If our best is always the best we can do, what is there left not to accept. So perhaps I had accepted her after all. Whatever our regrets, we had done the best we could do. We might keep on doing better, but whatever is better is not really better than we did before when we could only do what was best at the time. And since one of the things she had to do was to leave me, I had to accept that too. That seemed the most difficult part. I must have pretended she was not going to leave me after all. I took her for granted as always. I was not in touch with her for years, but I knew she was there if I wanted her. She was never there for me the way I wanted her to be, but she was there nonetheless. Then, in the last three years when I no longer wanted or needed her to be there the way I always had, I was accustomed to her bright happy hello whenever I called her and now I would never hear her voice again, at least in the physical plane of attachment. December 17 when I stood in her emptied apartment haranguing her friend, I must have been missing her. I took her watercolors and her family photos but I didn't want any of her other things. I wanted to resume our relationship and keep on making our lives better and more acceptable to each other. I stood facing her "good mother" in the form of her best friend, and I was still her "bad daughter" in only the initial stages of transformation. I would have to work the rest of it out myself. I had made my arm my bad baby, refusing to write or do very much for me, a useless appendage, a limp wing somebody called it, and at the end of December I went out to dinner with a friend whose father is a doctor who told me I'd better start using it or I wouldn't have one to use.

XII

January 15 I flew to California to see a specialist about my bad baby arm. By then I had seen two GPS, two chiropractors, one orthopedist and one healer. Naturally I was flying to California for more than my arm, but I had some feelings of certainty about an orthopedist in San Francisco recommended by a dancer there. The orthopedist I saw near home told me the same thing the orthopedist in San Francisco told me, but the orthopedist in San Francisco works closely with a physical therapist and doesn't like to administer drugs. They both said I had a disorder which is an inflammation called variously bursitis or brachila neuritis or adhesive capsulitis or a rotator cuff syndrome commonly affecting people like me whose mothers have just died. Actually they just said it was a common disorder of unknown origin affecting people over twenty or thirty. For a while I thought I had amyotrophic lateral sclerosis, otherwise known as Lou Gehrig's disease, which is fatal, at least for those who believe they have it. The chiropractors I went to told me I had pinched nerves and bad alignment and they wanted to know if I had had a fall. A friend told me chiropractors always say you have pinched nerves and bad alignment and they always ask you if you've had a fall. My dentist told me some people are helped by voodoo. I don't know if the chiropractors helped me or not. One of them told me time was the best healer, always a helpful thing to hear. But time was his limit it seemed, because after four visits he drove me away by saying I complained too much and I had no appreciation of chiropractors and was not grateful to the orthopedist in San Francisco, who provided a healer in the form of his physical therapist and also a more definite time of six months to a year to deal with all the stuff that surfaces when a mother dies. I was grateful for the time and all the remarks and recommendations and diagnoses and terminologies, which I believe I spun in a great mental web which began to look like a cure. Certain suggestions I never implemented, but I wove them into my web in the form of medicinal messages. One friend recommended more vitamin E. One said Siberian ginseng and niacinamide. One said hot comfrey root baths, and almost everyone mentioned Tiger Balm. The night before I left California I sat in a hot tub under a starless sky in the Topanga Canyon facing a vague outline of distant mountains. I was a vague outline in a tub regarded by distant mountains. I was a little girl like my mother in a faded photo of herself in an old-fashioned tub. I was an old mother mountain posing proudly in a fading photo over the tub with her little girl in it. I was an endless faded photo of mothers and little girls merging and separating—watching over each other like a mountain would a tub under a starless western sky.

Reflection

FICTIONS OF THE SELF IN THE MAKING

New York Times, April 25, 1993

I've read somewhere that women transform themselves, or set themselves on some path of achievement, only after an awakening. I don't know if this is so true any more. I'm sure it was generally true before the early 1970's. Before then I had two awakenings myself, both of them pertaining to the vocation of writing. Quite inconveniently, my first coincided with marriage and motherhood, causing a conflict of interest and a burden of responsibility that was simply untenable at the time without extraordinary support.

That was in 1957–58. My "calling" was to nothing more romantic than writing criticism. It was a powerful summons nonetheless, and I was undeterred in its pursuit for seven years (plying my trade in *The Village Voice* and *Art News*). In the end, my awakening helped to cost me my new family.

The conflict between personal achievement and family responsibility also contributed to my second awakening. Now it was the mid-60's, when waking up was a kind of epidemic, highly communicable and often fatal. It was nearly fatal for me. But since I survived, another career as a writer hove into view. This time my awakening was of an interior nature. I actually discovered just then that things were going on inside me, that I had a whole life of thoughts, feelings, attitudes, rooted in a past that had been conducting itself autonomously, disconnected from my surface life.

The subterranean thoughts that erupted at that moment consisted mostly of fantasies, centering on my long-dead father, whom I had never met, and who had never been married to my mother or even lived with her. Until his death when I was 21, he had always been described to me by my mother as already dead. My new introspection gave me for the first time the striking and novel idea that I had a story.

Until then, evidently, I thought only the world and other people had histories. Or else I thought histories were done deals, full of dead facts, not accounts that people had actually made up (and continue to make up, ever casting the same sets of facts into different accounts) or that I could make up myself. I had been given some facts. Nobody had made a "story" out of them. Somehow I sensed I had a mission here. And I became strongly motivated to write about myself instead of others, or rather the work of others. I converted my criticism for the newspaper into a personal anecdotal column, and by 1969 had signed my first book contract, with the working title of "Autobiography."

I've read somewhere that "the woman's quest for her own story" has been the subject of much literature in the past two decades. When I signed on to write my autobiography, I was sure I already had a story. Then it grew clear that I didn't know how to tell it, and that my "quest" would become the search for a method. Gradually I realized, in the course of three unsuccessful attempts (between '69 and '80) to fulfill three different book contracts, that the story and the means of telling it are one and the same. "History," Jacques Lacan said, "is not the past," or "is the past insofar as it is historicized in the present." Yet we may be missing essential facts from the past, making the creation of context difficult or impossible. In 1969, for instance, I had lots of facts about my life but I had yet to learn I was a woman, i.e. a member of a (disadvantaged) caste within a political system. This lack of a political vision meant that I didn't know how to assess the circumstances of my birth, much less the consequences of my father's abandonment or my mother's lie. Nor could I appraise the critical conflict I had experienced between family and career. Raised in an all-female family, with a mother who had a career, then sent to all-female schools, clearly once I entered the world of men through marriage, the domain of the father, I was going to find myself in a place I didn't understand. But in order to understand my lack of understanding I would first need to learn that women themselves did not have stories, or were not supposed to have them. That minorities and outsiders in general lacked stories.

The quest for a story is the quest for a life. The search itself is the subject of a new kind of literature, what might be called a "plebeian autobiography." This is a most significant cultural development, promising more fatal awakenings than have hitherto been imagined possible, especially once the form is canonized.

I've read that Roland Barthes called biography "a novel that dare not speak its name," and that the stories we tell ourselves about the past become the past. Eventually that is what I discovered for myself. Recently a friend wrote to me about his dead father, saying that at 30 he thought he was really beginning to understand him. Now, he says, at 65, he's finding ever-new aspects: that is, the facts he remembers are the same, but his present-day interpretations are different. His interpretation of the same event is different today from what it was in 1985, 1975, 1960, 1955, etc.

I wrote back saying how essential the facts are to me, as close as I can get them and maintain them—the birth, death and marriage dates, recent and ancestral; the names, places, vocations, career moves, travels, family upheavals, illnesses, anniversaries, celebrations; the feelings, the words both uttered and heard, books read, events in their minutiae as well as broad outlines, and so on. With the facts, we can endlessly move them around, make them do things, act on them, pitch them in different contexts.

As we remake the past, we alter the way we see ourselves in the present and the way we cast ourselves into the future. This is not the concept of the traditional autobiography, usually the prerogative of the famous or powerful, who look back at a life of accomplishment and tell a straight chronological and "factual" story. In 1989 in this publication a reviewer of Tobias Wolff's memoir "This Boy's Life" asked rhetorically: "Isn't it premature (if not presumptuous) for a young writer with three slim volumes (of fiction) under his belt to lapse into his anecdotage? Aren't memoirs, after all, the domain of elders . . . who are persuaded that a summing up is in order?" The judgment the question was playing off was that the life can't be written, it must be lived first, then written about—provided it meets certain standards of achievement and propriety. Of course when we write the life, we are making it up (not the facts but the ways of seeing and organizing them), and this is a political act of self-recognition.

I've read somewhere that a certain man—a writer on men's issues—saw the task of life as exchanging an unconscious myth with a conscious autobiography. He saw himself undoing the ways he had been taught to believe a man should be. I don't believe he thought this meant annulling his power, the one attribute on his list that, as a man, he might continue to take for granted. For a woman, a conscious autobiography means facing not only her past as a "female impersonator"—the realization that every accouterment of her sex has been culturally determined—but the ways in which she has been and continues to be victimized in that role, even when she no longer looks or acts or dresses or for that matter feels the part.

The efflorescence of autobiography in our time, plebeian by nature, is probably due to the tremendous outbreak of victim consciousness in America, arising from the political consensus developed by the civil rights and women's movements. The traditional autobiography has hardly ever been a medium for victims. On the contrary, it's been a repository for winners, those born that way or those who made it against the odds. Their subject is what has been done; the past is sealed in some achievement. In the new plebe autobiography, writing and self-creation are synonymous. Like Maya Angelou, the writer may create more than one autobiography, establishing a profession where none really exists. Reality is being construed, rather than merely reflected. Scribo ergo sum.

I've read somewhere that Käthe Kollwitz, when old, found familial ties growing slacker. She wrote that for the last third of her life there remained only her work as an artist. Possibly when I am really old I will find familial ties growing slacker. But in the last third of my life, these ties have tightened around me like the ropes of a racing sloop. I often feel in fact as if I'm in a race—against time. I have family business of a variety that is supposed to occur at a much earlier age. Anyway it's hard to imagine, like Kollwitz, a life of work not informed by family. To me, life and work are one body, and family is what shapes the life. Family would be powering my life, as it does everybody's, even if I remained oblivious to it. But family, the immediate extension of self, is obviously critical to any writer writing her life, any writer not writing about the life that has occurred already.

Most regular people writing their lives are not products of any intact patriarchal family, or else they have come to realize that what seemed ordinary in their backgrounds actually hid strange and unassimilable factors. The autobiographies of Geoffrey and Tobias Wolff—"The Duke of Deception" and "This Boy's Story"—told of a family sundered and a father who was a scam artist on a grand scale. Like the Wolffs, Richard Rhodes, author of "A Hole in the World" and one of two brothers abused as children, sought identity in an early disturbed history, long before achievement takes over as subject.

To establish the normality of every peculiar situation, to help show, in fact, that every situation is peculiar, to institute the centrality of every person, every kind of family, to celebrate difference, is the direction of the plebe autobiography. The woman-headed family, for instance, widespread as it now is, is still considered deviant. My postponed family business, focusing as it does on my two children, four grandchildren and female partner, has much to do with my struggle to embody an authority that was missing in my early history. My mother and grandmother were good caretakers, but they never assumed the authority of their absent fathers and husbands, could never step into that vacuum. Their lives lacked self-definition. They didn't have stories—or their stories were never constellated.

I've read Monique Wittig, the French feminist, who has said: "A text by a minority writer is efficient only if it succeeds in making the minority point of view universal, only if it is an important literary text. 'Remembrance of Things Past' is a monument of French literature even though homosexuality is the theme of the book." I would amend the first part of this statement to read, "A text by a minority writer only succeeds if it becomes an important literary text." Then we could say that the stigmatized subject (any minority) has been overlooked, forgiven, in being subsumed under the category of (great) literature. Wittig's comment about Proust bears this out. Proust's work "is a monument of French literature even though homosexuality is the theme." But Proust became a "monument" decades ago, long before the homosexuality in his text was decoded or widely recognized.

Around 1969, I found out that men ran the world, and that I was a member of quite a few minorities. My writing had been developing idiosyncratically, in a hermetic, personal, free-associative manner. Now I had to incorporate political exposition and diatribe. In my own view, politics definitely cramped my style. Between '69 and '75 or so I was split between the personal, the literary and the political, trying to crossbreed them in convincing new forms. I also had my hand at creating the "universality" of "the minority point of view" in "Lesbian Nation," a personal and political tract but not a unified text.

In my next book venture, my second attempt at writing an autobiography, I opted for literature, aiming to write the third unreadable book of the century—following "Finnegans Wake" and "The Making of Americans." After all, Gertrude Stein's monumentality was due largely to how she obscured her homosexuality by saying effectively nothing in a prolific and outstanding way.

My sexual orientation by now was no secret but my origins still were. Under contract with Random House in 1974–75 to write a book called "My Father in America," I delivered 430 pages in a single paragraph, all lower case, minimally punctuated. The book was jammed with appropriations (uncredited quotations) and studded with non sequitur, that smashing device for evasion, digression, obscuration, escape. At the end my editor was outraged that he couldn't find my father in it. Nor much of anything else, I wager.

I've read Carolyn Heilbrun on Dorothy Sayers. She wrote that Sayers believed her son's "illegitimate" birth to be sinful, and was afraid she might be found out. She also suggested that in her "sinfulness" Sayers's true destiny as a woman was revealed. What does this mean? My mother was eight years younger than Sayers, who was born in 1893, and she too was afraid, indeed in mortal fear, of the consequences of having a child out of wedlock. Living independently, outside the bonds of marriage, my mother was freer than other women to pursue her interests. Yet she found single motherhood very difficult. Living in fear, with a secret, under protection of a cover-up, in time she would regard me as integral to the problem of her choice, identifying me with her transgression. She had had to lie and present false credentials, and she could never take me into her confidence. She could never tell me the truth about my father. Her complicated conformity—to the social order that she had defied in having me—set her against me. And I, having no knowledge of the social order that guided her, naturally colluded in her judgment.

Here, I came to believe, was the essence of my story. The facts had accreted in a way that pointed to psychological and political truths. I had been stillborn, legally speaking, without male ancestry or inheritance rights. I was my mother's walking secret. I belonged to a huge unrecognized minority with untold stories. If I was going to exist (bring a story to light), it would only be by exposing my mother and the scheme of the fathers, by (re)creating my own "past."

In my mother's "sinfulness" lay my own true destiny. Here was an autobiography "that dare not speak its name," one with great novelistic potential. And I didn't have to make anything up, in the sense that fiction writers invent facts. I seemed ideally "dead" as a candidate for the new autobiography, in which the quest for a life is itself the subject. Where should such a story begin? For me, it began on paper. And in the 1980's, when finally I felt I had the method and a language, I called the second volume of my autobiography in progress "Paper Daughter."

I've read Clive James's "Unreliable Memoirs," in which he says that his ideal of autobiography had been set by Alfieri, the 18th-century Italian dramatist and poet, whose description of a duel he once fought in Hyde Park is mainly concerned with how he ran backward to safety. After 1975 I was definitely doing that, though it never seemed necessarily ideal. As I understand now, though, a war was over, and the losers—the backlash against the women's movement already apparent to some of us—had to jump ship and swim for their lives, or go down in a whoosh and bubbles of martyrdom. It was not hard for me to choose. Instinctively, I struck out for shore, not having the least idea what I would find there.

Cut adrift by my newspaper, at first I found no writing assignments at all. To the right of me, the establishment said no, they would not support me any longer in my outrages; to the left of me, the radicals whose causes I adopted and championed said no, they would not rescue me from the establishment.

WHILE my writing career hung in the balance, and the world was changing, my mother, from whom I had long been estranged, was getting ready to die. Evidently my renewed acquaintance with her reminded me of my conservative upbringing, because at length I sat down before a blank page and shaped a sentence, then another and another, as if I were writing a primer.

The pieces I wrote then were perhaps as close as writing can get to the still life. An excess of speed had turned into repose. I had reoriented myself to syntax and common usage. This was important for my autobiographical project because the improprieties of style to which I had become accustomed had not proven the best vehicle for getting my story across. In general, during the late 70's I was in revolt against my immediate past as an iconoclast. Nothing illustrated this better than my disowning a 1976 Canadian-made film about myself. Seeing myself cavort on screen like a child with no cause, no responsibility, no particular intelligence, I threatened the film makers with a libel suit if they tried to show it anywhere.

I've read that Henry James said, "The way to affirm one's self sur la fin is to strike as many notes, deep, full and rapid, as one can." In his old age, he felt that all of life was in his pocket, as it were, and he could "try everything, do everything, render everything—be an artist." I hardly feel that all my life is in my pocket. But I like the idea of striking "as many notes, deep, full and rapid," as one can. Implicit in the thought must be the assumption of having a good many notes to strike.

It's true that age brings deepening perspectives and the sense of a big palette. It should also bring, I believe, an increasing sense of the dimensions of what can never be known. When we're young, we think we know everything, and we're constantly surprised by the unimaginable. When we're older, we know we don't know much, and we're no longer surprised by new information. A certain boredom overtakes us. Convinced at last that we can't know very much, we become less avid to learn things, much more occupied going deeper into what we feel we already know. If we can't fit things into what we know, we forget them.

If we are striking many notes, they might be heard as one blended resonant deep chord. Struck therein should be the key note of compassion. In the New Agey 70's, in 1976 to be precise, during the time of my mother's dying, I was brought by the devotee of some guru to a reader of chakras—those points along the spine designated by yogis as centers of power. This reader told me that my "third" chakra—the one that corresponds in some way with the heart—was pretty faint, and that I was accustomed to drawing the energy up from that point into my head and astral region for intellectual purposes.

It was a fancy, and I suppose tactful, way of telling me I was still rather a merciless person. I took the reading to heart, dwelled on it, somehow let it act on me, giving my mother's death and my family issues a meaning they might never otherwise have had for me.

I read everywhere these days that the modern nuclear family is in disarray. This being true, it is also under reconstruction, and not, so far as I can tell, with any one design or blueprint to the exclusion of others. Our time is a pluralistic and experimental one. In my own case, the notion of re-creating the past through autobiography is inextricably tied up in family. Once I realized I was not alone (I did have relatives out there), a refugee from a broken family, blown forever into bits, I could imagine reassembling these parts of myself.

My mother's death planted the foundation of a new house. She had grown up in a large, coherent American family, coherent at least on her mother's side. (Her father had broken off from his side, becoming embedded in her mother's.) Then, with her own independence and a child who embarrassed her, she set the stage for a family inconceivable in her time. I am writing now of a family in the making, the product of a woman (myself) who once supplanted family with her own career of writing, for the reason that the traditional marriage she made, in 1958, flew contrary to the only model of family she knew: a daughter, a mother, a grandmother, and a mother's extended family, which by then was without a visible patriarch.

It's clear to see that women should not have to choose between family and career, that like men they should be free to have both. As women write (or otherwise construct, as in therapies) themselves into existence, reconstituting their own histories, just as clearly they will be inventing new families, reflecting their axial position in the creation process. Some of these new families may look traditional, with a Mom and Dad and the kids and all, but if the woman has succeeded in defining herself, the morphology will be decidedly different. The relationship of the parents to each other is likely to be that of siblings and friends rather than parent (husband) and child (wife), as traditionally understood. And the children are more likely to be recognized as people than treated as property or objects.

For myself, the Dad remains a shadowy figure, in my writing as in life. My plebe autobiography in progress has not encompassed him yet. He's in the works, though, and I've long considered him essential to understanding myself.

Nowhere have I read that autobiography might someday, perhaps soon, constitute a literary genre as persuasive as fiction has been. But even while fiction (and poetry) remain the standard for creative accomplishment in writing, a revolution is taking place, a form is under development, a challenge to the pre-eminence of fiction as the creative test for a writer. As the form grows, attracting more and more practitioners, I have to suppose that it will finally be recognized apart from the traditional autobiography. Change is at the heart of the new autobiography. It is never too late to be what you might have been.

As we write ourselves into existence, the class, race and sexual political structures of society inevitably change. The notion of who has rights, whose voice can be heard, whose individuality is worthy, comes under revision. Ideally, all will be heard and respected. The shame of difference will evaporate. Change will be as fundamental to our daily diet as bread. And as this happens the culture will expand. We associate culture with the achievers, the "stars," not with the people who live down the street. "Once the landscape is detailed and historicized," Carolyn Steedman writes in "Landscape for a Good Woman" (a narratively spare but interpretively rich English plebe autobiography that came out here in 1987), "the urgent need becomes to find a way of theorizing the result of such difference and particularity, not in order to find a description that can be universally applied (the point is not to say that all working class childhoods are the same, nor that experience of them produces unique psychic structures), but so that the people in exile, the inhabitants of the long streets, may start to use the autobiographical 'I,' and tell the stories of their life."

Appendix

ADDITIONAL WRITINGS BY JILL JOHNSTON

Books

Marmalade Me. New York: E. P. Dutton, 1971.

Lesbian Nation: The Feminist Solution. New York: Simon and Schuster, 1973.

Gullibles Travels. New York: Links, 1974.

Mother Bound: Autobiography in Search of a Father. New York: Knopf, 1983.

Paper Daughter. New York: Knopf, 1985.

Secret Lives in Art: Essays on Art, Literature, Performance. Chicago: a cappella books, 1994.

Jasper Johns: Privileged Information. New York: Thames and Hudson, 1996.

Admission Accomplished: The Lesbian Nation Years (1970–75). London: Serpents Tail, 1998.

At Sea on Land: Extreme Politics. New York: Print Means, 2005.

England's Child: The Carillon and the Casting of Big Bells. San Francisco: Cadmus Editions, 2008.

The Disintegration of a Critic. Berlin: Sternberg Press / Bergen, Norway, Bergen Kunsthall, 2019.

Articles, Chapters, Periodicals, Reviews

1957

"The Modern Dance—Direction and Criticisms." *Dance Observer*, April 1957.

1960

"Totem." *Village Voice*, February 3, 1960.

"Paul Taylor & Co." *Village Voice*, February 17, 1960.

"Merce Cunningham & Co." *Village Voice*, February 24, 1960.
"Aileen Passloff & Co." *Village Voice*, March 2, 1960.
"Joyce Trisler & Co." *Village Voice*, March 9, 1960.
"Jean Erdman." *Village Voice*, March 23, 1960.
"Merle Marsicano." *Village Voice*, April 6, 1960.
"Four Evenings at Juilliard." *Village Voice*, April 20, 1960.
"Katherine Litz & Co." *Village Voice*, May 18, 1960.
"Old Hat and New in Connecticut." *Village Voice*, September 8, 1960.
"Phoenix Series." *Village Voice*, December 8, 1960.

1961

"James Waring & Co." *Village Voice*, January 5, 1961.
"Paul Taylor & Co." *Village Voice*, January 26, 1961.
"Central European Group." *ARTnews*, February 1961.
"Echave." *ARTnews*, February 1961.
"Eleven by Vadeekay." *ARTnews*, February 1961.
"Felix Pasillis." *ARTnews*, February 1961.
"Priscilla Peek." *ARTnews*, February 1961.
"Shivitz." *ARTnews*, February 1961.
"Nikolais at Henry St." *Village Voice*, February 16, 1961.
"Brad Jernigan." *ARTnews*, March 1961.
"David Carnahan." *ARTnews*, March 1961.
"Edward Countey." *ARTnews*, March 1961.
"Hal Olsen's." *ARTnews*, March 1961.
"Masatoyo Kishi." *ARTnews*, March 1961.
"Norio Azuma and Minoru Saito." *ARTnews*, March 1961.
"R. Groll-Tyler." *ARTnews*, March 1961.
"Victor Brauner's." *ARTnews*, March 1961.
"Wolf Pogzeba." *ARTnews*, March 1961.
"Aileen Passloff." *Village Voice*, March 9, 1961.
"Five." *ARTnews*, April 1961.
"George Vranesh." *ARTnews*, April 1961.
"John Hoppe." *ARTnews*, April 1961.
"Lee Savage." *ARTnews*, April 1961.
"Marcia Marcus." *ARTnews*, April 1961.
"Nelson Seale." *ARTnews*, April 1961.
"Peter Forakis." *ARTnews*, April 1961.
"Robert Reid and James Russell." *ARTnews*, April 1961.

"Stanley Fein." *ARTnews*, April 1961.
"Susan Lewis." *ARTnews*, April 1961.
"Zdzislaw Salaburski." *ARTnews*, April 1961.
"Artists." *ARTnews*, May 1961.
"Audrey Skaling." *ARTnews*, May 1961.
"Calvert Coggeshall." *ARTnews*, May 1961.
"Ce Roser's." *ARTnews*, May 1961.
"Dan Flavin." *ARTnews*, May 1961.
"Eric Bass." *ARTnews*, May 1961.
"James Upham." *ARTnews*, May 1961.
"Martha Edelheit." *ARTnews*, May 1961.
"Marysole Worner Baz." *ARTnews*, May 1961.
"The City Center." *Village Voice*, May 11, 1961.
"Alan Kaprow." *ARTnews*, Summer 1961.
"Daniel Dickerson." *ARTnews*, Summer 1961.
"Irene Hamar." *ARTnews*, Summer 1961.
"Morris Gluckman and Sung Chae-Hyu." *ARTnews*, Summer 1961.
"Gino Hollander, Harry Whittemore and Carol Brodrick." *ARTnews*, October 1961.
"Joan Erbe." *ARTnews*, October 1961.
"Luis Seoane." *ARTnews*, October 1961.
"Mona Guibord and Richard tum Suden." *ARTnews*, October 1961.
"Robert Freimark." *ARTnews*, October 1961.
"Stan Sobossek." *ARTnews*, October 1961.
"Out of the Oven." *Village Voice*, October 12, 1961.
"Man About Town." *Village Voice*, October 26, 1961.
"Albert Alcalay." *ARTnews*, November 1961.
"Belle Golinka." *ARTnews*, November 1961.
"Ben Birillo." *ARTnews*, November 1961.
"Ernst Ludwig Kirchner." *ARTnews*, November 1961.
"Morris Kriensky." *ARTnews*, November 1961.
"Noboru Yamashita." *ARTnews*, November 1961.
"Noriko Yamamoto." *ARTnews*, November 1961.
"Riva Helfond." *ARTnews*, November 1961.
"Steve Lotz." *ARTnews*, November 1961.
"Vin Giuliani." *ARTnews*, November 1961.
"Arnold Treachtman." *ARTnews*, December 1961.
"'Art As Gaiety.'" *ARTnews*, December 1961.
"Arthur Woods." *ARTnews*, December 1961.
"Donald Fabricant." *ARTnews*, December 1961.

“Group.” *ARTnews*, December 1961.
“James Dignon and Philip Cherry.” *ARTnews*, December 1961.
“Lucas Samaras.” *ARTnews*, December 1961.
“Mixed Mediums.” *ARTnews*, December 1961.
“Sixteen.” *ARTnews*, December 1961.
“Life and Art.” *Village Voice*, December 7, 1961.
“Mr. Ailey.” *Village Voice*, December 21, 1961.

1962

“Abby Shahn.” *ARTnews*, January 1962.
“Alfred van Loen.” *ARTnews*, January 1962.
“American Group.” *ARTnews*, January 1962.
“Arthur Lineck.” *ARTnews*, January 1962.
“Carolyn S. Feldman.” *ARTnews*, January 1962.
“Doris Matthews.” *ARTnews*, January 1962.
“Drawings.” *ARTnews*, January 1962.
“Francis Jennings.” *ARTnews*, January 1962.
“Gallery Group 1962.” *ARTnews*, January 1962.
“Hilda O’Connell.” *ARTnews*, January 1962.
“Holiday Show.” *ARTnews*, January 1962.
“James Dine.” *ARTnews*, January 1962.
“James Snodgrass.” *ARTnews*, January 1962.
“June Hildebrand.” *ARTnews*, January 1962.
“London Sketch Club.” *ARTnews*, January 1962.
“Stephen Vasey.” *ARTnews*, January 1962.
“Environment, Uptown.” *Village Voice*, January 4, 1962.
“Alison Knowles.” *ARTnews*, February 1962.
“Bruce Beesley.” *ARTnews*, February 1962.
“Jules Olitski.” *ARTnews*, February 1962.
“Margaret Harris.” *ARTnews*, February 1962.
“Milton Avery.” *ARTnews*, February 1962.
“Robert Whitman.” *ARTnews*, February 1962.
“Roslyn Seelig Fearing.” *ARTnews*, February 1962.
“Sculpture and Paintings.” *ARTnews*, February 1962.
“Stanley Kearl.” *ARTnews*, February 1962.
“Tania.” *ARTnews*, February 1962.
“Wols.” *ARTnews*, February 1962.
“Waring & Passloff.” *Village Voice*, February 22, 1962.

"Armando Morales." *ARTnews*, March 1962.
"E.J. Stevens." *ARTnews*, March 1962.
"Elizabeth Chater." *ARTnews*, March 1962.
"Gino Hollander." *ARTnews*, March 1962.
"Guiton Knoop." *ARTnews*, March 1962.
"Hylozoists." *ARTnews*, March 1962.
"Johnny Friedlander." *ARTnews*, March 1962.
"Leo Russell." *ARTnews*, March 1962.
"Leon Horst." *ARTnews*, March 1962.
"Lin Show Yu." *ARTnews*, March 1962.
"Mary Darby and Mesh Katz." *ARTnews*, March 1962.
"Morris Brose." *ARTnews*, March 1962.
"Phryne Sapan." *ARTnews*, March 1962.
"Rhoda Kassof/Fritz Mooney/Azapain." *ARTnews*, March 1962.
"Sergio Chesini." *ARTnews*, March 1962.
"Tom Young." *ARTnews*, March 1962.
"Young Modern Masters." *ARTnews*, March 1962.
"Fresh Winds." *Village Voice*, March 15, 1962.
"Boiler Room." *Village Voice*, March 29, 1962.
"Albert Terris." *ARTnews*, April 1962.
"Bona." *ARTnews*, April 1962.
"Brook Artists Guild." *ARTnews*, April 1962.
"Christian d'Orgeix." *ARTnews*, April 1962.
"Christian Julia." *ARTnews*, April 1962.
"Claude Venot." *ARTnews*, April 1962.
"Eric Sloane." *ARTnews*, April 1962.
"Hasel Smith." *ARTnews*, April 1962.
"James Twitty." *ARTnews*, April 1962.
"Judith Rothschild." *ARTnews*, April 1962.
"League of Present Day Artists." *ARTnews*, April 1962.
"Marcia Marcus, Reuben Tato, Richard Boyce." *ARTnews*, April 1962.
"Oliver O'Connor Barrett." *ARTnews*, April 1962.
"Patrick Heron." *ARTnews*, April 1962.
"Peter Ruta." *ARTnews*, April 1962.
"Richard Hunt, Yutaka Ohashi, Nathan Oliveria." *ARTnews*, April 1962.
"Sally Hazelet Drummons." *ARTnews*, April 1962.
"Serena Rothstein." *ARTnews*, April 1962.
"Carl Plate." *ARTnews*, May 1962.
"Carroll Cloar." *ARTnews*, May 1962.

"Claes Oldenberg." *ARTnews*, May 1962.
"Colombo Mannelli." *ARTnews*, May 1962.
"Drawing Show." *ARTnews*, May 1962.
"Elvine Richard Rankine." *ARTnews*, May 1962.
"George Segal." *ARTnews*, May 1962.
"George Vander Sluis." *ARTnews*, May 1962.
"Group Show." *ARTnews*, May 1962.
"John Pike." *ARTnews*, May 1962.
"Jonah Kinigstein." *ARTnews*, May 1962.
"Libbie Mark." *ARTnews*, May 1962.
"Nina Jacobson." *ARTnews*, May 1962.
"Norma Jean Koplin." *ARTnews*, May 1962.
"Twelve NY Sculptors." *ARTnews*, May 1962.
"The Academy." *Village Voice*, May 17, 1962.
"Miss Marsicano." *Village Voice*, June 21, 1962.
"Mr. Hawkins." *Village Voice*, June 28, 1962.
"Albert Reid." *Village Voice*, July 5, 1962.
"New London." *Village Voice*, August 30, 1962.
"Bertie Kaplan." *ARTnews*, September 1962.
"Bob Thompson." *ARTnews*, September 1962.
"Hans Juergensen." *ARTnews*, September 1962.
"Peter Forakis." *ARTnews*, September 1962.
"New London: II." *Village Voice*, September 6, 1962.
"Central Park." *Village Voice*, September 20, 1962.
"Argentine Painters and Sculptors." *ARTnews*, October 1962.
"Bill Bray/Lynda McNeur/Rosalee Vogel/Geronimo Strassberg/William Jennings." *ARTnews*, October 1962.
"Evelyn Wilson." *ARTnews*, October 1962.
"Frances Manacher." *ARTnews*, October 1962.
"Frederick Wong." *ARTnews*, October 1962.
"Group Show." *ARTnews*, October 1962.
"Hugo Asbach." *ARTnews*, October 1962.
"M.C. Teitel." *ARTnews*, October 1962.
"Mimi Forstner and Berthold Mechur." *ARTnews*, October 1962.
"Recent American Drawings." *ARTnews*, October 1962.
"Arthur Herschensohn." *ARTnews*, November 1962.
"Boris Lurie." *ARTnews*, November 1962.
"Bernard Kassoy." *ARTnews*, November 1962.
"Claes Oldenberg." *ARTnews*, November 1962.

"Hayley Lever." *ARTnews*, November 1962.
"Hugo Weber." *ARTnews*, November 1962.
"James De Martis." *ARTnews*, November 1962.
"Jerome Paul Witkin." *ARTnews*, November 1962.
"John S. Anderson." *ARTnews*, November 1962.
"Kip Coburn/Caroline Clark Marshall/William Livingston/Paul Borsos/Judith Gerber/Albert Shape/Henry Almeida." *ARTnews*, November 1962.
"Leon Dolice." *ARTnews*, November 1962.
"Milos Jonic." *ARTnews*, November 1962.
"Robert Davison." *ARTnews*, November 1962.
"Phillip Wofford." *ARTnews*, November 1962.
"Tom Wesselman." *ARTnews*, November 1962.
"Victor de Pauw." *ARTnews*, November 1962.
"Vytautas Kasiulis." *ARTnews*, November 1962.
"William Giles." *ARTnews*, November 1962.
"Katherine Dunham." *Village Voice*, November 8, 1962.
"Paul Taylor." *Village Voice*, November 22, 1962.
"Andre Rancois." *ARTnews*, December 1962.
"Arnold Grossbuhler." *ARTnews*, December 1962.
"E.L. Mesens." *ARTnews*, December 1962.
"Gigi Ford." *ARTnews*, December 1962.
"Gwin Suttman." *ARTnews*, December 1962.
"Hubbard's." *ARTnews*, December 1962.
"Leif Anderson/Joan Bonagura/Joseph Barber/Richard Sala and Nong/Charles Lassiter/Carol Yudin and Rose Livingston." *ARTnews*, December 1962.
"Marcia Marcus." *ARTnews*, December 1962.
"Nikki de Saint-Phalle." *ARTnews*, December 1962.
"Paulo Buggaiani." *ARTnews*, December 1962.
"Sheldon Machlin." *ARTnews*, December 1962.
"Yves Klein." *ARTnews*, December 1962.
"Ximénez-Vargas." *Village Voice*, December 6, 1962.

1963

"Beate Hulbeck." *ARTnews*, January 1963.
"Arcadia Olenska." *ARTnews*, January 1963.
"Carmen Sherbeck and James Stwarky." *ARTnews*, January 1963.
"Cora Ward." *ARTnews*, January 1963.
"Gastone Nvelli." *ARTnews*, January 1963.

“Guido Molinari.” *ARTnews*, January 1963.
“Kaiko Moti.” *ARTnews*, January 1963.
“Malcolm Gordon Anderson.” *ARTnews*, January 1963.
“Michael Thompson.” *ARTnews*, January 1963.
“Vica Schniewindk.” *ARTnews*, January 1963.
“Getting Branded.” *Village Voice*, January 3, 1963.
“Schmidt, Widman.” *Village Voice*, January 10, 1963.
“Untitled (Jeff Duncan).” *Village Voice*, January 17, 1963.
“The Artist in the Coca-Cola World.” *Village Voice*, January 31, 1963.
“Anne Tabachnick.” *ARTnews*, February 1963.
“Carol Haerer and Hadar Frumkin.” *ARTnews*, February 1963.
“Helen Frank.” *ARTnews*, February 1963.
“Lewis Michael Stern.” *ARTnews*, February 1963.
“Ludmila Tcherine (Proscenium); Donn Russel (Caravan), Harvey Offenhartz (Aegis); Rod Rodgers (Studio Gallery); Louis Zansky (Caravan); I. Doctor (Milo); Eight French Artists (Gregory).” *ARTnews*, February 1963.
“Marguerite Wolff.” *ARTnews*, February 1963.
“Matta.” *ARTnews*, February 1963.
“Mel Fowler.” *ARTnews*, February 1963.
“Michael Black.” *ARTnews*, February 1963.
“Norma Jean Squires.” *ARTnews*, February 1963.
“Robert Whitman.” *ARTnews*, February 1963.
“Shirley Kaplan.” *ARTnews*, February 1963.
“Ursula Forster.” *ARTnews*, February 1963.
“Walter De Maria.” *ARTnews*, February 1963.
“Judson Concerts #3, #4.” *Village Voice*, February 28, 1963.
“Agnes Mills.” *ARTnews*, March 1963.
“Anne Truitt.” *ARTnews*, March 1963.
“Betty Lou/Edward Glannon/Marjorie Gehner/Zad rich Sala.” *ARTnews*, March 1963.
“Contemporary Art of Brazil.” *ARTnews*, March 1963.
“David Simpson.” *ARTnews*, March 1963.
“Evangelos Stephanos Phoutrides.” *ARTnews*, March 1963.
“Four-Man.” *ARTnews*, March 1963.
“Frederick Serger.” *ARTnews*, March 1963.
“George Curtis.” *ARTnews*, March 1963.
“Jim Dine.” *ARTnews*, March 1963.
“John Lindberg.” *ARTnews*, March 1963.
“New Works.” *ARTnews*, March 1963.
“Phillip Weichberger.” *ARTnews*, March 1963.

“Primitive Art.” *ARTnews*, March 1963.
“Rakoczi.” *ARTnews*, March 1963.
“Robert Andrew Parker.” *ARTnews*, March 1963.
“Ted Jacobs.” *ARTnews*, March 1963.
“William Barnett.” *ARTnews*, March 1963.
“Nikolais.” *Village Voice*, March 21, 1963.
“Untitled (James Waring Concert).” *Village Voice*, March 28, 1963.
“Carolyn Feldman.” *ARTnews*, April 1963.
“Gallery Group.” *ARTnews*, April 1963.
“Hugh Weiss.” *ARTnews*, April 1963.
“Jack H. Cornwell and Irmgard Mahler.” *ARTnews*, April 1963.
“Margarita Hahn Videl (Selected Artists), Albert Marcus (Forley and Wren), James Coggin (Carmel), William McCoy (Arkep), Clara Ledesma (Sudamericana), Stephen Kuzma (Fitzgerald), Mixed Group (Forley & Wren), Michael Kahn, John Masse, Charles Augustus Smith, Marguerite Wolf, C. F. Anthony.” *ARTnews*, April 1963.
“Nasos Dephanis.” *ARTnews*, April 1963.
“Peter Kahn.” *ARTnews*, April 1963.
“Rakoczi.” *ARTnews*, April 1963.
“Rauschenberg Paints a Picture.” *ARTnews*, April 1963.
“Richard Ahntholz.” *ARTnews*, April 1963.
“Robert A. Nelson.” *ARTnews*, April 1963.
“Rosalyn Drexler and Tom Doyle.” *ARTnews*, April 1963.
“Seven Painters, One Sculptor.” *ARTnews*, April 1963.
“Thomas W. Shields.” *ARTnews*, April 1963.
“Wong Keen.” *ARTnews*, April 1963.
“George Brecht.” *ARTnews*, May 1963.
“Abraham Walkowitz.” *ARTnews*, May 1963.
“Fletcher Benton and Robert Harvey.” *ARTnews*, May 1963.
“Four Man Show.” *ARTnews*, May 1963.
“Gerald Duff and Harvey Daniels.” *ARTnews*, May 1963.
“The Golden Horde.” *ARTnews*, May 1963.
“Gordon Press.” *ARTnews*, May 1963.
“Lillian Delevoryas.” *ARTnews*, May 1963.
“Marilyn Fein.” *ARTnews*, May 1963.
“Maryan.” *ARTnews*, May 1963.
“Phillip Russel.” *ARTnews*, May 1963.
“Robert Rauschenberg.” *ARTnews*, May 1963.
“Robert Whitman.” *ARTnews*, May 1963.

“Sally Cook.” *ARTnews*, May 1963.
“Silver and Judaica.” *ARTnews*, May 1963.
“Tako Yamaguchi.” *ARTnews*, May 1963.
“Thomas W. Orlando.” *ARTnews*, May 1963.
“Yvonne Rainer: I.” *Village Voice*, May 23, 1963.
“Al Newman.” *ARTnews*, Summer 1963.
“American Abstract Artists.” *ARTnews*, Summer 1963.
“Beniah Bassine.” *ARTnews*, Summer 1963.
“Boris Lurie.” *ARTnews*, Summer 1963.
“Giuseppe Napoli.” *ARTnews*, Summer 1963.
“Hal Toledo.” *ARTnews*, Summer 1963.
“Jack Roth.” *ARTnews*, Summer 1963.
“Jean Pierre Alaux.” *ARTnews*, Summer 1963.
“Jim Sterling.” *ARTnews*, Summer 1963.
“Malcolm Preston.” *ARTnews*, Summer 1963.
“Manual Hernandez/John J. Morris/Simone Ruyters Forthomme/Ann Thrope/Maria Fleischl.” *ARTnews*, Summer 1963.
“Martha Salemme.” *ARTnews*, Summer 1963.
“Mikhail Santaro.” *ARTnews*, Summer 1963.
“New Drawings.” *ARTnews*, Summer 1963.
“Norma Anderson.” *ARTnews*, Summer 1963.
“Pat Sloan.” *ARTnews*, Summer 1963.
“Rudolf Schoof.” *ARTnews*, Summer 1963.
“Three-Man Show.” *ARTnews*, Summer 1963.
“Yvonne Rainer: II.” *Village Voice*, June 6, 1963.
“Kings and Queens.” *Village Voice*, June 27, 1963.
“From Lovely Confusion to Naked Breakfast.” *Village Voice*, July 18, 1963.
“Judson Speedlimits.” *Village Voice*, July 25, 1963.
“Eight Abstract Painters.” *ARTnews*, September 1963.
“Four-Man Show.” *ARTnews*, September 1963.
“Giorgio Pagliari.” *ARTnews*, September 1963.
“Hilde Ward.” *ARTnews*, September 1963.
“Louis Burnett/Al Ruben/Beatrice Burke.” *ARTnews*, September 1963.
“Miriam Rogers.” *ARTnews*, September 1963.
“Nadia Gould.” *ARTnews*, September 1963.
“Tim Saska.” *ARTnews*, September 1963.
“Cunningham, Limón.” *Village Voice*, September 5, 1963.
“Owen Meiri.” *ARTnews*, October 1963.
“Robert Morris.” *ARTnews*, October 1963.

"The Black Watch." *Village Voice*, October 10, 1963.
"Fall Colors." *Village Voice*, October 31, 1963.
"Alberto Dutary." *ARTnews*, November 1963.
"Gene Hutner." *ARTnews*, November 1963.
"Helen Gerardia." *ARTnews*, November 1963.
"Hector Hill." *ARTnews*, November 1963.
"Jane Greenberg." *ARTnews*, November 1963.
"Marty Greenbaum." *ARTnews*, November 1963.
"Mary Mintz Koffler." *ARTnews*, November 1963.
"Michael Eastman." *ARTnews*, November 1963.
"Nicholas Roerich." *ARTnews*, November 1963.
"The NO Show." *ARTnews*, November 1963.
"Pablo Picasso." *ARTnews*, November 1963.
"Pierre Lesieur." *ARTnews*, November 1963.
"Ralph Chesse." *ARTnews*, November 1963.
"Robert Henry." *ARTnews*, November 1963.
"Robert Kampelis." *ARTnews*, November 1963.
"Roger Muhl." *ARTnews*, November 1963.
"Samuel Gelber." *ARTnews*, November 1963.
"Solomon Ethe." *ARTnews*, November 1963.
"Terry Hass." *ARTnews*, November 1963.
"William Harris." *ARTnews*, November 1963.
"Xavier Gonzalez." *ARTnews*, November 1963.
"Judson Collaboration." *Village Voice*, November 28, 1963.
"Agatha Wojciechowsky." *ARTnews*, December 1963.
"Antoine-Louis Bary." *ARTnews*, December 1963.
"August Madrigal and George Broadwell." *ARTnews*, December 1963.
"Barbro Östlihn." *ARTnews*, December 1963.
"Barrie McDowell." *ARTnews*, December 1963.
"Catherine Buxhoeveden." *ARTnews*, December 1963.
"Charles Sarka." *ARTnews*, December 1963.
"Claude Venard." *ARTnews*, December 1963.
"Clifford Johnson." *ARTnews*, December 1963.
"Enrico Donati." *ARTnews*, December 1963.
"Ernest Trova." *ARTnews*, December 1963.
"Graphics." *ARTnews*, December 1963.
"Masayuki Nagare." *ARTnews*, December 1963.
"Paul Moscatt." *ARTnews*, December 1963.
"Renato Guttuso." *ARTnews*, December 1963.

"William D. Gorman." *ARTnews*, December 1963.
"Motorcycle." *Village Voice*, December 19, 1963.

1964

"Antonella di Burgnana." *ARTnews*, January 1964.
"Bob Thompson." *ARTnews*, January 1964.
"Contemporary Painters and Sculptors." *ARTnews*, January 1964.
"Edward Andersian." *ARTnews*, January 1964.
"Edward Higgins." *ARTnews*, January 1964.
"Five Painters and Two Sculptors." *ARTnews*, January 1964.
"Irving Kriesberg." *ARTnews*, January 1964.
"J. Anthony Buzelli." *ARTnews*, January 1964.
"John Wesley." *ARTnews*, January 1964.
"Julia Papiroff." *ARTnews*, January 1964.
"Kasiulis." *ARTnews*, January 1964.
"Michael Goldberg." *ARTnews*, January 1964.
"Opening Exhibition: XX West." *ARTnews*, January 1964.
"Opening Exhibition: Willard." *ARTnews*, January 1964.
"Poet's Show." *ARTnews*, January 1964.
"Randi Aaroe/Marc Schiebman/Lewis Robert/Betty Thompson/T. Donleavy." *ARTnews*, January 1964.
"Sidney Klein." *ARTnews*, January 1964.
"Syvanita Molyneaux." *ARTnews*, January 1964.
"Thomas Locker." *ARTnews*, January 1964.
"$7.7 Million." *Village Voice*, January 16, 1964.
"Al Hansen." *ARTnews*, February 1964.
"Allen Blagden." *ARTnews*, February 1964.
"Benjamin Mendoza." *ARTnews*, February 1964.
"Eugenia Zundel." *ARTnews*, February 1964.
"Four Tennessee Primitives." *ARTnews*, February 1964.
"James Crum." *ARTnews*, February 1964.
"Kusama." *ARTnews*, February 1964.
"Margit Beck." *ARTnews*, February 1964.
"Norio Azuma." *ARTnews*, February 1964.
"Patricia Ladew/Sylvia Shliom/Sue Kleinman/Carolyn Ure/Denis Villard." *ARTnews*, February 1964.
"Paul England." *ARTnews*, February 1964.
"Robert Bolles." *ARTnews*, February 1964.

"Selina Trief and Nadine Valenti." *ARTnews*, February 1964.
"Sheldon Pennoyer." *ARTnews*, February 1964.
"Ten Realists." *ARTnews*, February 1964.
"Tom Cavanaugh." *ARTnews*, February 1964.
"Tom Morin." *ARTnews*, February 1964.
"Pain, Pleasure, Process." *Village Voice*, February 27, 1964.
"Amy Mendelson." *ARTnews*, March 1964.
"Anita Siegel." *ARTnews*, March 1964.
"Arthur Deshaies." *ARTnews*, March 1964.
"Bert Schwartz." *ARTnews*, March 1964.
"Consuelo Reyes." *ARTnews*, March 1964.
"Davis Paris." *ARTnews*, March 1964.
"Fay Gold." *ARTnews*, March 1964.
"Frederico Castellon." *ARTnews*, March 1964.
"Frederick Hobbs." *ARTnews*, March 1964.
"Gerald Fromberg." *ARTnews*, March 1964.
"Herbert B. Turner." *ARTnews*, March 1964.
"Jo Salwen & Molly Mcllree/Arijs Kellijs/Ralph Wehrenberg/William Meyer." *ARTnews*, March 1964.
"Leonard Rosenfeld." *ARTnews*, March 1964.
"Licio Isolani." *ARTnews*, March 1964.
"Max Spoerri." *ARTnews*, March 1964.
"Paul Hapke." *ARTnews*, March 1964.
"Peter Barnet." *ARTnews*, March 1964.
"Philip Orenstein and Stephen Vasey." *ARTnews*, March 1964.
"Phyllis Gordon and Karen Herzig." *ARTnews*, March 1964.
"Robert Kuhner." *ARTnews*, March 1964.
"Roger Bolomey." *ARTnews*, March 1964.
"Sari Dienes." *ARTnews*, March 1964.
"Seymour Leichmann." *ARTnews*, March 1964.
"Summer Gardens." *Village Voice*, March 12, 1964.
"The Gentle Tilt." *Village Voice*, March 26, 1964.
"Barbara Wasserman." *ARTnews*, April 1964.
"Bert Hasen." *ARTnews*, April 1964.
"Ce Roser." *ARTnews*, April 1964.
"Costas Coulentianos." *ARTnews*, April 1964.
"Dorothy Geyer and Rosette Jolis." *ARTnews*, April 1964.
"Helen Stoller." *ARTnews*, April 1964.
"James La Malfa and Raymond McNamara." *ARTnews*, April 1964.

"Lockspeiser." *ARTnews*, April 1964.
"Paul Seckel." *ARTnews*, April 1964.
"Pearl Shecter." *ARTnews*, April 1964.
"Tom Wesselman." *ARTnews*, April 1964.
"William Muir." *ARTnews*, April 1964.
"Cunningham in Hartford." *Village Voice*, April 9, 1964.
"American Primitives." *ARTnews*, May 1964.
"Anne Orling." *ARTnews*, May 1964.
"Art Beery." *ARTnews*, May 1964.
"Byron Browne." *ARTnews*, May 1964.
"Cecily Firestein." *ARTnews*, May 1964.
"Ch'i Pai-Shih." *ARTnews*, May 1964.
"Claes Oldenberg." *ARTnews*, May 1964.
"Elizabeth Frink." *ARTnews*, May 1964.
"George Abend/Three Man Show/Harry Marinsky/Ostor Glorig/Ellen Leelike/Constance Scharff/Ada Mende/Shirly A. Mason/Marjorie Windust/Ernestine Demuth." *ARTnews*, May 1964.
"Gerald Coarding." *ARTnews*, May 1964.
"Goldie Lipson." *ARTnews*, May 1964.
"Jean Messagier." *ARTnews*, May 1964.
"John J. Myers." *ARTnews*, May 1964.
"Max Benjamin and Ben Karnes." *ARTnews*, May 1964.
"Mixed Group." *ARTnews*, May 1964.
"Phillipe Sebastian Handenque." *ARTnews*, May 1964.
"Richard Powers." *ARTnews*, May 1964.
"Robert Cook." *ARTnews*, May 1964.
"Robert Wiegand." *ARTnews*, May 1964.
"Shizu Sugino." *ARTnews*, May 1964.
"Tom Gardner." *ARTnews*, May 1964.
"Umberto Romano." *ARTnews*, May 1964.
"Wait Dehner." *ARTnews*, May 1964.
"Anna Sokolow." *Village Voice*, May 28, 1964.
"20 Latin American Artists." *ARTnews*, Summer 1964.
"Ay-O." *ARTnews*, Summer 1964.
"Bruce Conner." *ARTnews*, Summer 1964.
"Carolee Schneeman." *ARTnews*, Summer 1964.
"Harvey Offenhartz." *ARTnews*, Summer 1964.
"Jack Squier." *ARTnews*, Summer 1964.
"Jean Cartier." *ARTnews*, Summer 1964.

"John Krushenick." *ARTnews*, Summer 1964.
"Neil Williams." *ARTnews*, Summer 1964.
"Three-Man Show." *ARTnews*, Summer 1964.
"Vincencia Blount." *ARTnews*, Summer 1964.
"Beverly Schmidt." *Village Voice*, June 11, 1964.
"'December' Romance." *Village Voice*, August 13, 1964.
"New London Revivals: Part I." *Village Voice*, August 27, 1964.
"Hannah Sandberg." *ARTnews*, September 1964.
"Lucas Samaras." *ARTnews*, September 1964.
"Monchito Carrasquillo." *ARTnews*, September 1964.
"Wilhelmina van Ness." *ARTnews*, September 1964.
"Al Svendsen." *ARTnews*, October 1964.
"Douglas Staten." *ARTnews*, October 1964.
"Georges Noel." *ARTnews*, October 1964.
"Group Show." *ARTnews*, October 1964.
"Lovis Corinth." *ARTnews*, October 1964.
"Malcolm Morley." *ARTnews*, October 1964.
"Rex Clawson." *ARTnews*, October 1964.
"Tobias Musicant." *ARTnews*, October 1964.
"Art Bevaqua." *ARTnews*, November 1964.
"Ayo." *ARTnews*, November 1964.
"Hilda O'Connell." *ARTnews*, November 1964.
"Jason Seley." *ARTnews*, November 1964.
"Lucio Pozzi." *ARTnews*, November 1964.
"Marcs MacAree." *ARTnews*, November 1964.
"Mariann Miller." *ARTnews*, November 1964.
"Paul Nuchims." *ARTnews*, November 1964.
"Robert Rutman." *ARTnews*, November 1964.
"Ruth Connery." *ARTnews*, November 1964.
"Three-Man Show." *ARTnews*, November 1964.
"Young Americans." *ARTnews*, November 1964.
"Judith Dunn." *Village Voice*, November 5, 1964.
"La Monte Young." *Village Voice*, November 19, 1964.
"Meat Joy." *Village Voice*, November 26, 1964.
"August Madrigal and Arthur Guagliomi." *ARTnews*, December 1964.
"Beula Bassine." *ARTnews*, December 1964.
"Elizabeth McFadden." *ARTnews*, December 1964.
"E.W. Eichel." *ARTnews*, December 1964.
"Giora Novak." *ARTnews*, December 1964.

"Gutman." *ARTnews*, December 1964.
"John Tham." *ARTnews*, December 1964.
"Maccabi Greenfield." *ARTnews*, December 1964.
"Nicholas Nappi." *ARTnews*, December 1964.
"Roy Lichtenstein." *ARTnews*, December 1964.
"Schlomo Zafrir." *ARTnews*, December 1964.
"William Anastasi." *ARTnews*, December 1964.
"William Clutz." *ARTnews*, December 1964.

1965

"Arnold Weber." *ARTnews*, January 1965.
"Barry McCallion." *ARTnews*, January 1965.
"Casto-Cid." *ARTnews*, January 1965.
"Dan Flavin." *ARTnews*, January 1965.
"David T. Smith." *ARTnews*, January 1965.
"Georges Rouault." *ARTnews*, January 1965.
"Hernando Isaza." *ARTnews*, January 1965.
"Ken Kadish." *ARTnews*, January 1965.
"Kuchi Inayama." *ARTnews*, January 1965.
"Lillian Delavoryas." *ARTnews*, January 1965.
"Maria St. Georges." *ARTnews*, January 1965.
"Max Ernest." *ARTnews*, January 1965.
"Tim Deverell." *ARTnews*, January 1965.
"Virbrations11." *ARTnews*, January 1965.
"Four-Men and Two Women." *ARTnews*, February 1965.
"June Hildebrand." *ARTnews*, February 1965.
"Larry Zox." *ARTnews*, February 1965.
"Marty Greenbaum and Lulu." *ARTnews*, February 1965.
"Quantum II." *ARTnews*, February 1965.
"The Shaped Canvas." *ARTnews*, February 1965.
"Thomas Nonn." *ARTnews*, February 1965.
"Wynn Chamberlain." *ARTnews*, February 1965.
"4-D." *ARTnews*, March 1965.
"Ann Freilich." *ARTnews*, March 1965.
"Claire Burch." *ARTnews*, March 1965.
"Don de Mauro." *ARTnews*, March 1965.
"Ernest Trova." *ARTnews*, March 1965.

"James Johnson." *ARTnews*, March 1965.
"Jean Dubuffet." *ARTnews*, March 1965.
"Lars-Bo." *ARTnews*, March 1965.
"Lei-Sun-Sen." *ARTnews*, March 1965.
"Lionel Kalish." *ARTnews*, March 1965.
"Mon Levinson." *ARTnews*, March 1965.
"Phyllis Agne and Robert Dunn." *ARTnews*, March 1965.
"Rex Gross." *ARTnews*, March 1965.
"Robert Broderson." *ARTnews*, March 1965.
"Chinyee." *ARTnews*, April 1965.
"David Leffel." *ARTnews*, April 1965.
"Doris Chase." *ARTnews*, April 1965.
"George Woodman." *ARTnews*, April 1965.
"Lucia Salemme." *ARTnews*, April 1965.
"Osamu Shimoda." *ARTnews*, April 1965.
"Paul Pollaro." *ARTnews*, April 1965.
"Walter Gutman." *ARTnews*, April 1965.
"Allan d'Arcangelo." *ARTnews*, May 1965.
"George Herms." *ARTnews*, May 1965.
"Jane Wilson." *ARTnews*, May 1965.
"Jean Tinguely." *ARTnews*, May 1965.
"Liliana Porter." *ARTnews*, May 1965.
"Noel Muir." *ARTnews*, May 1965.
"Robert Morris." *ARTnews*, May 1965.
"Sol Lewitt." *ARTnews*, May 1965.
"Morris-Childs." *Village Voice*, May 20, 1965.
"David Gray." *ARTnews*, Summer 1965.
"Frank Dudley Stepman/Dick Stark/Jane Echeverria/Vicki Rheubottom/Fred Adler." *ARTnews*, Summer 1965.
"Invitational." *ARTnews*, Summer 1965.
"Jeremy Comin." *ARTnews*, Summer 1965.
"Manus Pinkwater." *ARTnews*, Summer 1965.
"Tony DeLap." *ARTnews*, Summer 1965.
"Horizontal Baggage." *Village Voice*, July 29, 1965.
"Billy Klüver." *Village Voice*, August 12, 1965.
"Richard Smith." *ARTnews*, September 1965.
"Critics' Critics." *Village Voice*, September 16, 1965.
"Freedom for Action." *Village Voice*, October 14, 1965.

"Communications." *Village Voice*, November 4, 1965.
"Martha Graham." *Village Voice*, November 25, 1965.
"Three Theatre Events." *Village Voice*, December 23, 1965.

1966

"Claude Tousignant." *ARTnews*, January 1966.
"Grandma McCreary." *ARTnews*, January 1966.
"Guido Molinari." *ARTnews*, January 1966.
"Mark Fisher." *ARTnews*, January 1966.
"Michael Snow." *ARTnews*, January 1966.
"Wynn Aldrich and Carole Friedman." *ARTnews*, January 1966.
"Budd Hopkins." *ARTnews*, February 1966.
"Kenneth Campbell." *ARTnews*, February 1966.
"Piecework." *Village Voice*, March 24, 1966.
"Monk, Neville, King." *Village Voice*, May 5, 1966.
"Action." *Village Voice*, June 23, 1966.
"Pickled Alive." *Village Voice*, July 28, 1966.
"Interview with Judith Dunn." *Village Voice*, August 18, 1966.
"Robert Whitman." *Village Voice*, September 8, 1966.
"Post Mortem." *Village Voice*, December 15, 1966.
"Merce Cunningham." *Village Voice*, December 22, 1966.
"Murray Louis." *Village Voice*, December 29, 1966.

1967

"Judson 1964: End of an Era." *Ballet Review* 1, no. 6 (1967): 7–14.
"The New American Modern Dance." In *The New American Arts*, edited by Richard Kostelanetz, 162–93. London: Collier-Macmillan, 1967.
"Paul Taylor on Broadway." *Village Voice*, January 12, 1967.
"Notes on a Historian." *Village Voice*, January 19, 1967.
"Leatherman on Graham." *Village Voice*, January 26, 1967.
"Ballet Plus One." *Village Voice*, February 2, 1967.
"New Exposure." *Village Voice*, April 27, 1967.
"Two Concerts." *Village Voice*, May 11, 1967.
"Meredith Monk." *Village Voice*, May 18, 1967.
"Spring." *Village Voice*, June 1, 1967.
"Tudor." *Village Voice*, June 15, 1967.
"Weidman." *Village Voice*, June 22, 1967.

"Ship Ahoy!" *Village Voice*, October 5, 1967.
"Dancing Is a Dog." *Village Voice*, November 2, 1967.
"A Likely Story." *Village Voice*, November 9, 1967.
"Poets & Kings." *Village Voice*, November 16, 1967.
"Seated Forever." *Village Voice*, November 23, 1967.
"Take Me Disappearing." *Village Voice*, December 14, 1967.

1968

"Martha Graham: An Irresponsible Study: The Head of Her Father." *Ballet Review* 2, no. 4 (1968): 6–12.
"Where's Kenneth." *Village Voice*, January 18, 1968.
"Photoplay." *Village Voice*, February 1, 1968.
"Phone Sprawl." *Village Voice*, February 15, 1968.
"Well Hung." *Village Voice*, February 29, 1968.
"Intermedia." *Village Voice*, March 14, 1968.
"Rainer's Muscle." *Village Voice*, April 18, 1968.
"Pieces of Gene." *Village Voice*, April 25, 1968.
"Sheboygan." *Village Voice*, May 9, 1968.
"Once Twice." *Village Voice*, May 16, 1968.
"Okay Fred." *Village Voice*, May 23, 1968.
"To Whom It May Concern." *Village Voice*, May 30, 1968.
"Essays, Stories and Remarks about Merce Cunningham." *Dance Perspectives*, no. 34 (Summer 1968): 20–21.
"Cultural Gangsters." *Village Voice*, June 6, 1968.
"rr." *Village Voice*, June 13, 1968.
"The Grandest Tiger." *Village Voice*, June 20, 1968.
"Return of a Perplexed Native." *Village Voice*, July 11, 1968.
"Getting Batter All the Time." *Village Voice*, July 18, 1968.
"Il n'y a pas de quoi." *Village Voice*, August 8, 1968.
"Vive George." *Village Voice*, August 22, 1968.
"Celebrating People Places & Things." *Village Voice*, September 26, 1968.
"Light Years Away." *Village Voice*, October 3, 1968.
"Tornado in a Teacup." *Village Voice*, October 24, 1968.
"Angel Anyone?" *Village Voice*, October 31, 1968.
"Any Time." *Village Voice*, November 7, 1968.
"Not in Broad Daylight." *Village Voice*, November 21, 1968.
"Credo Qui Absurdum." *Village Voice*, November 28, 1968.
"Marmalade Me." *Village Voice*, December 12, 1968.

"Holy Christometer." *Village Voice*, December 19, 1968.
"Soft in the Head." *Village Voice*, December 26, 1968.

1969

"Casting for 69." *Village Voice*, January 9, 1969.
"About the Ash Tree." *Village Voice*, January 23, 1969.
"Do It Yourself." *Village Voice*, January 30, 1969.
"Ice Blue Secret." *Village Voice*, February 6, 1969.
"What Sin a Name." *Village Voice*, February 6, 1969.
"You Got Me." *Village Voice*, February 20, 1969.
"Threes and Fours." *Village Voice*, February 27, 1969.
"Pubis Est Veritas." *Village Voice*, March 6, 1969.
"Tapioca State Pudding." *Village Voice*, March 13, 1969.
"Come Seven." *Village Voice*, March 15, 1969.
"Non Noto." *Village Voice*, March 20, 1969.
"Ergo Sum." *Village Voice*, March 27, 1969.
"O Saisons, O Chateaux!" *Village Voice*, April 3, 1969.
"All the Ooze That's Fit to Print." *Village Voice*, April 10, 1969.
"477 Years Later." *Village Voice*, April 24, 1969.
"Letters from Camp." *Village Voice*, May 1, 1969.
"Helas." *Village Voice*, May 8, 1969.
"The Belles in the Towers (1)." *Village Voice*, May 22, 1969.
"The Belles in the Tower (2)." *Village Voice*, May 29, 1969.
"Each to All the Other." *Village Voice*, June 5, 1969.
"Entrer sans frappe." *Village Voice*, June 12, 1969.
"Loobie Loo." *Village Voice*, July 3, 1969.
"Ere Midsummer." *Village Voice*, July 17, 1969.
"Ben." *Village Voice*, July 24, 1969.
"Down to the Hilt." *Village Voice*, August 7, 1969.
"Jotsam & Feltchup." *Village Voice*, October 9, 1969.
"For His After Life." *Village Voice*, October 30, 1969.
"Horses Teeth." *Village Voice*, December 11, 1969.
"Until We're 90." *Village Voice*, December 25, 1969.

1970

"Holier Than Me." *Village Voice*, January 15, 1970.
"Thanks for the Zonkers." *Village Voice*, January 22, 1970.

“Now a Butterfly Dreaming.” *Village Voice*, February 5, 1970.

“Now I Lama Down to Sleep.” *Village Voice*, February 12, 1970.

“They Considered It Prudent to Return.” *Village Voice*, February 26, 1970.

“A Wha?” *Village Voice*, March 12, 1970.

“Okafanokee.” *Village Voice*, March 19, 1970.

“Who Turned Out to Be.” *Village Voice*, March 26, 1970.

“He Who Keeps the Sun.” *Village Voice*, April 9, 1970.

“Short and Fat and Adorable.” *Village Voice*, April 16, 1970.

“Not to Worry Laddy.” *Village Voice*, April 23, 1970.

“And Now It’s Friday.” *Village Voice*, April 30, 1970.

“Springjoyce.” *Village Voice*, May 7, 1970.

“Ching Chock Crazy.” *Village Voice*, May 21, 1970.

“As Everybody Says.” *Village Voice*, May 28, 1970.

“Canyonder.” *Village Voice*, June 5, 1970.

“Stupor Star.” *Village Voice*, June 11, 1970.

“Garookuh.” *Village Voice*, July 9, 1970.

“Hasten Slowly.” *Village Voice*, July 16, 1970.

“Begin a New Page.” *Village Voice*, July 23, 1970.

“Begin at Home.” *Village Voice*, July 30, 1970.

“Summore Treasures.” *Village Voice*, August 6, 1970.

“The Tuesday Afternoon Miracle.” *Village Voice*, August 20, 1970.

“Untitled (Gregory Battcock).” *Village Voice*, August 27, 1970.

“The Crooked Road to the Center.” *Village Voice*, September 10, 1970.

“Of Herselves the King.” *Village Voice*, September 17, 1970.

“All My Engauzements.” *Village Voice*, October 1, 1970.

“Illegal, However Paternal.” *Village Voice*, October 15, 1970.

“Mater Sui.” *Village Voice*, October 22, 1970.

“The Kingdom of Holy Insecurity.” *Village Voice*, October 29, 1970.

“Can You Hide Me?” *Village Voice*, November 5, 1970.

“The Roles of the Passion.” *Village Voice*, November 12, 1970.

“For an Improper Person.” *Village Voice*, November 19, 1970.

“Anatomy of a Cross-Country Junket.” *Village Voice*, December 3, 1970.

“The Shape of the Wind.” *Village Voice*, December 17, 1970.

“Here We Are (Not).” *Village Voice*, December 24, 1970.

1971

“Wild the Way It Was.” *Village Voice*, January 7, 1971.

“Ladies & Genitals Mexico Is a Man.” *Village Voice*, January 21, 1971.

"The Cadaver Sits Up & Screams Bloody Murder." *Village Voice*, February 4, 1971.
"The Wong Sisters." *Village Voice*, February 11, 1971.
"If She Was a Whale with Hands." *Village Voice*, February 25, 1971.
"Sigmund: An Analysis of a Case of His-Teria." *Village Voice*, April 1, 1971.
"Ecce the Sapphic Swimmer!" *Village Voice*, April 8, 1971.
"The Media Macho." *Village Voice*, April 15, 1971.
"Germaine & Guillaume in Baltimore." *Village Voice*, April 22, 1971.
"On a Clear Day You Can See Your Mother." *Village Voice*, May 6, 1971.
"I Suppose She Was Born." *Village Voice*, May 13, 1971.
"16 More Women, Each for a Night!" *Village Voice*, June 3, 1971.
"Hic et ubique." *Village Voice*, June 10, 1971.
"Who Is the Father of Her Child?" *Village Voice*, June 24, 1971.
"It's Been a Wild Summer, Thank God." *Village Voice*, July 22, 1971.
"Oh vader & moeder goddelijk." *Village Voice*, July 29, 1971.
"Could I Kiss His Wife?" *Village Voice*, August 5, 1971.
"All the Women are Bernadette." *Village Voice*, August 12, 1971.
"Descent to Olympus." *Village Voice*, August 19, 1971.
"Zelda, Zelda, Zelda." *Village Voice*, August 26, 1971.
"Serial Monogamy with Raisins & Honey." *Village Voice*, September 2, 1971.
"Quam erroris viam apellamus." *Village Voice*, September 9, 1971.
"For All in Fence and Porpoises." *Village Voice*, October 7, 1971.
"Anybody Dying of Love." *Village Voice*, October 14, 1971.
"Of Death in Living Color." *Village Voice*, October 21, 1971.
"And They Ain't Gonna Love You Right." *Village Voice*, October 28, 1971.
"Ave atque vale, guillaume in pax." *Village Voice*, November 4, 1971.
"Movement Schmoovement." *Village Voice*, November 11, 1971.
"Nihil no interim est." *Village Voice*, November 18, 1971.
"Paddling Across the Ocean." *Village Voice*, November 25, 1971.
"Gayer Than Thou." *Village Voice*, December 2, 1971.
"Her Command of Impermanence." *Village Voice*, December 9, 1971.
"An Amazon in the White House." *Village Voice*, December 16, 1971.
"A Fish & a Bird a Girl Riding a Dolphin." *Village Voice*, December 30, 1971.

1972

"Dada and Fluxus." In *Neo-Dada Redefining Art 1958–62*, ed. Susan Hapgood, 85–101. New York: American Federation of Arts, 1972.
"The Second Sucks & the Feminine Mystake." *Village Voice*, January 6, 1972.
"Stamp Out Clitoral Imperialism." *Village Voice*, January 13, 1972.

"Some Bad-Assed Dyke." *Village Voice*, January 20, 1972.
"The Genius I've Squandered in Bed." *Village Voice*, January 27, 1972.
"That Nape of the Woulds." *Village Voice*, February 17, 1972.
"Lesbians are Homosexuals Too." Reviews of *Homosexual: Oppression and Liberation*, by Dennis Altman, *Dancing the Gay Lib Blues: A Year in the Homosexual Liberation Movement*, by Arthur Bell, *Society and the Healthy Homosexual*, by George Weinberg. *New York Times*, February 20, 1972.
"Your Guernica Is Very Good Looking." *Village Voice*, February 24, 1972.
"Films Out of Focus." *Village Voice*, March 2, 1972.
"Lesbian Mothers Ltd." *Village Voice*, March 9, 1972.
"The Myth of Motherhood." *Village Voice*, March 16, 1972.
"The Ague of Enblightenment." *Village Voice*, March 23, 1972.
"Atkinson: Lesbianism and Feminism." *Village Voice*, March 30, 1972.
"The Strategy of It All." *Village Voice*, April 6, 1972.
"Fanatica, Femina Fatiloqua." *Village Voice*, April 13, 1972.
"Yogurts & Poets & Flower Boys." *Village Voice*, April 20, 1972.
"Letters to the Editor: Mating Game." *Village Voice*, April 27, 1972.
"Now There Are Six of Her." *Village Voice*, April 27, 1972.
"Avocados and Rainstorms." *Village Voice*, May 11, 1972.
"Survival Plan Number One." *Village Voice*, May 18, 1972.
"Schizofrenzier Than Thou." *Village Voice*, May 25, 1972.
"She Apparently Died a Virgin." *Village Voice*, June 1, 1972.
"Call It a Day & a Day It Was." *Village Voice*, June 8, 1972.
"The Moon in Pieces on the Street." *Village Voice*, June 15, 1972.
"The Holy Spirit Lucid in New York." *Village Voice*, June 22, 1972.
"Hordes of Dykes and Faggots." *Village Voice*, June 29, 1972.
"Their Inappropriate Manhood." *Village Voice*, July 6, 1972.
"In Excessive Deo." *Village Voice*, July 13, 1972.
"Gullible's Travels." *Village Voice*, July 27, 1972.
"Strage degli innocenti." *Village Voice*, August 3, 1972.
"Post eventum placentum." *Village Voice*, August 10, 1972.
"Slouching Towards Feminism." *Village Voice*, August 17, 1972.
"Unidentified Flying Information." *Village Voice*, August 31, 1972.
"Return of the Amazon Mother." *Ms. Magazine*, September 1972.
"Writing into the Sunset." *Village Voice*, September 7, 1972.
"xxxxxxxxxxxxxxxxxxxxx." *Village Voice*, September 14, 1972.
"Letters to the Editor: Press & Oppression." *Village Voice*, September 14, 1972.
"Could I Have a Light." *Village Voice*, September 28, 1972.
"Quid Pro Quaquaquaquaqua." *Village Voice*, October 5, 1972.

“Dyke Nationalism & Heterosexuality.” *Village Voice*, October 12, 1972.
“‘A Woman Like Bella.’” *Village Voice*, October 19, 1972.
“The Yearly Mellowdrama.” *Village Voice*, October 26, 1972.
“Off to the Bewilderness.” *Village Voice*, November 9, 1972.
“The Virgins of the Stacks.” *Village Voice*, November 16, 1972.
“R. D. Laing: The Misteek of Sighcosis.” *Village Voice*, November 30, 1972.
“A Stray Case of Normality.” *Village Voice*, December 7, 1972.
“Delitism, Stardumb, & Leadershit.” *Village Voice*, December 14, 1972.
“Mary Kissmas, Hippy Nude Year.” *Village Voice*, December 21, 1972.

1973

“The Red Baroness in America.” *Village Voice*, January 11, 1973.
“As Anybody Lay Dying.” *Village Voice*, January 25, 1973.
“Great Expectorations.” *Village Voice*, February 1, 1973.
“A Lot More Lesez Faire.” *Village Voice*, February 8, 1973.
“Like Grendel & Beowulf Somehow.” *Village Voice*, February 15, 1973.
“Time Wounds All Heals.” *Village Voice*, February 22, 1973.
“Mother & the Midwest Passage.” *Village Voice*, March 1, 1973.
“There’ll Awe Ways be an England.” *Village Voice*, March 9, 1973.
“Who Was Virginia Woolf Afraid Of?” *Village Voice*, March 15, 1973.
“Free Kids! Free You & Me!” *Village Voice*, March 22, 1973.
“Palindrome & Tintinnabulum.” *Village Voice*, March 29, 1973.
“Babbling into yr Shopping Bag.” *Village Voice*, April 12, 1973.
“Feud and Variations in a Flat.” *Village Voice*, April 19, 1973.
“The Rightful Air to the Thrown.” *Village Voice*, April 26, 1973.
“Busted: Illegal Attire in the First Degree.” *Village Voice*, May 3, 1973.
“The Venus Flytrap of Feminism.” *Village Voice*, May 10, 1973.
“Kraut Fishing in Amerika.” *Village Voice*, May 17, 1973.
“Years of the Kozmic Lavenders.” *Village Voice*, May 24, 1973.
“Vest Coastal Media Trip.” *Village Voice*, June 7, 1973.
“Lady Macbeth with a Rubber Dagger.” *Village Voice*, June 14, 1973.
“Lesbians, (Wo)men, Faggots, Witches, etc.” *Village Voice*, June 21, 1973.
“Chairs in the Erogenous Zone.” *Village Voice*, June 28, 1973.
“Going Down with Peggy & Janis.” *Village Voice*, July 5, 1973.
“Women & Film.” *Village Voice*, July 12, 1973.
“A Fair to Meddling Story.” *Village Voice*, July 19, 1973.
“A Straight Wall of China.” *Village Voice*, July 26, 1973.
“More Orphan Than Not.” *Village Voice*, August 2, 1973.

"Sharks Names Birds Giants Toys . . ." *Village Voice*, August 9, 1973.
"Elektra Reconsidered." *Village Voice*, August 16, 1973.
"The End of the World Is Eminent." *Village Voice*, August 30, 1973.
"Resurrection for 40 Cents." *Village Voice*, September 6, 1973.
"At the Crotch of Dawn." *Village Voice*, September 27, 1973.
"Imported Cycle Parts." *Village Voice*, October 4, 1973.
"The Mothers." *Village Voice*, October 11, 1973.
"Untitled (Food and Variations on a Stein)." *Village Voice*, October 25, 1973.
"If You Want Me You Can Halve Me." *Village Voice*, November 1, 1973.
"The Princess and the Pauper." *Village Voice*, November 8, 1973.
"Nanny Goat Eat This Can." *Village Voice*, November 15, 1973.
"Oh Well Who Can Do Better." *Village Voice*, November 29, 1973.
"Between Scylla and Charybdis: Janis Joplin." *American Poetry Review* 2, no. 6 (November/December 1973): 10–16.
"Airheart Was Merely Felled." *Village Voice*, December 6, 1973.
"Admission Accomplished." *Village Voice*, December 13, 1973.
"The Mothers, Con't." *Village Voice*, December 20, 1973.
"Love Letters in the Strand." *Village Voice*, December 27, 1973.

1974

"A Child's Christmas in Whales." *Village Voice*, January 3, 1974.
"Lebensweischeitspielerei." *Village Voice*, January 17, 1974.
"Living Heavily Ever After." *Village Voice*, January 25, 1974.
"Only the Raccoon Lady Knows." *Village Voice*, January 31, 1974.
"Each Beaver a Loved One." *Village Voice*, February 7, 1974.
"Leaving Oklahoma to You." *Village Voice*, February 14, 1974.
"Valentein for Stine." *Village Voice*, February 21, 1974.
"Kansas Wheat, Steak, & Beautiful Dykes." *Village Voice*, February 28, 1974.
"Come Health or High Waffles." *Village Voice*, March 7, 1974.
"Feminism on the Road." *Village Voice*, March 14, 1974.
"Vita and the Virgin." *Village Voice*, March 28, 1974.
"All the Ooze That's It to Print." *Village Voice*, April 4, 1974.
"The Mother Takes a Wife." *Village Voice*, April 25, 1974.
"Normals & Other Sorts of Rejects." *Village Voice*, May 9, 1974.
"The Wrongs of Spring." *Village Voice*, May 16, 1974.
"Inseparable Particles." *Village Voice*, June 13, 1974.
"Pushing as Supine Success." *Village Voice*, June 20, 1974.
"'Lesbian Nation' Reviewed." *Village Voice*, June 27, 1974.

"'Lesbian Nation' (Con't)." *Village Voice*, July 11, 1974.
"'Exposure Will Weaken Yr Power.'" *Village Voice*, July 18, 1974.
"The Decline & Rise of Everybody." *Village Voice*, July 25, 1974.
"The King Must Dial." *Village Voice*, August 1, 1974.
"Technologies for Ascent." *Village Voice*, August 8, 1974.
Crowe, F. J. [pseud.] "Crowes Next." *Majority Report*, August 8, 1974.
"Letters to the Editor: Lower-Case in Point." *Village Voice*, August 15, 1974.
"While I'm Still Behind." *Village Voice*, August 15, 1974.
"Kvinderlejr by the Sea." *Village Voice*, September 5, 1974.
"Kvinderlejr by the Sea (Continued)." *Village Voice*, September 12, 1974.
"Slouching into Antwerp." *Village Voice*, September 19, 1974.
"Diagknowsis: Varicose Brains." *Village Voice*, September 26, 1974.
"Igmoodlence Yum Saxon Phonac." *Village Voice*, October 3, 1974.
"In the Pleasant Tense." *Village Voice*, October 10, 1974.
"From Chaos with Love: A Tribute to Sue." *Village Voice*, November 7, 1974.
"Tribute to Sue (Cont'd.)." *Village Voice*, November 14, 1974.
"Par for the Whole." *Village Voice*, November 21, 1974.
"The Voice Is Interested in This Woman and I Am Too but Probably Not for the Same Reason." *Village Voice*, December 2, 1974.
"Mother Vehicle Bureau." *Village Voice*, December 9, 1974.
"If Anyone Loves You as Much as I Do I Want to Meet Her." *Village Voice*, December 15, 1974.
"A Critique of Male Voices." *Village Voice*, December 23, 1974.

1975

"Media Knots and Future Shots." *Village Voice*, January 6, 1975.
"The Value of a Crossing and Other Mystery Stories." *Village Voice*, January 20, 1975.
"Trick or Trek." *Village Voice*, February 17, 1975.
"Time Warp to the Fifties." *Village Voice*, February 24, 1975.
"The Myth of Bonnies without Clydes: Lesbian Feminism and the Male Left." *Village Voice*, April 28, 1975.
"Lesbian Feminism Isn't a White Male Trip." *Berkeley Barb* 21, no. 17 (May 9–15, 1975): 5, 9.
"Already Moribund." *Village Voice*, May 12, 1975.
"Woman's Words." *Village Voice*, May 19, 1975.
"Are Lesbians 'Gay'?" Review of *Out of the Closets: Voices of Gay Liberation*, by Karla Jay and Allen Young. *Ms. Magazine*, June 1975.

"Being Beyond Doing." *Village Voice*, June 2, 1975.
"Write About Face." *Village Voice*, June 9, 1975.
"Patriarchum Patriarchus." *Village Voice*, June 30, 1975.
"A Cavalier in America." *Village Voice*, July 7, 1975.

1977

"On Dance." In *A Voice in the Village Howard Moody: Twenty Years on Washington Square*, edited by Annette Kuhn, 25. New York: Judson Memorial Church, 1977.
"The Farm: The Friendliest Place in America." *Village Voice*, January 3, 1977.
"Pick It Cover It or Kiss It Goodbye." *Village Voice*, January 10, 1977.
"Au fond du monstre: Another Look at Beaubourg." *Village Voice*, March 7, 1977.
"The Structure of Winter and the Intentions of Trees." *Village Voice*, March 21, 1977.
"Death & Transfiguration on the Speaking Circuit." *Village Voice*, April 25, 1977.
"The Company of the Short-Distance Runner." *Village Voice*, May 30, 1977.
"Rape and Resolution on the Northeastern Seaboard." *Village Voice*, June 27, 1977.
"I'll Never Go Back to Western Massachusetts." *Village Voice*, July 25, 1977.
"Woman Flesh, Woman Bones." *Village Voice*, August 29, 1977.
"Et tu roote." *Village Voice*, October 3, 1977.
"Can You Catch a 40-Pound Blue with a Four-Word Haiku?" *Village Voice*, October 31, 1977.
"How I Became an Art Critic and How I Do It Now." *Village Voice*, November 5, 1977.
"The New Age Climbs the Beanstalk." *Village Voice*, November 21, 1977.

1978

"Of Course, Martha Graham—but Especially Doris Humphrey." *Ms. Magazine*, December 1978.

1979

"Sexuality and All That." *Village Voice*, July 23, 1979.

1980

"Writers Go Naked for Love & Money." *Village Voice*, July 1, 1980.
"Hair: A Shortcut to the Queen." *Village Voice*, October 1, 1980.

1981

"Judson the Sixties." *New Dance USA/Walker Arts Center*, October 1981.

1982

"Lesbian/Feminism Reconsidered." *Salmagundi*, no. 58/59 (Fall 1982–Winter 1983): 76–88.

1983

"Cage, John (Milton, Jr.)." In *Thinkers of the Twentieth Century, A Biographical, Bibliographical and Critical Dictionary*, edited by Elizabeth Devine, Michael Held, James Vinson, and George Walsh, 105–6. London: Macmillan, 1983.

1984

"Edwin Denby Remembered Part II." *Ballet Review* 12, no. 2 (1984): 27–28.
"Hardship Art." *Art in America*, September 1984.

1985

"Has Modernism Failed?" Review of *Has Modernism Failed?* by Suzi Gablik. *Art in America*, June 1985.
"Letters to the Editor: Burdens of Illegitimacy." *New York Times*, August 4, 1985.
"The Myth of Women's Masochism." Review of *The Myth of Women's Masochism*, by Paula J. Caplan. *New York Times*, December 22, 1985.

1986

"Herself Explained." Review of *For Sylvia: An Honest Account*, by Valentine Ackland. *New York Times*, July 13, 1986.
"Imagine a New Kind of TV Soap: Bloomsbury Comes to Dallas." *New York Times*, August 24, 1986.
"The Punk Princess and the Postmodern Prince." *Art in America*, October 1986.
"Family Spectacles." *Art in America*, December 1986.

1987

“Jigs, Japes and Joyce.” *Art in America*, January 1987.

“Sins of the Fathers.” *Ms. Magazine*, February 1987.

“Letters to the Editor: A Good Story.” *New York Times*, March 15, 1987.

“Walking into Art.” *Art in America*, April 1987.

“Psychoanalyzing Psychoanalysis, by Marie Balmary.” Review of *Psychoanalyzing Psychoanalysis*, by Marie Balmary. *Women’s Review of Books* 4, no. 10/11 (July–August 1987): 17.

“Tracking the Shadow: Jill Johnston on Jasper Johns.” *Art in America*, October 1988.

“‘Cursed Oaf’ Strikes Back.” Review of *Gabriel’s Lament*, by Paul Bailey. *New York Times*, October 18, 1987.

1988

“The Inner Life: When Reality Fails.” *Ms. Magazine*, January 1988.

“Elena’s Aria.” *Art in America*, January 1988.

“Intimate Moves.” *Art in America*, January 1988.

“Jasper Johns le puzzle de Grünewald.” *Art Press*, June 1988.

“Divided Against Her Father.” Review of *My Father’s House: A Memoir of Incest and of Healing*, by Sylvia Fraser. *New York Times*, October 2, 1988.

“Jasper Johns’ Artful Dodging.” *ARTnews*, November 1988.

“Living on Borrowed Importance.” Review of *Night Studio: A Memoir of Philip Guston*, by Musa Mayer. *New York Times*, December 18, 1988.

1989

“A Fluxus Funeral.” *Art in America*, March 1989.

“A View from the Top of the Dump.” *Binnewater Tides*, Fall 1989.

“Painting Charleston.” *Art in America*, December 1989.

1990

“liar! liar! liar!” Review of *Daddy, We Hardly Knew You*, by Germaine Greer. *New York Times*, January 28, 1990.

“Biography.” Review of *Carrington: A Life*, by Gretchen Holbrook Gerzina. *Art in America*, February 1990.

“The Mod Squad.” Review of *Cage, Cunningham, Johns: Dancers on a Plane*, by Susan Sontag et al. *New York Times*, December 16, 1990.

1991

"Trafficking with X." *Art in America*, March 1991.

"How Dance Artists & Critics Define Dance as the Political." *Movement Research Journal*, Winter/Spring 1991.

"Remembering Charlotte Moorman." *Village Voice*, December 10, 1991.

1992

"Why Iron John Is No Gift to Women." Review of *Iron John*, by Robert Bly. *New York Times*, February 23, 1992.

"The World Outside His Window." *Art in America*, April 1992.

"Lies My Mother Told Me." Review of *One of the Family*, by Wendy W. Fairey. *New York Times*, May 17, 1992.

"Men and Their Myths." Review of *Women Respond to the Men's Movement: A Feminist Collection*, edited by Leigh Hagan. *Women's Review of Books* 10, no. 1 (October 1992): 8–9.

"Letters to the Editor: Gay Politics Goes Mainstream." *New York Times*, November 1, 1992.

1993

"The Artist as Social Worker." Review of *The Reenchantment of Art*, by Suzi Gablik. *Art in America*, February 1993.

"Fictions of the Self in the Making." *New York Times*, April 25, 1993.

1994

"Ages of the Avant-Garde." *Performing Arts Journal* 16, no. 1 (January 1994): 29–31.

"John Cage: Music for Museums." *Art in America*, January 1994.

"Flux Acts." *Art in America*, June 1994.

"Wedding in Denmark." *Art in America*, June 1994.

"Becoming Her Father's Child." Review of *Uncommon Knowledge*, by Judy Lewis. *New York Times*, August 21, 1994.

"Picasso's Visitor." Review of *Picasso and Dora: A Personal Memoir*, by James Lord. *Art in America*, November 1994.

1995

"Untitled (Letter to the Editor)." *Artforum International*, March 1995.

"Between the Buttons." *Artforum International*, April 1995.

"Deep Tapioca." *On the Issues* 4, no. 3 (July 31, 1995): 24.

"Death of a Mother: Daughters' Stories." Review of *Death of a Mother: Daughters' Stories*, edited by Rosa Ainley. *British Medical Journal* 311, no. 7012 (October 1995).

1996

"$500 with interest: The author, who never knew her father, has a score to settle." *On the Issues* 5, no. 2 (April 30, 1996): 44.

"The Cyclops of Fountainebleau." *Art in America*, June 1996.

"Self-Portrait." Review of *The Diary of Frida Kahlo*, by Harry N. Abrams. *Art in America*, July 1996.

"Rutgers Artists at the Mason Gross School of the Arts Gallery." *Art in America*, October 1996.

1997

"As if Moms Don't Know Beans." *On the Issues* 6, no. 1 (January 31, 1997): 48.

"Report from Basel: Rebel's Memorial." *Art in America*, March 1997.

"Dunn Deal." *Movement Research Performance Journal*, Spring 1997.

1998

"Foreword: I. Closet Criticism." In *Footnotes: Six Choreographers Inscribe the Page*, edited by Elena Alexander, ix–xii. London: Routledge, 1998.

"David Bourdon 1934–1998." *Village Voice*, April 14, 1998.

1999

"Mad For Her." In *A Woman Like That: Lesbian and Bisexual Writers Tell Their Coming Out Stories*, edited by Joan Larkin, 18–27. New York: Avon Books, 1999.

2001

"Artist's Gift to Hannover." *Art in America*, March 2001.
"Tehching Hsieh: Art's Willing Captive." *Art in America*, September 2001.
"Baryshnikov Dancing Judson." *Art in America*, December 2001.

2003

"Dance Quote Unquote." In *Reinventing Dance in the 1960s: Everything Was Possible*, edited by Sally Banes, 98–104. Madison: University of Wisconsin Press, 2003.
"In the Meantime, Art Was Happening." In *Critical Mass: Happenings, Fluxus, Performance, Intermedia and Rutgers University 1958–1972*, edited by Geoffrey Hendricks, 168–71. New Brunswick, NJ: Rutgers University Press, 2003.

2004

"Billy Klüver, 1927–2004." *Art in America*, March 2004.

2005

"David Bradshaw at Mad Brook Farm." *Art in America*, January 2005.
"Agnes Martin: 1912–2004." *Art in America*, March 2005.
"Airborne Abstraction." *Art in America*, December 2005.

2006

"Was Lesbian Separatism Inevitable?" *Gay and Lesbian Review* 13, no. 2 (March/April 2006): 36.
"George Brecht, the Philosopher of Fluxus." *Art in America*, April 2006.

2007

"'Beauty Will Save the World.'" *Gay and Lesbian Review* 14, no. 1 (January/February 2007): 16–18.

Index